Tocharian and Indo-European Studies

Founded by Jörundur Hilmarsson

Edited by

Birgit Anette Olsen (executive editor)

Hannes Fellner · Michaël Peyrot

Georges-Jean Pinault

VOLUME 21 · 2022

Museum Tusculanum Press

2022

Tocharian and Indo-European Studies, Vol. 21

ISSN 1012 9286
ISBN 978 87 635 4700 0
https://doi.org/10.55069/gyi10854

Published with support from the Department of Nordic Studies and Linguistics, University of Copenhagen

Museum Tusculanum Press
Rådhusvej 19
2920 Charlottenlund
Denmark
www.mtp.dk

Contents

DOUGLAS Q. ADAMS
A note on the name of a Tocharian B divinity 1

TIMOTHÉE CHAMOT-ROOKE
Back to the caustic lye stream. A revision of the Tocharian fragment A 226 from the *Maitreyāvadānavyākaraṇa* 5

ILYA B. ITKIN
Nouvelles formes tokhariennes B extraites des fragments de Berlin I. Quelques formes nominales nouvelles ou « oubliées » 97

VÉRONIQUE KREMMER
In too deep: the tale of Vyāsa and Kāśisundarī in Tocharian A. A new reading of THT 743 and 744 (A 110–111) 107

SERGEY V. MALYSHEV
Tocharian A leaf A 429 in light of its parallels in the Kṣudrakavastu 143

MICHAËL PEYROT
Notes on Tocharian A *o(k)* 'snake', A *oram* and B *ṣorromp* 'down', B *oṣno*, B *nanāmo* 'recognising', B *pāwe*, and B †*tsəwm-* 'trickle' 163

MAKSIM VYZHLAKOV
Telling, explaining, and instructing in Tocharian A: the semantics of the verbs *ākl-*, *āks-*, *en-*, *eśe yäp-*, *kärsā-* (caus.), *ṣärp-* 179

A note on the name of a Tocharian B divinity

Douglas Q. Adams

It is proposed here that the Tocharian B divine name *wekārsa* is a variant spelling of **wekkārsa*, or rather **wek-kārsa* 'voice-knowing' or '±eloquent.' Similar compounds in Sanskrit are epithets of *Bṛhaspati* or *Sarasvatī*.

The divine name *Wekārsa* occurs only twice in Tocharian B, in lines a4 and a6 of PK AS 17A a4, a6^{C} (Pinault, 1984: 169; also now CEToM), a translation of the B(H)S play *Supriyanāṭaka*.[1] The relevant lines of PK AS 17A are given below as they appear in CEToM and are followed by the English translation (by Georges-Jean Pinault, Theresa Illés, and Michaël Peyrot) provided there:

tumeṃ supriye cakravārtti walo ṣleṃtse kre[a3]*ntauna yumāne tatāka(r w)ekārsasa pilko śeśśamu weṣṣäṃ* || *putropatne* ||
añmaññemar sä(s)w(eṃmpa) pūrvavedīdvīpne ce$_{u}$ «:»
ya[a4]*tsi ārwer ptākas yes snai enerke palskosa* :
kre(ṃ)t yāmorne aiśaumye manta tākoy enerke :
alāläcc(e pa)lskos(a su yär)p(o)nta kraupoytür 1
[a5] || *tumeṃ supriye cakravārt(t)i (wa)lo te ka ārs(k)ormeṃ weṃ(ts)i – – reye wekārsa iprerne plyewsa kau(c) yāmu ṣukt naumīyenta kauṃ-pi*[a6]*(r)k(o)ṣṣai k(al)ym(ine) ma(sa) c(akravārt)t(i) w(a)lo ra* ||

---

1 I am indebted to comments received when this paper was read at the "Tocharian in Progress" conference in Leiden, December 2020, particularly those of Michaël Peyrot and Georges-Jean Pinault. I am also indebted to the comments of an anonymous TIES reviewer. Remaining infelicities are my own.

> "Then, the cakravartin king Supriya, having fixed his gaze on Wekārsa, says about the ripening of the virtues of the mountain || in [the tune] Putropat[2] ||:
>
> "I wish to go together with the lord to this Pūrvavedīdvīpa.
> You, be ready, with a mind without hesitation.
> In doing good [lit. a good deed] the wise should never hesitate:
> with an indefatigable mind (this one) should accumulate merits."
>
> Then the cakravartin king Supriya, having hardly finished saying this, ... Wekārsa floated in the sky.[3] Having lifted up the seven jewels he went in the direction of the rising sun, like a cakravartin king."

This play is set in India, but the divine name *Wekārsa* is clearly not Indian but Tocharian. I said in the second edition of my *Dictionary of Tocharian B* (Adams 2013: 660–661), "[i]f we knew the Indian name that *Wekārsa* replaces, we would know more about the *interpretatio indica* of native Tocharian divinities." Indeed, we would, but I think now that the story is both simpler and more complex than my brief 2013 interpretation.

Unremarked upon in 2013 is the anomalous phonological shape of the word. For a word of long-standing in Tocharian B we would expect to find the effects of *a*-umlaut in the first syllable and thus ***wakārsa* (/wākā́rsā/) rather than the attested *wekārsa*. The easiest way to account for this anomaly, I think, is to assume that <wekārsa> is a "defective" spelling for <wekkārsa> or rather a compound *wek-kārsa* 'speech-knowing' or the like, since *ā*-umlaut does not spread across compound boundaries.[4]

2 Consisting of four lines/pādas of 14 syllables each (rhythm 7/7).

3 Pinault (2020, p.c.) suggests that the literal 'floated in air' should be taken as having the metaphorical meaning 'had great joy.' Compare English the metaphorical meaning of 'floating on air.'

4 In the usual compounds in Tocharian B the stress is on the last syllable of the first member. Therefore, we might have expected ***wék-karsa* or ***weká-karsa*, depending on what the underlying form of surface *wek* was. Perhaps the solution is that at the stage where the shape was **-käkā-* the **-kä-* was lost by a sort of haplology. (In which case *wekārsa* may not be a defective spelling at all.) In any case, one should note that the second member of this putative compound, *-kārsa* is very much paralleled by the *-tsaika* of *lwaksātsaka*

Immediately, this analysis suggests the numerous B(H)S compounds beginning with *vāk-* (or sandhi variants *vāg-* or *vāṅ-*) that are alternative names or epithets of Bṛhaspati, the god of wisdom and eloquence, or of Sarasvati, the goddess of speech and learning. For the former we have *vāg-īśa-* 'master of speech,' *vācás-pati-* 'lord of speech,' *vācasām-pati-* 'id.,' and for the latter we have *vāg-īśvarī-* 'lady of speech,' *vāgdevī-* 'goddess of speech,' *vāg-devatā-* 'id.,' *vāg-vādinī-* '±speech-producing,'[5] *vāṅmayī-* 'delighting in speech,' and *vāṅ-mūrti-* 'embodiment of speech.' None of these match Tocharian B **wek-kārsa* exactly, but something like 'having knowledge/understanding of speech [and thus eloquence]' would seem a quasi-match for the B(H)S series. The form of *-kārsa* is epicene in Tocharian B, so we cannot tell whether the reference is to the male Bṛhaspati or the female Sarasvatī.[6]

Lacking any knowledge of the original Buddhist (Hybrid) Sanskrit original, this purely Tocharian-internal argument remains hypothetical, but it would seem that Tocharian B *Wekārsa* (better *Wek-kārsa*?) is not an ancient name for a Tocharian god, pressed into service to match a Buddhist one, but rather a post-Buddhist, inner Tocharian creation, a (semi-) calque of a B(H)S name of a Buddhist god.

[RECEIVED: FEBRUARY 2021]

'potter' (literally 'pots-former'). *-tsāika* is the same sort of deverbal adjective, derived from the subjunctive stem, as *-kārsa* is.

5 Or perhaps 'causing speech to be produced'. Monier-Williams (1899) simply says 'name of goddess' with no specific reference to Sarasvatī.

6 It is just possible that the unreconstructible word which precedes *Wekārsa* in line a6 is an adjective modifying *Wekārsa* (the translators' placement of a comma before it suggests that is the solution they prefer). If so, *Wekārsa* is a masculine noun and we have a possible Tocharian B equivalent of *Bṛhaspati*. However, it is at least equally possible that – – *reye* is an adverb modifying *weṃtsi* 'to speak' –and that frankly seems the more likely scenario to me, as it keeps the modified and the modifier in the same pāda. And, if that is the case, we have no data about the gender of *Wekārsa*.

Department of English
University of Idaho
Moscow, Idaho 83843
United States
dqadams@uidaho.edu

References

Adams, Douglas Q. 2013. *Dictionary of Tocharian B.* 2nd ed. Leiden: Rodopi.

Monier-Williams, Monier (1899). *English-Sanskrit Dictionary.* Oxford: Oxford University.

Pinault, Georges-Jean. 1984. “Fragment d’un drame bouddhique en Koutchéen.” *Bulletin des Études Indiennes* 2: 163–191.

Back to the caustic lye stream

A revision of the Tocharian fragment A 226 from the *Maitreyāvadānavyākaraṇa*[1]

Timothée Chamot-Rooke

Ma ficca li occhi a valle, ché s'approccia
la riviera del sangue in la qual bolle
qual che per vïolenza in altrui noccia
Dante, *Inferno* XII, 46–48

Two important manuscripts from the Berlin collection (A 219–238 and A 239–242) contain a long Buddhist poem in Tocharian A entitled *Maitreyāvadānavyākaraṇa* (MAV). This article provides a revision with new restorations and a philological commentary of fragment A 226, which corresponds to the end of MAV chapter 22 and beginning of chapter 23. The new interpretation of this fragment relies on an unnoticed parallel with a passage from the 'hell chapters' of the Old Uyghur *Maitrisimit nom bitig* (MNB). Like its Old Uyghur equivalent, the Tocharian text describes scary metamorphoses in the 'Caustic Lye Stream' (Skt. *kṣārodakā nadī*). The existence of this parallel raises important questions about the composition of the Tocharian *Maitreyasamitināṭaka* (MSN).

1 This publication belongs to the research conducted under the HisTochText project. This project has received funding from the European Research Council (ERC) under the European Union's Horizon 2020 research and innovation programme (grant agreement No. 788205). I thank Georges Pinault, Nalini Balbir, Sylvie Hureau, Jens Peter Laut, Jens Wilkens, and Athanaric Huard for their extremely precious remarks on an earlier draft of this paper. I am also indebted to the anonymous reviewer for pointing out new restorations in the Uyghur text, and to Hannes Fellner, Michaël Peyrot and Thomas Olander for their careful reading and editorial suggestions.

1 Introduction

This article presents a revision of the Tocharian fragment A 226 (THT 859) with translation and commentary. This fragment belongs to one of the two fragmentary manuscripts of the *Maitreyāvadānavyākaraṇa* (hereafter, MAV) discovered near Šorčuk and edited by Sieg and Siegling in 1921.[2] Together with the Tocharian A *Maitreyasamitināṭaka* (hereafter, MSN) and its translation in Old Uyghur, the *Maitrisimit nom bitig* (hereafter, MNB),[3] this long poem of 23 chapters in *kāvya*-like style is connected to an ensemble of various works related to the legend of Maitreya, the future Buddha.[4] Written in various Central Asian languages such as Chinese, Khotanese, Old Uyghur, Tocharian A, Tocharian B, Tibetan, these texts have influenced each other through translation or free adaptation – ultimately from Indian models.[5] Fragment A 226 contains the end of chapter 22 and the beginning of chapter 23 of the MAV. Unfortunately, the original manuscript itself is lost: only the old black and white photograph reproduced by Sieg and Siegling in *Tocharische Sprachreste* is extant (plate

2 One manuscript of the MAV corresponds to fragments A 219–238 (Sieg & Siegling 1921: 107–119); the other manuscript corresponds to fragments A 239–242 (Sieg & Siegling 1921: 119–121). The fragments of both manuscripts are available in transcription and transliteration on the CEToM website.

3 For the MSN, see Ji, Winter & Pinault (1998) (manuscript from Yanqi). For the MNB, see Geng & Klimkeit (1988) (manuscript from Hami, ch. 1–5); Geng, Klimkeit & Laut (1998) (manuscript from Hami, ch. 20–27); Tekin (1980) (manuscripts from Sängim and Murtuk); Laut & Wilkens (2017) (authoritative catalogue of Sängim and Murtuk fragments).

4 In chapter 23, the author of the MAV refers to his own work as a *kāvviṣi retwe* '*kāvya* composition'. See the partial edition and translation of fragments A 229, A 230, and A 236 already by Sieg (1918), revised and discussed by Bailey (1937: 908–913).

5 For a presentation of Maitreya literature, see Kumamoto (2002) and Beih. II (12–18). Concerning the MSN, Lévi was the first to point out the close connections between this work and a collection of Avadānas translated in Chinese under the title 'Sūtra of the Wise and the Fool' (Lévi 1925). Similar connections between the MAV and Avadāna literature is evident from the title of the work itself.

35 in plate volume). The text is rather fragmentary and is difficult to understand. There is no complete translation available.

As this article will show though, a careful comparison between the text of A 226 and a passage belonging to the 'hell chapters' (ch. 20–25) of the Uyghur MNB sheds a new light on its contents.[6] The Uyghur passage in question, located in MNB chapter 24, shows several exact correspondences with the Tocharian text. Both texts describe a fantastic hellish torment. As strange as it is, the beings who endure it have their bodies metamorphosed in daily life objects (especially vessels and jewels) and immersed in the corrosive waters of an infernal river, the 'Caustic Lye Stream' (Skt. *kṣārodakā nadī*).[7] In fact, since MNB 'hell chapters' abound with scary metamorphoses of this kind and since the MNB is translated from Tocharian A, we expect such hellish descriptions to be found in Tocharian A texts. Some of them are indeed attested in various fragments belonging to the MSN.[8]

What is more surprising is to find them in the MAV too. This discovery confirms the existence of very close connections between the MSN and the MAV, as recently shown by Huard (2020: 8–13) and Pinault (2020a). The interrelations between the Uyghur MNB and the Tocharian MSN have been explored since the beginning of tocharology (Müller & Sieg 1916) and have been further clarified after the discovery of new

6 Within non-Tocharian Maitreya literature, there is nothing comparable to MNB 'hell chapters'. For a general presentation of these chapters, see Laut (2013) and Geng, Klimkeit & Laut (1998: 3–20). For a classification of the sins described in MNB 'hell chapters' and the corresponding punishment, see Laut (2000). On chapter 24 in particular, see Laut (1996) and Laut (2002).

7 I borrow the translation 'Caustic Lye Stream' from Zieme (2021), who discusses the few Uyghur sources related to this theme (including MNB 24). I thank G.-J. Pinault for bringing this paper to my attention. On this infernal river, see also Van Put (2015: 193–194, s.v. 'Caustic River').

8 In contrast to the relative abundance of Uyghur fragments, only a dozen Tocharian fragments of the MSN belonging to 'hell chapters' (ch. 20–25) are extant (Pinault 1999: 204). Recently, new fragments have been identified as belonging to MSN 20 (Itkin & Kuritsyna 2017), MSN 23, and MSN 25 (Itkin, Kuritsyna & Malyshev 2017).

manuscripts in both languages through several publications cowritten by tocharologists and turcologists.[9] On the other hand, the MAV somewhat stayed in the shadow of these two monumental works. By drawing more attention on the MAV and on its fascinating content, the present article also aims to contribute to a better understanding of the place and role of this poem in the evolution of Maitreya literature and related Buddhist ideas.

The existence of the parallel discussed in this article tends to prove that MSN 'hell chapters' were not created *ex nihilo*, but that they result from the readaptation of older textual material.[10] More generally, and to anticipate an important conclusion that ought to be confirmed by the philological analysis of other parallels, the existence inside the MNB of Uyghur passages parallel to the MAV shows either that some material from the MAV was included into the Tocharian MSN,[11] from which the MNB was quite faithfully translated into Uyghur probably around the 9th century CE (Pinault 1999: 190), or that the MSN and the MAV borrowed from a common (Sanskrit?) source. The first hypothesis — which I believe is the correct one — has far-reaching consequences, for it implies that the MSN was composed not only from Indian sources, as the MNB colophons claim,[12] but also from Tocharian sources.

The present article is divided into three parts. In order to situate the texts in the broader framework of Buddhist literature and to better appreciate their mutual affinities, the first part discusses their Buddhist content (2.1 and 2.2). The correspondences between the texts are given in the synoptic table (2.3). In the second part, the Uyghur text is given in transcription with a translation reproduced from Geng, Klimkeit &

9 See for example Geng, Laut & Pinault (2004a); Geng, Laut & Pinault (2004b); Peyrot & Semet (2016).

10 Cf. the literary process referred to by Pinault as 'collage': 'Inserting pieces of different texts of Sanskrit origin in the main text of the story.' (Pinault 2020a).

11 Since the linguistic features of the MAV are especially archaic (Itkin 2002), which is not the case of the MSN, it is very likely that the composition of the former pre-dates that of the latter (see 3.2).

12 On this question, see recently Mair (2013: 109–111).

Laut (1998; 3.1). The Tocharian text is given in a revised transliteration, with a transcription including new restorations, and a complete translation (3.2). The third part consists of a philological commentary of stanzas 80–87 of the Tocharian text (4).

2 Content

2.1 Content of MNB 24

The following paragraphs provide a discussion of the main Buddhist motifs developed in MNB 24 and aim to clarify issues related to its hellish cosmological background.

2.1.1 *A demonstration of how karma works*

As the other 'hell chapters', MNB 24 relates an encounter with hellish beings, a popular theme often associated in Avadāna literature with the figure of Maudgalyāyana ~ Mulian 目連 (see Teiser 1988: 124–130). As Rotman has shown for the *Divyāvadāna*, Avadāna hell and ghost stories always imply some kind of visual experience, but such a visual experience has to be explained by words in order for the viewer to grasp its significance and to develop *śraddhā* ('faith') (Rotman 2009: 53–59). In the *Koṭikarṇāvadāna* for example, Koṭikarṇa sees iron cities full of hungry ghosts (*pretas*), but he still needs someone to explain him what he is seeing. In this context, the explanation of visions by a special character (often Maudgalyāyana) is referred to by the Sanskrit verb *darśayati*, lit. 'he causes to see', hence 'he proves, he demonstrates, he explains' (Rotman 2009: 55). This very idea is expressed in the title of MNB 24 by the Uyghur term *körgitmäk*,[13] which is the transposition of TA *nidarśaṃ*, itself borrowed from Skt. *nidarśana-* 'demonstration' (Pinault 1999: 204). In the

13 The Uyghur word *körgitmäk* is the verbal noun based on the causative verb *körgit-* ~ *körkit-* 'show, display' (HWAU: 409a, s.v. *körgit-*), ultimately from the root *kör-* 'see' (for the formation, see Erdal 1991: 778).

titles of MNB 'hell chapters', the terms *körgitmäk* (~ Skt. *nidarśana-*) or *körmäk* (~ Skt. *darśana-*) are used indifferently, referring to the 'demonstration' by Maitreya to his followers of the system of *karma* affecting beings who behaved badly in a former life.[14] In MNB 24, Maitreya exhibits the infernal beings to his followers by splitting the earth open with his hand.[15] This exhibition is accompanied by a sermon (Uygh. *y(a)rlıg*).

2.1.2 *The problem of 'little hells'*

The mention of 'little hell beings' (Uygh. *kičig tamuluglar*) in the title of MNB 24 raises interesting issues concerning the cosmological background of our texts. As a glance on the titles of 'hell chapters' reveals, most of them – ch. 24 included – are concerned with *kičig tamular* 'little hells' (ch. 20–24), as opposed to *ulug tamular* 'great hells' (addressed in ch. 25). Such an importance given to 'little hells' in the MSN / MNB is intriguing. As is well known, the traditional hell system as described in the third chapter, the *Lokanirdeśa*, of the *Abhidharmakośabhāṣya*, a text belonging

14 The titles of the 'hell chapters' – quoted hereafter from Laut (1986: 41, note 2, 3, 4, and 42, note 1; 1996: 128, note 35, and 130) and Tekin (1980: 188) – are: ch. 20 *egil karte kišilär [körklüg] kičig tamulug ätözläri[n körgit]mäk* '[Das Zeigen] der Körper von Wesen in den Kleinhöllen, die eine Laien$_2$-[Gestalt] haben' (transl. Geng, Klimkeit & Laut 1998: 85); ch. 21 … *[-la]rıg körgitm[äk]* (the rest is lost), cf. MSN 21 (the only title of the 'hell chapters' preserved in Tocharian): *gr̥hast(h)apravrajitanirayanidarśaṃ* 'the showing of hells for householders and religious mendicants' (transl. Carling 2009: 189b, s.v. *gr̥hastapravrajitanirayanidarśaṃ*); ch. 22 *toyın š(a)mnanč körklüg kičig tamuluglarıg körmäk* 'Das Sehen der Kleinhöllen-Wesen in Mönchs- und Nonnengestalt' (transl. Geng, Klimkeit & Laut, 1998: 95); ch. 23 *[adrok] adrok körklüg kičig tamuluglarıg körmäk* 'Das Sehen von Kleinhöllen-Wesen in verschiedenster Gestalt' (transl. Geng, Klimkeit & Laut 1998: 102); ch. 24 *[az bili]g kököüzlü[g kičig tamulugl]arıg körgitmäk* 'Das Zeigen von [Kleinhöllenwe]sen mit [Gier$_2$]-Āśaya' (transl. Geng, Klimkeit & Laut 1998: 112); ch. 25 *ulug tamuluglarıg körgit[mäk]* 'Das Zeig[en] von Großhöllen-Wesen' (transl. Geng, Klimkeit & Laut 1998: 126).

15 The same pattern can be observed in the story surrounding the *parinirvāṇa* of Kāśyapa, as related by Xuanzang's (quoted by Huard 2020: 14).

to the Sarvāstivāda school, distinguishes between three main categories of hells, all located under the Jambudvīpa continent:[16] 1. the eight 'great hells' or 'hot hells' (Skt. *mahānarakāḥ* or *uṣṇanarakāḥ*); 2. the eight 'cold hells' (Skt. *śītanarakāḥ*); 3. the infernal 'annexes' or 'supplementary hells' (Skt. *utsadāḥ* or *utsedhāḥ*, Pa. *ussadā*). The *Abhidharmakośabhāṣya* lists four infernal 'annexes': 1. Kukūla 'Pit of Live Embers'; 2. Kuṇapa 'Swamp of Filth'; 3. Kṣuramārga 'Road of Razor Blades', Asipattravana 'Forest with Leaves Like Swords', Ayaḥśālmalīvana 'Forest of Iron Spikes' (these three form a single annex); 4. Kṣārodakā nadī 'Caustic Lye Stream'. These four infernal places are located at each door of each 'great hell', amounting to sixteen (4 × 4) 'annexes' for each 'great hell', i.e., 128 'annexes' (8 × 16).[17]

In the *Abhidharmakośabhāṣya* (ad AK 3.59a–c), *utsada*s are conceived as obligatory places for the sinners to pass through after their stay in one of the eight 'great hells' (see La Vallée Poussin 1926: 152). Since in the MNB sinners are often said to be reborn in *kičig tamular* after being reborn in *ulug tamular*, Laut identifies *kičig tamular* as the 'sub-hells' (Germ. 'Nebenhöllen') of the eight 'great hells', i.e., *utsada*s (Laut 2013: 26, see also Geng, Klimkeit & Laut 1998: 13–14). Furthermore, as the authors of *Eine buddhistische Apokalypse* note in their translation of MNB 24, the 'Caustic Lye Stream' (Uygh. *čad(ı)r ügüz*) in which beings are immersed corresponds to Kṣārodakā nadī, the fourth *utsada* according to the *Abhidharmakośabhāṣya* (Geng, Klimkeit & Laut 1998: 109).

However, the equation between *kičig tamular* and *utsada*s conceived as places adjacent to the eight 'great hells' is not straightforward. Especially, the fact that *kičig tamular* (ch. 20–24) are described at length before *ulug tamular* (ch. 25) is to be explained, since in most sources on hells the

16 For a general presentation of hells in ancient Buddhism, see Tiefenauer (2018: 86–146). Van Put (2007) distinguishes three stages in the development of Buddhist hells: 1. the early Āgama *sūtra*s, 2. the early cosmologies (ca. 100 BCE–200 CE), 3. the later cosmologies (ca. 200 CE–500 CE). The *Abhidharmakośabhāṣya* corresponds to the third stage.

17 On *utsada*s, see Van Put (2015: 52–55 and 243, s.v. *Utsada*). The *Saddharmasmṛtyupasthānasūtra* attributes a specific name to each of the 128 infernal annexes (see Demoto 2009).

'annexes' are logically described *after* the 'great hells'. Moreover, far from playing any structuring role in 'hell chapters' 20–24, the *utsadas* other than the Kṣārodakā nadī are neither mentioned nor alluded to, nor are found the narrative elements traditionally associated with them. Therefore, the cosmological background of 'hell chapters' 20–24 only superficially fits in the traditional threefold division between 'great hells', 'cold hells', and 'annexes'.

So, if not *utsadas stricto sensu*, what kind of hells are described in MNB 'hell chapters' 20–24? On the one hand, Uygh. *ulug tamular* must translate TA *śāwaṃ ñareyntu* 'great hells' (attested in A 309 b3), obviously referring to the eight 'great hells' (Skt. *mahānarakāḥ*). But crucially, on the other hand, Uygh. *kičig tamular* does not seem to be the literal translation of a Tocharian expression meaning 'little hells', hypothetically TA *mkältont ñareyntu*. This is in line with the fact that in Sanskrit and Pali sources on hells, no such category as 'little hells' or 'minor hells' exists *per se*. In fact, Uygh. *kičig tamular* is a gloss of the Tocharian A ~ Sanskrit term referring to such hells in the MSN, i.e., TA *prattikañare* ~ Skt. *pratyekanaraka-* (Laut 2003: 20).[18] This term, which literally means 'individual hell', was independently borrowed into Uyghur as *pratikañ(a)re* (← TA) or *pratikanarak* (← Skt.), so that the Uyghur translator of the MSN had the choice between using the loanword or its gloss, or even both in a binomial and bilingual fixed phrase.[19] In Tocharian A, the word *prattikañare* is mostly found in the MSN; no Tocharian B match is known.

The Sanskrit compound *pratyekanaraka-* (from Skt. *pratyeka-* 'each single one' and *naraka-* 'hell') mainly occurs in Sanskrit Avadāna and Abhidharma literature. There is no clear equivalent in the Pali canon.

18 According to Laut, this is a case of 'Lehnübertragung', i.e., 'die Verbindung einer Teilübersetzung des Fremdwortes unter Beibehaltung eines Fremdbestandteils' (Laut 2003: 14). Note that the rendering of TA *prattika°* (cf. Skt. *pratyeka-* 'each single one' (MW: 664b, s.v. *pratyeka*) by Uygh. *kičig* 'little' may be due to the following analogy: *śāwaṃ ñareyntu* : *prattika-ñareyntu* :: *ulug tamular* : X, where X = *kičig tamular*.

19 Uygh. *pratikanarak* (cf. Skt. *pratyekanaraka-*), combined with *kičig tamu*, forms the binomial fixed phrase *pratikanarak kičig tamu* (HWAU: 560b, s.v. *pratikanarak*). For an example, see below Uygh. 85–86.

The notion has received little attention from scholars working on Buddhist ancient sources. In her book on Buddhist hells, Van Put does not mention *pratyekanarakas* (Van Put 2015). Rotman however, commenting on the use of Skt. *pratyekanarakeṣu* in the *Saṃgharakṣitāvadāna*, writes: 'The meaning of this expression is unclear. In the *Divyāvadāna*, the term seems to mean 'personal hell' – a hell realm of particular design for particular individuals. According to Edgerton's extensive note (BHSD), this hell realm 'seems clearly to be a place of less severe punishment than a (*mahā*-, or regular) [hell realm].' The *Mahāvyutpatti* (4944) explains this as *nyi tshe ba'i*, perhaps in the sense of 'ephemeral'.' (Rotman 2017: 381–382, note 380).

In the passages from the *Saṃgharakṣitāvadāna* (Divy, ch. 23 and 25) where it occurs, Skt. *pratyekanaraka*- refers to undetermined hells intended for evil monks. These hells are described as isolated monasteries located on the fringes of the human world, without connection with the traditional cosmology of the subterranean 'great hells' and their 'annexes'.[20] Although not referred to as such in the Sanskrit text, the iron cities full of hungry ghosts of the *Koṭikarṇāvadāna* (Divy, ch. 1), also located on the surface of the earth, are explicitly regarded as *pratyekanarakas* in a 13th century Tibetan commentary entitled *Exposition of Abhidharmakośa Arranged in Chapters and Called 'Ornament of Abhidharma'* (Berounský 2012: 29–32 and 41). Similarly, the isolated iron city inhabited by a lonely man tormented by a blazing iron wheel in the *Maitrakanyakāvadāna* (Divy, ch. 38) is referred to as a *pratyekanaraka* in the *Karmavibhaṅga* (Lévi 1932: 53 [text], 125 [transl.]). Comparable hells are also described in the *Dvāviṃśatyavadānakathā* (ch. 10).

Moreover, a consistent scholastic corresponding definition of *pratyekanarakas* is attested in Sanskrit Abhidharma literature. The passage in question is from the *Abhidharmakośabhāṣya* (ad AK 3.59). It is quoted by Tiefenauer in his book on Indian hells (Tiefenauer 2018: 140). However,

20 See the translation of the whole scene in Rotman (2017: 143–155). The *Saṃgharakṣitāvadāna* was popular among Tocharians. It is quoted in A 371 a3 (*saṅgharakṣite avatāṃ*), and a version of it is extant in Tocharian B (see Ogihara 2016).

because the text is singularly corrupt, Tiefenauer fails to see that the passage refers to *pratyekanarakas* as a distinct, fourth category of hells (AKB 165,4–7):[21]

> *itīme ṣoḍaśa narakāḥ sarve* {emend to *sarva°*} *sattvakarmādhipatya-nirvṛttāḥ* | *pratyekaṃ narakās* {emend to *pratyekanarakās*} *tu svaiḥ svaiḥ karmabhir abhinirvṛttāḥ* | *bahūnāṃ sattvānāṃ dvayor ekasya vā* | *teṣām anekaprakalpo bhedaḥ sthānaṃ cāniyataṃ nadīparvatamaru-pradeśeṣv anyeṣu vā 'dhaś ca bhāvāt*
>
> 'That being said, these sixteen hells [scil. the eight 'hot hells' plus the eight 'cold hells'] develop from the dominance (*ādhipatya*)[22] of the deeds committed by all the beings [collectively]. On the other hand, *pratyekanarakas* result from each individual deed (*svaiḥ svaiḥ karma-bhir*), those of numerous beings, two beings, or one being. Their variety is adapted to many, and their location is not determined, because they are found in places like rivers, mountains, deserts, or elsewhere, and below.' (my transl.).

Since the main characteristic of the numerous hells called *prattika-ñareyntu* described in MSN 20–24 is that they are particular to the individual faults of the sinners, as shown in detail by Laut (2000), and since

21 In the passage in question, *pratyekaṃ narakās* as per Pradhan (AKB 165,5) should be emendated to *pratyekanarakās* (as per Mimaki 2000: 98). Therefore, the expression is not to be understood as 'each [great] hell', pace Tiefenauer, but as 'individual hells'. Also, *sarve* should be corrected to *sarva°* (belonging to the following compound) in order to match the Chinese version (translated in La Vallée Poussin 1926: 155).

22 The word *ādhipatya* 'dominance' is connected to the difference made by Sarvāstivādins between the result of collective *karma* (Skt. *adhipatiphala-* 'fruit of dominance') and the result of personal *karma* (Skt. *vipākaphala-* 'retribution fruit') (see Dhammajoti 2015: 205–208). The AKB associates *pratyekanarakas* with the latter. One may compare *Mahāvastu*, chapter 2 (Mvu I 16,10–13 and passim): *evaṃ khalu punaḥ ādhipateyamātram etaṃ tatropapatteḥ* | *tatropapannā anyeṣāṃ pi pāpakānām akuśalānāṃ karmāṇāṃ vipākaṃ pratyanubhavanti* 'But this is no more than the principal cause of rebirth in this hell [scil. Saṃjīva]. Those reborn here reap the fruit of still other wicked and sinful deeds.' (transl. Jones 1949: 14).

their location is not specified, the AKB definition of *pratyekanarakas* would apply to them without difficulty. As we shall see, the hell described in the passage under study of MAV 22 also displays all the characteristics of *pratyekanarakas*.

2.1.3 *The importance of having a pure mind*

The expression *az bilig köküzlüg* 'mit Gier$_2$-Āśaya' (transl. Laut) in the title of MNB 24 gives the main reason for the rebirth of beings in the Caustic Lye Stream. In this chapter, the noun *köküz* is explicitly associated with the notion referred to in Uyghur by the technical term *ašay* '[mental] disposition', a loan (probably via Tocharian) from Skt. *āśaya-*.[23] The concept of *āśaya* (Uygh. *ašay*) is developed in MNB 24 through scholastic expositions uttered by Maitreya to his followers (see sections *b* and *s* in the synoptic table). Interestingly, TA *āśai* '[mental] disposition' (< Skt. *āśaya-*) is exclusively found in the MSN and in the MAV.[24] Though it is not attested in fragment A 226, it especially occurs in a fragment belonging to MAV 23, dealing with rebirth in the eight 'great hells'.[25]

In MNB 24, the term *āśaya* is deeply intertwined with the well-known concept of *kuśalamūlas* ('roots of goodness') according to Vaibhāṣikas' theories. According to a Vaibhāṣika threefold typology, the second type of *kuśalamūlas* is called *mokṣabhāgīyakuśalamūlas* 'roots of goodness associated with liberation'. This term is matched by TA *tsälpāluneyac kuśalamūläntu* (A 320 b8, see also A 299 a2).[26] In an article dealing with Buddhist soteriology according to the *Abhidharmamahāvibhāṣā*,

23 Ch. 24, folio 5 recto, lines 20 ff. (MaitrSängim, Kat.-Nr. 159 ~ Taf. 80 + 59) (Laut 1986: 204): *[ka]ltı köŋüli köküzi artamıš k(ä)rgäks(i)z* [21] *[y]avaz ašayl(ı)g tınlıglar ärsär* '(Dies ist der Fall), wenn es Lebewesen mit mißratenem Herzen$_2$, (d.h.) mit nutzlosem, schlechten Āśaya sind.' (transl. Geng, Klimkeit & Laut 1998: 108).

24 The translation 'asylum, retreat' in Carling (2009: 55a, s.v. *āśai*) is incorrect.

25 Fragment A 234, line a4. According to Sieg & Siegling (1921: 117), A 234 belongs to folio 127, which corresponds to MAV 23.

26 On *mokṣabhāgīyakuśalamūlas*, see Dhammajoti (2015: 494–496): 'Those who have not planted the *kuśala-mūla*-s of *mokṣa-bhāgīya* are said to be 'stream-

a massive treatise on Abhidharma belonging to the Vaibhāṣika school, Buswell analyses the factors that prevent beings from attaining liberation. He summarises the doctrine of the *Abhidharmamahāvibhāṣā* concerning *mokṣabhāgīyakuśalamūlas* as follows: '[Wholesome roots associated with liberation] can be planted by acts that are based on nongreed [Skt. *alobha-*], nonhatred [Skt. *adveṣa-*], and nondelusion [Skt. *amoha-*], such as giving, keeping precepts, or learning the dharma; however, the number and type of wholesome actions necessary to ensure the implantation of this root vary and depend on the mentality (*āśaya*, *yìlè* [意樂]) of the individual.' (Buswell 1992: 110). Accordingly, in MNB 24, the fundamental factor causing 'wholesome roots' to be eradicated, thus triggering rebirth in the Caustic Lye Stream, is 'greed', the opposite of *alobha-*.

The Uyghur expression *az bilig* modifying *köküzlüg* in the title corresponds to Skt. *tṛṣṇā-* (~ *lobha-*) 'thirst, greed' (Röhrborn 2017: 103, s.v. *az*). MNB 24 insists on the fact that the *āśaya* of beings must be purified in order for them to be freed from the Caustic Lye Stream. Purification of mind is explicitly associated with 'caustic lye' (Skt. *kṣārodaka-*) in the Mahāyānic 'allegory of the unpurified Vaiḍūrya stone', as described in the *Dhāraṇīśvararājasūtra*, quoted in the *Ratnagotravibhāga*. The beginning of the allegory runs as follows:

> 'O noble youth, take for instance a skilful jewel-maker who knows quite well how to purify precious stones. Having taken out an unpurified precious stone from the mine, and <u>having washed it with acid salt water</u> [*tīkṣeṇa khārodakena*], he then polishes it by rubbing with blackhair cloth. […]' (transl. Takasaki 1966: 150–151).

The text goes on comparing living beings to unpurified precious stones. Since in our texts, beings are reborn in the Caustic Lye Stream with bodies in the shape of jewels, the same metaphor is probably at work.[27]

accordants (*anu-srota*); those who have done so, stream-discordants (*pratisrota*). 'Stream' here refers to *saṃsāra*.' (Dhammajoti 2015: 495).

27 On the Caustic Lye Stream, see also below under 4.2.1.

2.2 Content of MAV 22

Since the text of the end of MAV 22 largely overlaps with that of MNB 24 (see the synoptic table below), most of the Buddhist motifs discussed above are common to both chapters. In the following, I will focus on the title of MAV 22, i.e., *āgārikanarakopapatti*.

In Sanskrit Buddhist literature, the compound *narakopapatti-* usually means 'rebirth in hell' or 'rebirth among hell beings', by contrast to the other four kinds of destinies (Skt. *gati-*): *tiryagupapatti-* 'rebirth among animals', *pretopapatti-* 'rebirth among hungry ghosts', *manuṣyopapatti-* 'rebirth among human beings', *devopapatti-* 'rebirth among gods'. The compound *āgārikanarakopapatti-* is likely to refer to some hell specifically intended for *āgārika*s: 'rebirth in the hell for *āgārikas*'. The name of this hell, unknown in Sanskrit sources, points to an 'individual hell' (Skt. *pratyekanaraka-*).

The Sanskrit term *āgārika-* (m.), based on *āgāra-* (n.) 'house', means 'someone who lives at home, i.e., who stays in the worldly life' (SWTF I: 230a, s.v. *āgārika*). In the context of MAV 22, it probably denotes a spiritual status rather than a merely socio-economical one. Since monks share the same fate in hell as householders in MAV 22 (see the translation of the Tocharian text under 3.2.4), the hell in question is by no means intended for householders exclusively. If the title of MAV 22 is in adequation with its content, this fact suggests that the meaning of the term *āgārika-* in our context is broad enough to apply to certain kinds of bad or false monks, obviously *behaving like* householders. This theme is associated with the decline of the Dharma in Mahāyāna literature (Nattier 1991: 124–125). Such false monks are described in the TB *Udānālaṅkāra* as follows:

THT 31 b5–6

> *ṣeṃ ywārc ostmeṃ ltweṣ pudñäkteś (…) tärkoṣ ārte alloṅkna cmela triwoṣ attsaik kattākeṃmp// eṣe* **:** *riṃne k$_u$ṣaiṃne ostwane ṣek yeyeṃ ceṃ lkatsi*[28]

28 Misspelling for *lkātsi*.

> 'They were [only] halfway gone from the house to the Buddha … indifferent to the other births, mingling only with householders, they were always going to cities, villages [and] houses in order to see those [scil. the householders]' (transl. after Stumpf 1971: 45).

The meaning of *āgārika-* can also be compared to that of the TB adjective *ostaññe*. Although a relational adjective based on *ost* 'house', this word may refer to ascetics:

PK AS 18A b2–3

> *tum(eṃ) cai ostaññi nāksante-ne skarāre-ne kampāl mā päst kalatar matsisa kauc laṅkäm-cä*
> 'Thereupon these *ostaññi* [= the Ājīvikas] blamed him [and] they threatened him: '[If] you don't bring back the cloak, we will hang you up by your hair!' (transl. Pinault in CEToM).[29]

In this context, *ostaññi* cannot refer to 'householders' in a restrictive sense.[30] Rather, it seems to be a pejorative term referring to Ājīvikas' householder-like behaviour, as they try to get back some expensive cloth. Thus, *ostaññi* may be translated as 'house-oriented, house-minded individuals, materialists'. Similarly, in the compound *āgārikanarakopapatti-*, the word *āgārika-* would mean 'a house-oriented, worldly-minded person'.

A Mahāyānic *sūtra*, the *Ratnarāśisūtra*, quoted in the *Śikṣāsamuccaya* of Śāntideva, mentions a *pratyekanaraka* whose name is formed on the same model as *āgārika-naraka-*, i.e., *śramaṇa-varṇa-pratirūpaka-(naraka-)* '(hell) for those who counterfeit the appearance (lit. 'colour') of monks' (ŚS 76,7–9):

> *tatra kāśyapa pratyekanarake śramaṇarūpapratirūpeṇa tāḥ kāraṇāḥ kāryante ādīptacailā ādīptaśīrṣā ādīptapātrā ādīptāsanā ādīptaśayanāḥ | yaḥ kaścit tatra teṣām upabhogaparibhogaḥ, sa sarva*

29 The translation of *ostaññe* by 'housemate' in CEToM – 'commensaux' according to Pinault (2008: 76) – is not very cogent in the context.

30 The householders are referred to in the same text as *kattāki*, cf. PK AS 18A a4.

> *ādīptaḥ saṃprajvalita ekajvālībhūtaḥ | tatra taiḥ śramaṇavarṇarūpeṇa duḥkhāṃ vedanām anubhavantīti*
> 'Kāśyapa, those who counterfeit the appearance of religious wanderers undergo the following torments in that individual hell: burning clothes, burning heads, burning begging-bowls, burning seats, and burning beds. Whatever luxuries and comforts they have there are burning, blazing, one single flame. There, those counterfeit religious wanderers experience painful sensations.' (transl. Goodman 2016: 132, slightly modified).

The title of MAV 22 could thus be translated: 'rebirth in the hell for worldly-minded ones'.

2.3 Synoptic table

The synoptic table below gives the textual correspondences between the Tocharian fragment A 226 and the Uyghur fragments of MNB 24. In order to highlight its progression and structure, the text is divided into sections which are assigned a letter from *a* to *u*, with a summary of the main events. In the table the narrative situation is specified in the right column by a capital letter: narrative passage = N, direct speech uttered by Maitreya = M, direct speech uttered by Maitreya's followers = F. Four types of interrelations between the Tocharian and Uyghur texts can be observed: 1. (underlined) structural correspondences (sometimes with minor differences): sections *h*, *k*, *l*, *o*; 2. (in italic script) displaced correspondences: sections *j* ~ *e*, *n* ~ *t*; 3. interpolations: sections *i*, *q*, *r*, *s*; 4. suppressions: sections *g*, *m*. These kinds of interrelations point to a rearrangement of the MAV stanzas by 'collage'. This is perhaps what lies behind the famous use in MNB colophons of the Uyghur term *yaratmıš* 'composed', referring to the *creation* (as opposed to the *translation*) of the Tocharian MSN.

There are no correspondences in the Tocharian MAV for sections a–f of the Uyghur MSN.

	Mss	Stanza	MAV 22 (Toch. A) Summary	
g	A226 a1	80	(Continued?) Relative clause describing infernal beings (fragmentary).	M
h	A226 a1–2	81	Identification of some of the infernal beings as monks in a previous life and explanation of the sins committed by them.	M
i	–	–	–	M

	Mss/folio	Cont.	MSN 24 (Uygh.) Summary	
a	Säng. 1r-v Säng. 4r-v		Beginning of the chapter. The location of the scene is near Mount Kukkuṭapāda. (Important lacuna.) With a good *āśaya*, beings will be able to see Maitreya.	N
b	Säng. 5r-v Säng. 6r-v Murt. 325v		Didactic exposition in the form of a scholastic dialogue between Maitreya and his followers about the acts 'committed' (Skt. *kr̥ta-*) and 'accumulated' (Skt. *upacita-*). The importance of *āśaya*.	M + F
c	Säng. 8r01–04	01–04	Maitreya's followers express the wish to see the infernal beings.	F
d	Säng. 8r04–12	04–12	Maitreya splits the earth open with his hand. The 'Caustic Lye Stream' (*kṣārodakā nadī*) appears to his followers.	N
e	Säng. 8r12–16 Säng. 8v01–03 Murt. 327r01–11	12–36	*Description (with lacuna of 15 lines) of the fantastic bodies of the beings immersed in the Caustic Lye Stream and of their sufferings (cf. j).*	N
f	Murt. 327r12–26	37–51	Shocked reaction of Maitreya's followers. They ask Maitreya to identify the sinners and to explain the sins committed by them.	F
g	–	–	–	–
h	Murt. 327r28 Murt. 327v01–06	53–59	Identification of some of the infernal beings as monks in a previous life and explanation of the sins committed by them.	M
i	Murt. 327v06–16	59–69	The monks have developed a greedy mind, so that they have forgotten that they were monks.	M

	Mss	Stanza	MAV 22 (Toch. A) Summary	
j	A226 a3–5	82–83	*Description of the fantastic bodies belonging to other infernal beings immersed in the Caustic Lye Stream (cf. e).*	M
k	A226 a5–6	84	Identification of the other infernal beings as householders in a previous life and explanation of the sins committed by them.	M
l	A226 a6–7	85ab	Conclusive sentence on the rebirth in hell of householders.	M
m	A226 a7	85cd	Exhortation addressed to householders and monks in general (fragmentary).	M
n	A226 b1–2	86	*Beatification of some of Maitreya's followers in the future tense: the monks (?) obtain the dignity of Arhat (fragmentary) (cf. t).*	N
o	A226 b2–3	87	Conversion of some of Maitreya's followers in the future tense: they become monks (fragmentary).	N
p	A226 b4		End of chapter 22 (colophon).	N

There are no correspondences in the Tocharian MAV for sections q–s of the Uyghur MSN.

			MSN 24 (Uygh.)	
	Mss/folio	Cont.	Summary	
j	–	–	–	–
k	Murt. 327v16–29 Murt. 328r01–02	69–84	Identification of the other infernal beings as householders in a previous life and explanation of the sins committed by them.	M
l	Murt. 328r02–05	84–87	Conclusive sentence on the rebirth in hell of householders.	M
m	–	–	–	–
n	–	–	–	–
o	Murt. 328r05–12	87–94	Conversion of some of Maitreya's followers in the present tense: they become monks.	N
p	–	–	–	–
q	Murt. 328r12–17	94–99	End of the description of the infernal beings immersed in the Caustic Lye Stream.	N
r	Murt. 328r17–29 Murt. 328v01		Question by Maitreya's followers about why these infernal beings are unable to get themselves out of the Caustic Lye Stream.	F
s	Murt. 328v01–23 Säng. LastFr01–16 Hami LastF01–12		The cause of having a bad *āśaya* is greed.	M

	Mss/folio	Cont.	MSN 24 (Uygh.) Summary	
t	Hami LastF12–16		*Beatification of some of Maitreya's followers in the present tense: the monks obtain the dignity of Arhat (fragmentary) (cf. n).*	N
u	Hami LastF16 Säng. Last-Fv12–17		End of chapter 24 (colophon).	

There are no correspondences in the Tocharian MAV for sections t–u of the Uyghur MSN.

3 Texts

3.1 The Uyghur text

In the following, the Uyghur passage from MNB 24 is reproduced starting with the wish expressed by Maitreya's followers to see the infernal beings (section *c* in the synoptic table) up to the end of the description of the infernal beings immersed in the Caustic Lye Stream (section *q* in the synoptic table).[31]

The text of the scene combines seven fragments from three different leaves, corresponding to the following numbers in Laut and Wilkens' catalogue: Kat.-Nr. 160 (Mainz 893 + Mainz 1208 + Mainz 1035), Kat.-Nr. 234 (= U 3716 + U 1965), and Kat.-Nr. 235 (= U 3724 + U 1153). The three leaves belong to two different manuscripts: Kat.-Nr. 160 belongs to Sängim manuscript (ch. 24, folio 8), whereas Kat.-Nr. 234 and Kat.-

31 The attribution of the quoted fragments to MNB 24 and their ordering is due to Geng, Klimkeit & Laut (1998: 109–111) and Laut & Wilkens (2017). The following synthesis relies upon these scholars.

Nr. 235 belong to Murtuk manuscript (folios 327 and 328).[32] Kat.-Nr. 160, Kat.-Nr. 235, and part of Kat.-Nr. 234 have been edited by Tekin as Taf. 105, Taf. 226, and Taf. 218 (Tekin 1980: 229–230, 230–231, and 262–263, respectively).

	Manuscript	Kat.-Nr.	Fragments	Folio-Nr.	Tafel-Nr.
1	Sängim	160	Mainz 893 + Mainz 1208 + Mainz 1035	8	105 (= Mainz 893)
2	Murtuk	234	U 3716 + U 1965	327	218 and Beih. II: 83–85
3	Murtuk	235	U 3724 + U 1153	*328	226

Concerning Kat.-Nr. 234, Taf. 218 facsimiles only a small piece (6 lines) of the fragment originally discovered, for which an old transcription by v. Le Coq is fortunately extant, reproduced in Beih. II (Laut 2002: 167, note 20). The reason for this discrepancy is that the original fragment suffered additional damages during the war (Beih. II: 79). However, although U 3716 (= Taf. 218) was long believed to be the only piece left from the original fragment, a second piece (U 1965) was rediscovered by Wilkens in 2002 (Laut & Wilkens 2017: 264, note 1642). The most complete source for the text of this fragment remains v. Gabain's reproduction of v. Le Coq's transcription (Beih. II: 83–85).[33] A similar problem applies to Kat.-Nr. 235 (see Zieme 2021: 218).

32 Laut has shown that there is no reason to make a differentiation between several Murtuk manuscripts (Laut 1986: 46–48). Note that unlike the Sängim manuscript, in the Murtuk manuscript the pagination ignores the chapter division, and the chapter number is not specified (Laut 2002: 167, note 16).

33 Unfortunately, since the dimensions of the original fragment are unknown, it is unclear whether the text at the end of the recto is directly linked to the beginning of the verso, and whether the end of the verso corresponds to the end of the leaf, hence the mention 'Ende der Seite?' with question mark in Beih. II (84–85).

The text of Murtuk manuscript overlaps with that of Sängim manuscript at folio 8 verso, end of line 03 of the latter (Uygh. *amarıları äränčü*), which corresponds to folio 327 recto, beginning of line 01 of the former (Uygh. idem).

3.1.1 *Transcription*

Ch. 24, folio 8 recto + verso, lines 01–03[34]

(MaitrSängim, Kat.-Nr. 160 ~ Taf. 105)
[transcription based on Tekin 1980: 229–230]

Recto

Pag. [tört otuzunč] ülüš säkiz p(a)t(a)r
01 ulug münin kadagların tägi[ng]äli [ama]rı- 01
02 lar[ı] inčä tep ötünürlär küsäyü täginü[r]- 02
03 biz ayagka tägimlig t(ä)ŋrim .. bäkiz 03
04 [täg]i[nü]r biz atı kötrülmiš t(ä)ŋrim .. anta 04
05 [ötrü t]ükäl bilgä maitre burhan [ ] 05
06 [ ]/ZWN ⊙ altun ö[ŋlüg] 06
07 el[ig]in k[raža] ⊙ tonın /// 07
08 RWP č(a)k(i)r lak[šanın] ⊙ yaratıglıg [ ] 08
09 elig üzä yerig bürtä [ ] 09
10 ötrü yer yarılıp ötrü tigi čo[gı] 10
11 birlä čadır suvlug ulug ügü[z bälgülüg] 11
12 bolur .. ötrü ol ügüz suvı k[ayınar čok-] 12
13 rayur .. kap kara tägzinč [ ] 13
14 oŋaru tägz[inür] 14
15 YW sekriyü //[ ] 15
16 sanınča P/[ ] 16
17 T/[ ]//[ ] 17

34 Lines 03–26 are parallel to Murtuk manuscript, folio 327 recto, 01–24.

18 TW[ ] 18
19 käyirkänči[g] 19
20 LRRR .. T'/[ ] 20
21 toyın š(a)m[nanč] 21
22 //[ ] 22

Verso

23 //SW L/[ ]/ ätözlüglär amarıları //// 01
24 kičig yumuz yančuk kur osuglug 02
25 (ä)tözlüglär .. (…) 03

Ch. 24, folio 327 recto + verso

(MaitrMurtuk, Kat.-Nr. 234 ~ Taf. 218)
[Beih. II: 83–85, see also Tekin (1980: 230–231)]

Recto

26 amarıları äränčü[35] bibru üm tärlik 01
27 ätözlüglär amarıları yarık ıšıık 02
28 osuglug ätözlüglär amarıları 03
29 yer-suv bag borluk yayl(a)g kıšl(a)g[36] 04
30 kalık ısırka ävbark osuglug-g 05
31 ätözlüglär ⊙ ol örtlüg 06
32 yalınl(ı)g čad(ı)r ⊙ ügüz ičintä 07
33 yokaru kudı yüzä altın tüpin 08
34 tägmädin ikidin sıŋar kıdıgıŋa 09
35 yakmadın bıčıšu osušu ärüyü sizä 10
36 ulıyu müŋräyü ämgäk ämgänürlär .. 11
37 anı körüp ol ärüš üküš yıgılmıš 12
38 tınlıglar sansarka korkınč köŋül 13

35 So to be read according to HWAU (67b, s.v. *artču* †), not *artču* (as per Geng, Klimkeit & Laut, 1998: 109, note 1).
36 *yıšl(a)g* as per Beih. II is to be read *kıšl(a)g* (HWAU: 901a, s.v. *yıšl(a)g* †).

39 öritirlär .. inčä tep teyürlär (..) yar- 14
40 sınčıg ok ärmiš artamıš köŋüllüg 15
41 bolmak .. kim tınlıglar ayıg yavlak 16
42 tsui erinčü kılıp bo muntag ačıg 17
43 ämgäkin kötürürlär .. ötrü toyın 18
44 kuvrag ayaların kavšurup t[ükäl] 19
45 bilgä maitre burhanka ayıtu ötünür- 20
46 lär .. ayagka tägimlig t(ä)ŋrim (..) bolar 21
47 čad(ı)r ügüz ičintä örtänü yala 22
48 kayına čokrayu ämgäk ämgändäčilär 23
49 kimlär ärki .. ymä nä ayıg kılınč 24
50 küčintä bo muntag körksüz ažun- 25
51 larda tugmıšlar ärki .. ötrü 26
52 bilgä maitre burhan [inčä tep] 27
53 y(a)rlıkayur (..) bolar ʾM/[ ] 28
(End of the folio?)

Verso

Pag. üč yüz yeti otuz
54 šazanınta amarıları šakimuni burhan 01
55 šazanınta toyın š(a)mnanč ärdilär (..) k(ä)ntü 02
56 tonları idiš tavarları üzä aŋsız 03
57 yapıšmıš bodulmıš[37] ärdilär (..) turkaru nom- 04
58 suz törösüzin ton pat(i)r tiläyür 05
59 //YQʾRLʾR ärdi (..) ⊙ bulmadok ädtavar(ı)g 06
60 ///WT avant- ⊙ ta azıp 07
61 ////g kataglan- ⊙ makın bulgalı 08
62 tiläyürlär ärdi (..) bulmıš idiš tavar- 09
63 ları üzä yapıšmak köŋülläri 10
64 küčlüg ärdi .. az almır köŋülläri 11
65 (a)rtok üčün toyın dentar bolmıš- 12
66 ların unıtı ıdıp üč ärdnig tapın- 13

37 *bodulup* as per Beih. II is to be read *bodulmıš* (Tekin 1980: 231, note 168).

67 madılar udumadılar .. todunčsuz kanınč- 14
68 sız köŋülin anta ölüp bo kičig 15
69 [tamu]da tugdılar .. kim ymä egil karte 16
70 /////g idiš tavarları osuglug 17
71 [ätöz]lüg üzütlär ärsär bolar 18
72 [ ] öŋrä ažunlarda ärklig elig- 19
73 [lär] bäglär buyruklar bayagutlar ärti- 20
74 [lär] (..) balık uluštakı tınl(ı)glar(ı)g ämgätip 21
75 törösüzin kuna tarta agı bar(ı)m 22
76 äd tavar yıgdılar kazgantılar ärdi (..) 23
77 k(ä)ntü tavarl(ı)g bay bädük bolmıšlarıŋa 24
78 törösüz kazganmıš ton ätük etig 25
79 yaratıgın ätözlärin etip yaratıp 26
80 [ ]/D/[ ]/ilärig tuṭ tolvı 27
81 [ ]L’R ärdi .. ädläri-i 28
82 [ ] bulguča sakınıp 29
(End of the folio?)

Ch. 24, folio 328 recto, lines 01–17

(MaitrMurtuk, Kat.-Nr. 235 ~ Taf. 226)
[transcription based on Tekin 1980: 262]

Recto

83 bir tanču aš täŋinčä buši berip 01
84 buyan ädgü kılınč kılmadılar .. ol-l 02
85 tıltagın anta ölüp amtı bo pr(a)ti- 03
86 kan(a)rak kičig tamuda tugmıš ärür- 04
87 lär .. ol y(a)rl(ı)g äšidip sansız tümän 05
88 ol kuvragdakı ⊙ tınl(ı)glar kop 06
89 ilig tutug ⊙ saranlanmak 07
90 yapıšmak köŋül- ⊙ lärin kodup 08
91 ıdalap tükäl bilgä maitre burhan 09
92 [no]mınta toyın bolurlar [alku niz-] 10

93 [va]nilark(a) arıtıp arhant kut[ıŋa] 11
94 [tägi]rlär .. ötrü ol tamuluglar [ür] 12
95 [keč ü]dün ol čad(ı)r ügüz [suvınta] 13
96 [kayınıp] bıšıp ämgäk ämgänip [bir ymä] 14
97 [tamulu]g tınl(ı)g tašgaru [ünmädin-n] 15
98 [ikilä] čad(ı)r ügüz [suvı birlä yerkä] 16
99 [kirdilär ..] (…) 17

3.1.2 *Translation*[38]

(01–02) … (Um die Höllenwesen[?] und) ihre großen Sünden$_2$ [schauen zu dürfen(?)], bitten [einige] von ihnen (d.h. der versammelten Gemeinde) folgendes: (02–03) 'Wir bringen ergebenst [unseren] Wunsch dar, unser verehrungswürdiger Gott! (03–04) Wir sind (jetzt) manifest,[39] unser Bhagavat!'

(04–12) Dann$_2$ … der vollkommen weise Buddha Maitreya … mit seiner gold[farbenen] Hand [zog(?)] sein k[āṣāya] Gewand an,[40] (und) als er mit seiner Hand, die mit dem Cakra[lakṣaṇa] geschmückt ist, die Erde berührt, da spaltet sich diese und mit Lärm und Krach [erscheint] der große Strom aus Ätzlauge (Skt. *kṣārodakā nadī*).

(12–17) Dann [brodeln$_2$] die Wasser dieses Flusses und ein pechschwarz Strudel … [wirbelt] rechtsherum[41] … springend … zahl[los viele(?)] … [Lacuna of about 15 lines] (23–31) … [Einige von ihnen] haben Körper wie …, einige von ihnen haben Körper wie kleine runde[42] Säcke

38 The translation reproduced here is from *Eine buddhistische Apokalypse* (Geng, Klimkeit & Laut 1998: 109–111).

39 Translation modified after the alternative reading *bäkiz* (line 03) proposed by the anonymous reviewer.

40 Translation modified after the alternative reading *altun ö[ŋlüg] el[ig]in k[raža] tonın ///*RWP (lines 06–08) proposed by the anonymous reviewer.

41 Translation modified after the alternative reading *kap kara tägzinč […] oŋaru tägz[inür]* (lines 13–14) proposed by the anonymous reviewer.

42 Translation modified after the alternative reading *yumuz* (line 24) proposed by the anonymous reviewer. On this word, see Clauson (1972: 940a, s.v. *yumuz*).

und Gürtel, einige von ihnen haben Körper wie eine Jacke,[43] wie eine Hose,[44] wie eine Unterhose[45] und wie ein *tärlik*,[46] einige von ihnen haben Körper wie Panzer und Helme, einige von ihnen haben Körper wie Erde, Gärten, Weingärten und Paläste$_2$ und Häuser für Sommer und Winter. (31–36) In jenem glühenden$_2$ Strom aus Ätzlauge erleiden sie Qualen, indem sie auf und ab schwimmen, ohne unten den Boden berühren oder sich den beiden Ufern nähern zu können, und indem sie sich wehklagend$_2$ gegenseitig zerschneiden$_2$ und (dabei) zerschmelzen$_2$.

(37–39) Als sie das sehen, erschrecken die zahlreich$_2$ versammelten Lebewesen vor dem Saṃsāra und sprechen folgendermaßen: (39–43) 'Wie widerwärtig ist es doch, einen mißratenen Āśaya zu haben, aufgrund dessen Lebewesen (solche) üblen$_2$ Sünden$_2$ begehen und solch bitteres Leid ertragen!' (43–46) Dann legt die Mönchsgemeinde ihre Handflächen zusammen und fragt den [vollkommen] weisen Buddha Maitreya ehrerbietig: (46–49) 'Unser verehrungswürdiger Gott, wer sind diese wohl, die in dem Strom aus Ätzlauge brennend$_2$ und brodelnd$_2$ Qualen erleiden? (49–51) Und kraft welcher Sünden sind sie wohl in derart häßlichen Existenzen wiedergeboren worden?'

(51–53) Darauf geruht der vollkommen weise Buddha Maitreya [folgendermaßen zu sprechen]: (53) '(Von) diesen lei[denden Wesen(?)] [End of the folio?] (54–55) (sind manche) in der Disziplin (des Buddha …) und manche von ihnen in der Disziplin des Buddha Śākyamuni Mönche und Nonnen gewesen. (55–59) Sie hingen$_2$ sehr an ihren Gewändern, ihrem Geschirr und an ihrer (sonstigen) Habe und ständig verlangten$_2$ sie gesetzwidrig[47] nach (neuer) Kleidung und Bettelschalen.

(59–62) Die nichterlangte Habe verfehlten sie durch die [ ] Ursache(?) und wünschten, sie durch [ ] Anstrengung zu erlangen(?). (62–64) Ihre

43 Translation modified after HWAU (111b, s.v. *äränčü*). On this term and the following three, see Nugteren & Wilkens (2019: 154–155, note 1).

44 Translation modified after HWAU (166b, s.v. *bıbru*).

45 Translation modified after HWAU (824b, s.v. *üm*).

46 Translation modified after HWAU (703a, s.v. *tärlik*).

47 Or, 'improperly' according to Wilkens (p.c.).

durch die erlangte Habe (entstandene) Gesinnung des Anhaftens war stark. (64–67) Da ihre Gier$_2$ übermäßig war, vergaßen sie völlig, daß sie Mönche waren, und sie verehrten$_2$ die 'Drei Juwelen' nicht (mehr). (67–69) Unbefriedigten$_2$ Herzens starben sie dort und wurden in diesen Kleinhöllen wiedergeboren.

(69–74) Diejenigen (Höllen)-Geister, die haben Körper wie [ ] Geschirr und Habe von Laien$_2$,[48] die waren in früheren Existenzen mächtige Könige, Befehlshaber$_2$ und Begüterte. (74–76) Sie quälten die Bewohner im Reich$_2$ und eigneten sich (deren) Schätze$_2$ und Besitztümer$_2$ an, indem sie sie gesetzwidrig[49] konfiszierten. (77–82) Dadurch (nun) selber begütert$_2$ und groß geworden, schmückten$_2$ sie ihre Körper mit den gesetzwidrig[50] angeeigneten Kleidern, Schuhen und Schmuckgegenständen und … die … waren sie … verächtlich$_2$[51] … dachten, es seien ihre Besitztümer, (aber in ihrem Geiz?) [End of the folio?] (83–84) haben sie nicht (einmal) soviel wie einen Bissen Speise als Almosen gespendet und haben (somit) keine verdienstvollen Werke$_2$ ausgeführt. (84–87) Aus diesem Grunde starben sie dort und wurden jetzt in diesen Pratyekanaraka (genannten) Kleinhöllen wiedergeboren.'

(87–92) Als sie diese Predigt gehört haben, geben die unzähligen$_2$ Lebewesen dieser Versammlung ihre Gesinnungen des 'Anhaftens', des 'Greifens' und des 'Geizigseins' auf$_2$ und werden Mönche in der Lehre des vollkommen weisen Buddha Maitreya. (92–94) Sie reinigen [alle Kleśa]s und [gelangen zur] Würde eines Arhat.

(94–99) Daraufhin [brodeln] und kochen jene Höllenwesen [lange] Zeit [im Wasser] jenes Stroms aus Ätzlauge und erleiden Qualen, und

48 Translation modified after the alternative reading *[ätöz]lüg* (line 71) proposed by Wilkens (p.c.).

49 See preceding note.

50 See preceding note.

51 Translation modified after the alternative reading *tuṭ tolvı* (line 80) proposed by the anonymous reviewer.

[ohne daß irgendeines der Höllen]wesen herauskommt, gehen sie [noch einmal mit dem Wasser] des Stroms aus Ätzlauge [zum Land].[52]

3.2 The Tocharian text

The manuscript A 219–238 has 55 *akṣaras* per line (Sieg & Siegling 1921: 107). As shown by Itkin (2002), this manuscript as well as the other manuscript of the MAV (A 239–242) both contain archaic linguistic features and dialectal innovations.[53] Since such features are absent in MSN manuscripts (Itkin 2002: 13), we are justified to suppose that the manuscripts of the MAV predate the manuscripts of the MSN. Therefore, it is reasonable to suppose that the composition of the MAV also predates the composition of the MSN.

The original fragment A 226 being lost, the plate reproduced by Sieg and Siegling in *Tocharische Sprachreste* (plate 35 in plate volume) is authoritative. The transcription available on CEToM is based on Sieg and Siegling's edition with some corrections retrieved from Siegling's personal copy of the *Tocharische Sprachreste*. The pagination of the leaf is lost, but recoverable from the pagination of the next fragment as 124 (A 227/8 = leaf 125, beginning of MAV 23) (Sieg & Siegling 1921: 112). On the verso, the empty space in the middle of the leaf interrupting the text and bounded by two vertical zigzag lines (represented below by the symbol ⦚ ⦚) signifies the end of a chapter. A small fragment on the right (a4–5 and b3–4, reproduced below in roman type) was identified by Sieg and Siegling only after the photograph of the plate was done (Sieg & Siegling

52 Translation modified after the restoration of this passage by Zieme (2021: 218–219).

53 Archaic linguistic features mentioned by Itkin are: lack of assimilation of clusters containing a sibilant followed by yod, *pyāpyāñ* 'flowers' written with a single *p* (instead of 'standard' *pyāppyāñ*), special inflectional paradigm for *kapśañi* 'body', i.e., acc. sg. *kapśaṃ*, gen. sg. *kapśäññe* (instead of 'standard' acc. sg. *kapśañi*, gen. sg. *kapśiññis*), etc.; dialectal innovations: *āneṃśi* for *āneñci* as here in b5, frequent use of the 'truncated' *-e* form of subjunctive 3pl. in place of the usual *-eñc* form, as here *yā(m)e* in b1 and *tāke* in b2.

1921: 112). Consequently, for this small fragment we cannot compare Sieg and Siegling's transliteration with the photograph. The identification of the Uyghur parallel calls for a number of minor corrections, which are discussed below (see 3.2.2).

3.2.1 *Transliteration*

Recto

a1 - - - - - - - - - *t nu ālkonṯ\ saṃ neñc^{ä}\ leṯa̱ḵ\ leṯa̱ḵ\ wäknantyo : ṣāmañ[i] yap̱\ pari - - - - - ·[ā]mañi : toṣ̱ṃ̱a̱ḵ\ toṣ̱ṃ̱a̱ḵ\ wäknaṃt[yo]* /// {lacuna of about 12 akṣ.}[54]

a2 *·[ā]śyapi p̱a̱ttāṃñäkte ṃ̱a̱rkamplaṃ : wa̱ṣ̱ṯa̱ṣ̱ laltuṣ ṣeñc^{ä}\ ṣome śākyamūniṣ̱\ ṃ̱a̱rkamplaṃ : - swa wsā[l]· - - - - [r]·ṣkāraṃ tattṟa̱ṅkuṣ̱\ : kṟa̱ntsonā[ṣ̱]* /// {lacuna of about 11 akṣ.}[55]

a3 *tāṃ̱a̱[ḵ]\ āpaṃ ālyek nuṃ wrasañ^{ä}\ tāloṣ̱\ klopasuṣ̱\ : k· - - - [wa]mpeṣi - - - - [l]·kā ceṃ̱\ : mahurṣi lekā ṣome pu* /// {lacuna of about 11 akṣ.}[56]

a4 *mokśi kṣurași lek⸗ ālyek saṃ : 80 2 hārṣi wakaḻ\ hārași mu - - rṣi wäṯḻa̱kṣi : ka[t]· - - p̱a̱rsānṯ\ lekā kontāl lekā ṣome saṃ* (:) - - - - - leṯa̱ḵ\ leṯa̱ḵ\ - - -

a5 *r·i̱ṉa̱ṣ̱\ : s̱a̱lpiñc^{ä} śkaṃ ·l·ma·yo utkraṃ klopanṯ\ [w]ärpnānṯa̱ṟ\ 80 3 ceṃ ṣeñc^{ä}\ kātkāñ^{ä}\ neṣ̱\ cmolwaṃ wramaṃ prāḵa̱ṟ\ tattṟa̱ṅkuṣ̱\ : kropñā* - - - - - - - lā sne [p]lā pe - (:)

a6 *śātoneṣiṃ trekeyo trikoṣ̱\ - - nṯ\ āñc [ṣa]kkatṣ̱\ : ypā - [ā]ly[e]ḵa̱ṣ̱\ āp̱p̱a̱rmāṯ\ mā eḻ\ eṣāṟ\ mā pñi ypānṯ\ 80 4 c·m lyalypū yāmūṟa̱ṣ̱* /// {lacuna of about 14 akṣ.}[57]

---

54 'Es fehlen etwa 12 *akṣ.*, Ende von Str. 80 und Anfang von 81.' (Sieg & Siegling 1921: 112, note 1).

55 'Es fehlen 11 *akṣ.* und die Strophenzahl 81.' (Sieg & Siegling 1921: 112, note 3).

56 'Es fehlen 11 *akṣ.*' (Sieg & Siegling 1921: 112, note 4).

57 'Es fehlen etwa 14 *akṣ.*' (Sieg & Siegling 1921: 112, note 6).

a7 *[nt]·[ṃ] ta̱m̱a̱nṯˎ tos̱a̱ṃ klopanṯˎ lkeñc^{ä}ˎ : [ṯa̱] - - - - - - - ·[e] - [l]kā kātkāśśi : - - - - - - - - - - nṯ(ˎ) cesmi p̱a̱l·o̱ṟa̱ṣ̱ˎ : 8o (5) ///* {lacuna of about 14 akṣ.}[58]

Verso

b1 *a̱ḵa̱ntsūne ṯa̱rkoṟa̱ṣ̱ˎ yā·e spa[lk/n/t·] - - - - - - - - (wa) ⁞ ⁞ wikūṟa̱ṣ̱ˎ ārāntiśpa ///* {lacuna of about 12 akṣ.}[59]
b2 *rṣināṣ̱ klop̱a̱ntwäṣ̱ˎ : 8o (6) - pat nu kātkāñ^{ä}ˎ tāke kākr[opu]ṣ̱ˎ ⁞ ⁞ tā[m] praṣtaṃ : cem penu lyut· ///* {lacuna of about 10 akṣ.}[60]
b3 *[w]ṣeññe cem̱ˎ raryūṟa̱ṣ̱ˎ - - [wa]ṣ̱ṯa̱ṣ metraknac^{ä}ˎ ske ⁞ ⁞ spalṯa̱k śkaṃ yāmūṟa̱ṣ̱ˎ tā[k(·)e] - - - - -* [8o] 7 || maitreyā(va)-
b4 *dānavyākaraṇaṃ āgārikanarak[o]papatti ñomā ⁞ ⁞ wikiwepiñci pāḵˎ :* · || (|| - - -) [kk]atseḵˎ ime - -
b5 *c^{ä}ˎ ā[n]eṃśi : puḵˎ āñmaṣ̱ˎ ḵa̱ryāṣ̱ˎ tāṣ̱ˎ plāc^{ä}ˎ ṣa ⁞ ⁞ kkatṣ p̱a̱klyoṣ̱a̱ṣ̱ˎ sne wyākṣe ///* {lacuna of about 13 akṣ.}[61]
b6 *- rsatsi ṯa̱rkāc^{ä}ˎ ke-ne āñcäm̱ˎ kulypal tāṣ ṣakkatseḵˎ : 1 ke pa ⁞ ⁞ t nu krī tāṣ̱ˎ ñareyäntwaṣ̱ˎ ///* {lacuna of about 11 akṣ.}[62]
b7 *- - - - - - - - (:) ke pat nu saṃ krī ñäkcī suḵˎ ṉa̱ṣ ḵa̱lpīmāṟˎ : ke ⁞ ⁞ pat nu ākāḻˎ ñäkci napeṃṣi ā ///* {lacuna of about 11 akṣ.}[63]

3.2.2 *Textual notes*

a1 *neñc^{ä}ˎ*

The choice between the reading *neñc^{ä}ˎ* and *teñc^{ä}ˎ* is difficult. Both forms are grammatically possible, i.e., the present active 3pl. of *nas-* 'be' (*neñc*), or the subjunctive active 3pl. of the same verb (*teñc*). Although Sieg and Siegling edit *teñc^{ä}ˎ*, since the left part of the letter is erased, it is impos-

58 'Es fehlt der erste *pāda* von Str. 86.' (Sieg & Siegling 1921: 112, note 7).
59 'Es fehlen etwa 12 *akṣ.*' (Sieg & Siegling 1921: 113, note 1).
60 'Es fehlen 10 *akṣ.*' (Sieg & Siegling 1921: 113, note 3).
61 'Der dritte (12-silbige) *pāda* fehlt.' (Sieg & Siegling 1921: 113, note 5).
62 'Es fehlen etwa 11 *akṣ.*' (Sieg & Siegling 1921: 113, note 6).
63 'Es fehlen etwa 11 *akṣ.* (Ende von Str. 2 und Anfang von 3).' (Sieg & Siegling 1921: 113, note 7).

sible to determine with certainty whether the part continued, in which case one should read <ta>, or not, in which case one should read <na>. The probable meaning of the sentence favours an indicative form rather than a subjunctive form, but an eventual meaning cannot be excluded.

a1 *ṣāmañ[i] yap̱*

A different segmentation from that of Sieg and Siegling should be adopted. The presence of a short *a* weakens the hypothesis of a gen. sg. form in *-yāp*. It is preferable to segment this sequence into two separate words.

a1 *·[ā]mañi*

The continuation of the upper part of the vowel is visible. It can be *ā* or *o*. Reading *///omañi* would imply a segmentation *///o mañi* with *mañi*, pl. of *mañ* 'month', which would make no sense in the context (for possibilities for *///mañi*, see the philological commentary to THT 1306 by Pinault, Burlak & Peyrot in CEToM).

a1 *wäknaṃtyo*

The spelling *wäknaṃtyo* with *anusvāra* is an exception in this manuscript, where alt. nouns inflected in a secondary case usually have the spelling <nt>: *-ntu*, *-ntwaṃ*, *-ntwäṣ*, etc.

a2 *·[ā]śyapi*

The restitution *(k)[ā]śyapi* suggested by Sieg & Siegling (1921: 112, note 2) is certain, especially since the upper part of <kā> is visible.

a2 *[r]·ṣkāraṃ*

The *akṣara* is most likely *r* and not *k*. The head is too small in height to be that of a <ka>, compare the <ka> of *lekā* just below in a3.

a3 *[l]·kā*

The restitution is due to Sieg and Siegling; it is impossible to verify it, as the vertical line has been erased. In any case, the word *lekā* is very likely, for the syntax is parallel to the other occurrence of *lekā* in the same line and to the other three occurrences of the same word in the next line.

a4 *ālyek saṃ*

Edited in one word by Sieg and Siegling. Actually, the two terms of this sequence composed of *ālak* 'other' in the nom. pl. masc. and of the indefinite *saṃ* in the nom. are not separated in the spelling by a *virāma*, unlike *ālkont̠*\ *saṃ* (nom. pl. fem.) in a1. There is no doubt that this analysis in two words should be preferred to the analysis of **ālyeksaṃ* as the loc. pl. of *ālak* (pace Sieg, Siegling & Schulze 1931: 193, note 1, §323). Similarly, *ṣomesaṃ* in a4 must be segmented into two words, *ṣome saṃ*, which is the semantical match of TB *ṣemi ksa* (see Chamot-Rooke 2021: 222–223).

a4 *ka[t]·*

Again, it is difficult to choose between the reading *[t]·* and *[n]·*. The sequence *ka[n·]* as edited by Sieg and Siegling would imply the following possibilities: *kanak* 'cotton garment' (or derivative), *Kanaṣke* 'Kaniška', *kanti* 'gong, cymbal', *kanweṃ** 'knees' (or derivative). According to the context, a derivative of *katu* 'jewellery' is rather expected.

a5 *·l·ma·yo*

The manuscript is torn, but *la* in ligature and *y* (vertical line on the right) are clearly visible. The restitution *(s)l(a)ma(s)yo* suggested by Sieg & Siegling (1921: 112, note 5) is therefore very likely.

a6 *nt̠*\ *āñc [ṣa]*

This reading is due to Sieg and Siegling. One does not see much on the plate. Although *ā* is no longer visible, *ñc* appears relatively safe.

a7 *[nt]·[ṃ]*

The reading can be improved. We would expect *-ntwaṃ*, ending of loc. pl. of *ñare* 'hell'.

a7 *nt̠*(\)

The sign of *virāma* must have disappeared in the lacuna.

a7 *·[e]*

Given the height of the traces, they can only match the vocalization sign *e*. The *akṣara* in question is located two *akṣaras* before the next visible one.

a7 ***[l]kā***

The reading *[l]* is due to Sieg and Siegling, but the *l* is no longer visible on the photograph.

b2 ***nu kā***

Given the poor visibility on the photograph for the *akṣaras* in question, one should rely on the reading suggested by Sieg and Siegling.

b2 ***tā[m] praṣtaṃ***

The reading *pra* is safe, but the beginning of the *akṣara* is hard to read because its seems that the manuscript has been erased.

b3 ***tā[ke]***

A slight reading improvement can be made compared to Sieg and Siegling's edition. One reads *[k(·)e]* or *[n(·)e]*, i.e., *tā-ne* 'where' or *tāke* = *tākeñc*, subjunctive active 3pl. of *nas-* 'be'. Syntactically, the second solution is better since we expect a subjunctive form.

3.2.3 Transcription and metrical restoration

The metre is 4×14 (7/7) syllables, mostly 4¦3/4¦3, sometimes 3¦4/4¦3. The next chapter (ch. 23) has a metre of 12 + 15 + 12 + 15 = 5/7 + 5/7/3 + 5/7 + 5/7/3 syllables. Despite the relatively fragmentary character of the text, the comparison with the Uyghur parallel allows of a number of restitutions (for justifications, see below the philological commentary under 4).

– – – – – – – – ; – [a1] – – – – – – – : [80a]
(ke pa)t nu ¦ ālkont saṃ neñc ; letäk letäk ¦ wäknantyo : [80b]
ṣāmañi yap- ¦ pari(ṣkār ; kāṣāri-wsāl ¦ ṣā)mañi : [80c]
tosmäk tosmäk ¦ wäknaṃtyo ; (utkraṃ klopant ¦ wärpnāmāṃ : *80)*
(cem ṣeñc ṣome ¦ [a2]*kā)śyapi ; pättāṃñäkte ¦ märkamplaṃ* : [81a]
waṣtäṣ laltuṣ ¦ ṣeñc ṣome ; śākyamūnis ¦ märkamplaṃ : [81b]
(kā)swa-wsāl(u ¦ bhājantu ; pari)ṣkāraṃ ¦ tatträṅkuṣ : [81c]
kräntsonā(s ¦ wsālu pātär ; skam prakṣār mā ¦ märkamplā : *81)*
[a3]*tāmäk āpaṃ ¦ ālyek nuṃ ; wrasañ tāloṣ ¦ klopasuṣ* : [82a]
k(apśño nāṃtsuṣ) ¦ wampeṣi ; (ñemintwāṣi) ¦ l(e)kā cem : [82b]

mahurṣi ¦ lekā ṣome ; pu(skāṣi lek⁄ ¦ ālyek saṃ :) [82c]
(– – – – ¦ –) [a4]*mokśi ; kṣurași lek⁄ ¦ ālyek saṃ : 82*
hārṣi wakal- ¦ hāraṣi ; mu(ktihā)rṣi ¦ wätläkṣi : [83a]
kat(uṣi) ¦ pärsānt lekā ; kontāl lekā ¦ ṣome saṃ (:) [83b]
(puk wäknantyo ¦ cem)[64] *letäk ; letäk (nāṃtsuṣ*[65] *¦ po)*[a5]*r(ṣ)inäs :* [83c]
sälpiñcä śkaṃ ¦ (s)l(a)ma(s)yo ; utkraṃ klopant ¦ wärpnāntär 83
ceṃ ṣeñc kātkāñ ¦ neṣ-cmolwaṃ ; wramaṃ prākär ¦ tatträṅkuṣ : [84a]
kropñā(nt ālu ¦ niṣpalntu ; kältsā)lā[66] *sne- ¦ plā pe(nu :)* [84b]
[a6]*śātoneṣiṃ ¦ trekeyo ; trikoṣ (tamä)nt ¦ āñc ṣakkats :* [84c]
ypā(nt) ālyekäs ¦ āppärmāt ; mā el eṣār ¦ mā pñi ypānt 84
c(a)m lyalypū ¦ yāmūräṣ (puk ; tämyo antuṣ ¦ waluräṣ :) [85a]
(cem prattika- ¦ ñare[a7]*ntw)aṃ ; tamänt tosäṃ ¦ klopant lkeñc :* [85b]
tä(myo skenal ¦ sparcwatsi ; sne-k)e(n-pä)lkā ¦ kātkāśśi : [85c]
(ṣāmnāśśi śkaṃ ¦ puk āñmaṣ ; nākma)nt«†ä» cesmi ¦ päl(k)oräṣ : 8(5)
(k$_u$ce-ne ṣāmnāñ ¦ aśyāñ śkaṃ ; tāṣ plāc klyoseñc ¦ tām praṣtaṃ :) [86a]
[b1]*akäntsūne ¦ tärkoräṣ ; yā(m)e spal(täk ¦ ske śkaṃ cem :)* [86b]
(puk kleśās ¦ wa)wikūräṣ ; ārāntiśpa(rn ¦ kälpānträ :) [86c]
(tsälpe śkaṃ cem ¦ traidhātuk ; saṃsā)[b2]*rṣinās ¦ klopäntwäṣ : 86*
(k$_u$ce) pat nu ¦ kātkāñ tāke ; <ṣyak> kākropuṣ ¦ tām praṣtaṃ : [87a]
cem penu ¦ lyut(ār memaṣ ; puttiśparnac ¦ spaltkasuṣ :) [87b]
(waṣt-)[b3]*wṣeññe cem ¦ raryūräṣ ; (läñce) waṣtäṣ ¦ metraknac «:»* [87c]
ske spaltäk śkaṃ ¦ yāmūräṣ ; tā(ke cem poñś ¦ ārāntāñ) : 87 ||

maitreyā(va)[b4]*dānavyākaraṇaṃ āgārikanarakopapatti ñomā wikiwepiñci pāk : • || (||)*

(yas pe ṣa)kkatsek ; ime (ppāṣā)[b5]*c āneṃśi :* [1a]
pūk āñmaṣ käryāṣ ; tāṣ plāc ṣakkats päklyoṣäs ; sne wyākṣe(p :) [1b]
(– – – – – ; – – – – – – – – :) [1c]
([b6] *mä)rsatsi*[67] *tärkāc ; ke-ne āñcäm kulypal tāṣ ; ṣakkatsek : 1*

---

64 Restoration according to Pinault (p.c.).
65 Restoration according to Pinault (p.c.).
66 Restoration of *kältsālā* according to Pinault (p.c.).
67 The restitution of the substantivized infinitive *märsatsi* 'forgetfulness', though unattested elsewhere in TA, would fit the context, expressing the same idea as the phrase *sne wyākṣe(p)* 'without distraction' in the same *pāda*. Although

ke pat nu krī tāṣ ; ñareyäntwaṣ (śalpatsi **:**)[68] [2a]
(– – – – – ; – – – [b7] – – – – – ; – – – **:**) [2b]
ke pat nu saṃ krī ; ñäkcī suk näṣ kälpīmār **:** [2c]
ke pat nu ākāl ; ñäkci napeṃṣi ā(wās[69] *; yomnāssi* **:** 2)

3.2.4 *Translation*

… or (those who) have the other [bodily forms], each in a different way: [in the shape of] a monk's barley uten(sil, of a m)onk's (reddish robe, enduring excruciating pains) in each of these ways, [80]

(some of these) [had left the house] under the law of Buddha (Kā)śyapa; some had left the house under the law of Śākyamuni. Attached to (beau)tiful clothe(s, vessel, [and] ut)ensils, (they were constantly asking for) beautiful (clothes and for a [new] alms bowl improperly). [81]

In that same stream [there are] still other beings, miserable [and] suffering. Those (have) b(odies) in the shape of ornaments, (of jewels), some in the shape of a diadem, (some in the shape of a) gar(land,) the others in the shape (of …), of a knife, of a razor, [82]

some in the shape of a necklace, of a half-necklace, of a pea(rl necklace), of a *wätläk*, of a gold(smith piece of work), of a gemstone, of an earring. (They have all become) each one in a different way, and they burn in flames of (fire), [and] they endure excruciating pains. [83]

Those were householders in previous births, firmly attached to possession; they were (constantly) amass(ing other people's riches) through (oppression), and also improperly. Intoxicated by the intoxication of wealth, they are necessarily (reb)orn down [in hell], for they were despising others, they were not giving alms, they were not performing meritorious deeds. [84]

---

the TA root *märs-* gives a present 6 in TA (A 318 a7 *märsneñc*) and not a present 3, the latter is expected and attested in TB. If this restitution is correct, the word *märsatsi* would confirm that the present 6 in TA is secondary, as per Schmidt (1974: 34, note 1).

68 Restoration according to Peyrot (2013: 268).

69 Restoration according to Pinault (p.c.).

Having committed (all) these deeds, (therefore having died [and passed away] from here, they) are reborn in (individual hells), [and] they suffer those pains. Th(erefore) the householders (and the monks should strive with all their heart to behave) according to the absence of false view, having seen the (sin)s of these. [85]

(The monks and nuns who will hear this speech at that time), having abandoned their possessions, will make effo(rt and zeal). Having expelled (all the *kleśas*), (they will attain) the dignity of Arhat, (and they will be freed) from the pains of the (threefold) Saṃ(sāra). [86]

As for the householders (who) will be gathered <together> at that time, they too exceed(ingly zealous to obtain the rank of Buddha), having abandoned dwelling (in a household, they will leave) the house for Maitreya, and having made effort [and] zeal, they (will all) beco(me Arhats). [87]

In the *Maitreyāvadānavyākaraṇa*, chapter 22 entitled 'Rebirth in the hell for house-minded ones' [is finished].

(You too,) definitely (prote)ct your mind carefully! Listen to this sermon with all your heart [and] with all your will, without distraction! (If you …, then) you will dismiss the (forgetful)ness (of …). He who definitely has the heart [and] the desire to … , [01]

or he who has the will (to be freed) from the hells … or he who has this will: 'May I obtain divine happiness!', or he who (has) the wish (to reach) a divine [or] human a(bode), [02] …

4 Philological commentary

This part consists of a philological commentary of the end of chapter 22 of the Tocharian MAV (stanzas 80–87). Its main purpose is to provide the reader with philological justifications for all the restitutions proposed above. This commentary strongly relies on the Uyghur parallel text as well as on intra-Tocharian (TA and TB) phraseological comparison. Sanskrit and Pali texts are also adduced when relevant for the explanation of Tocharian expressions. All German translations from Uyghur without reference are from *Eine buddhistische Apokalypse* (Geng, Klimkeit & Laut 1998).

The most exact overlaps between the Uyghur and the Tocharian text are stanzas 81 and 84 of the latter (sections *h* and *k* in the synoptic table). This fact is very likely not accidental, since these stanzas are parallel to each other,[70] and they both play a structuring role in the progression of the text. They are explanatory keys that not only shed light on the identity of the sinners who have just been described, but also explain the causes for their infernal rebirth (i.e., the sins committed by them). Stanza 81 identifies the first group of sinners as monks having 'left home' in a previous life (*waṣtäṣ laltuṣ ṣeñc* 'they had left home', cf. Uygh. 55 *toyın š(a)mnanč ärdilär* '(sind) … Mönche und Nonnen gewesen'), while stanza 84 identifies the second group as 'householders in previous births' (*ceṃ ṣeñc kātkāñ neṣ-cmolwaṃ* 'those were householders in previous births', cf. Uygh. 71–74 *bolar öŋrä ažunlarda ärklig eliglär bäglär buyruklar bayagutlar ärtilär* 'die waren in früheren Existenzen mächtige Könige, Befehlshaber₂ und Begüterte'). Stanzas 85, 86, and 87 form the end of MAV 22. These stanzas probably describe the reaction of Maitreya's followers, which appears as the logical consequence of his speech. Although these stanzas contain many lacunas, their formulaic and cliché character allows quite safe restitutions.

The structure of the text can be divided into three parts: 1. the monks (stanzas 80–81), 2. the householders (stanzas 82–85), 3. the followers' reaction (stanzas 86–87).

4.1 The monks: stanzas 80–81 (sections **g–i**)

4.1.1 *Stanza 80 (not reflected in the Uyghur text)*

a1 *(ke pa)t nu … neñc* 'or those who have'

70 Both stanzas have a *pāda* ending with *tatträṅkuṣ* 'attached'.

[tnu] forms a single *akṣara*. The sequence of particles *pat nu* 'or' may be restored, possibly preceded by the gen. sg. of the relative pronoun *kus-ne*, i.e., *ke-ne* or *ke* without relative particle: 'or [those] to whom belong (the others) [scil. bodily forms?]' = 'or those who have (the others) [scil. bodily forms?]'.[71] This restitution is unproblematic from a grammatical point of view, since in the case of a disjunctive structure with two or more members coordinated by a conjunction, the relative particle *-ne* is omitted after all *ke* except the first one (Sieg, Siegling & Schulze 1931: 177, §299).[72] The Uyghur text corresponding to the beginning of Maitreya's speech shows no trace of relative clause: 53–55 *bolar ʾ*M*/[ ] šazanınta amarıları šakimuni burhan šazanınta toyın š(a)mnanč ärdilär* '(Von) diesen [ ] (sind manche) in der Disziplin (des Buddha …) und manche von ihnen in der Disziplin des Buddha Śākyamuni Mönche und Nonnen gewesen.'[73] This passage closely corresponds to stanza 81 of the Tocharian text, so that stanza 80 is not reflected in the Uyghur text. However, relative clauses are well attested in the MNB in similar contexts, when Maitreya speaks in order to identify the sinners and to explain the sins committed by them ('those who … those were in a previous existence …').[74] The following example is

71 For the syntax, cf. A 17 b2: *ke-ne pñintu neñc cami s$_u$kuntu ṣñ⸗ akälyme* 'he who possesses virtue, this one owns the goods of happiness' (transl. CEToM after Sieg 1944: 20–21). For the idea of 'bodily forms', see below, s.v. a1 *ālkont ṣaṃ*.

72 The same expression with disjunction of the relative pronoun in the gen. is attested later in the fragment (A 226 b6). See also the following fragment: A 227/8 a5 *ke-ne… ke pat nu…* 'wessen… oder wessen…' (transl. Sieg, Siegling & Schulze 1931: 177, §299).

73 According to the translation by Geng, Klimkeit & Laut, the text belonging to the last line of the recto (*bolar ʾ*M*/[ ]*) and the text belonging to the first line of the verso (*šazanınta*) of folio 327 form one and the same sentence. On the basis of the Tocharian parallel, Wilkens (p.c.) now proposes to restore the text as follows: 53–55 *bolar am[arıları kašip burhan] šazanınta amarıları šakimuni burhan šazanınta toyın š(a)mnanč ärdilär* '(of) these some were monks or nuns under the law of Buddha Kāśyapa, some under the law of Buddha Śākyamuni' (see below under 4.1.2).

74 For the syntax of *kim* in relative clauses, see Erdal (2004: 443–448). In the example quoted, *kim olarnaŋ ara* literally means 'those among them (who)'

from MNB 23, folio 9 verso, lines 18 ff. (MaitrSängim, Kat.-Nr. 150 ~ Taf. 74; Tekin 1980: 193):

> *kim olarnaŋ ara ät yumgak* [19] *ätözlüglär .. tämir tumšuklug*[75] [20] *kargalar kuzgunlar örtlüg* [21] *yalınlıg ätözin ät yumgak* [22] *ätözlügärig soka tarmayu* [23] *yeyürlär ärsär .. olar öŋrä ažun-* [24] *da koyn ölürgüči ätčilär ärdi*
> 'Diejenigen unter [ihnen] mit Körpern wie Fleischklumpen, deren fleischklumpige Körper eisenschnäblige Raben₂ mit flammenden₂ Körpern zerstückeln₂ und fressen, die waren in früheren Existenzen Schafschlächter und Fleischer.' (transl. Geng, Klimkeit & Laut 1998: 100).[76]

Another example, also from MNB 23, is folio 11 recto, lines 26 ff. (MaitrSängim, Kat.-Nr. 152 ~ Taf. 202; Tekin 1980: 253):

> *kim ymä ol tälim üküš uzun* [27] *tonlug käntü sačlarınta yörgänmiš* [28] *kunčular ičtin sıŋar ätözlärintä* [29] *kurt kovšayu örtänü köyürlär*[77] [30] *ärsär .. olar amarıları adın amrakın*
> 'Und was jene zahlreichen₂, langröckigen, in ihre eigenen Haupthaare gehüllten Frauen betrifft, die brennen₂, während in ihrem Körperinneren Würmer wühlen: Von diesen [haben] einige die Geliebten anderer [abspenstig gemacht(?)] ...' (transl. Geng, Klimkeit & Laut 1998: 102).

with *olarnaŋ* (~ *olarnıŋ*) in the gen. pl. and *ara* postposition, meaning 'among'.

75 The manuscript has TWMŠWQ LWQ L'R, but L'R is a mistake (Tekin 1980: 193, note 140; Laut 2000: 139–140, Sünde B3, Strafe).

76 As the anonymous reviewer points out, the syntax of the sentence is curious. One has to assume that a relative sentence is embedded without being indicated in the text itself.

77 KWYN'RL'R as per Tekin is to be read *köyürlär*.

Interestingly, the same syntactic structure is attested in a TB fragment of the *Saṃgharakṣitāvadāna*.[78] In the Sanskrit version of this Avadāna,[79] the monk Saṃgharakṣita, awakening in a strange world inhabited by monstrous monks, witnesses fantastic scenes of monks slaying each other inside monasteries – actually not monasteries, but *pratyekanarakas* 'individual hells'. The TB fragment THT 431 preserves the Buddha's explanation for such punishments (text and transl. Ogihara 2016: 135–137):

> [a2]*/// [cai] ñake ṣamāñe erepatesa tsäksenträ* 6 || *k$_u$ce cewne no* {emend to *k$_u$ce cew nano*} *sa(ṅkrāmne)* [a3]*/// -mane* <*p*>*älwāmane kwasnāmane cey rano nauṣ kāśyā*<*p*> *pa(ñäkte)*
> 'they now are burning in the form of monks.[80] 6 || 'Again those whom (you saw) in the monastery […] ?-ing, wailing and mourning […], but they (were disciples of(?)) Kāśyapa-Buddha before […]'.

In our text, the syntax of stanza 80 must be similar to that of the examples quoted above, namely, a relative clause resumed by an anaphoric demonstrative. Concerning the verb *neñc*, although Sieg and Siegling adopt the reading *teñc* (subjunctive), a present form *neñc* (indicative) is more appropriate for the descriptive context (the beings in question are currently suffering, cf. *tosäṃ klopant lkeñc* 'they see (indicative) those pains' in stanza 85). On the other hand, a subjunctive form *teñc* could be justified by the eventual value of the relative clause (see Peyrot 2013: 255–256).

a1 *ālkont saṃ* 'the others'

This locution in the nom. pl. containing the pronoun *ālkont* doubled by the enclitic indefinite *saṃ* (obl. *caṃ*) is the fem. counterpart of masc. *ālyek saṃ* 'the others' as opposed to *ṣome saṃ* 'the ones' (see Chamot-Rooke 2021: 220–225). It may belong to the end of an enumeration, parallel to that of stanzas 82–83 (see under 4.2.1 and 4.2.2): 'the ones … the others … the others …', cf. Uygh. 23–28 *amarıları … amarıları* 'einige …

78 Text identified and edited by Ogihara (2016).

79 One version of this Avadāna is part of the *Divyāvadāna* (ch. 23 and 25), another is extant in Gilgit manuscripts (*Pravrajyāvastu* section of the *Vinayavastu*).

80 Alternatively, 'in the form of a monk's …', for the sentence may not be complete.

einige'. Due to the gender agreement, the referent of *ālkont saṃ*, which is the grammatical subject of the verb *neñc*, should be a substantive of alt. or fem. gender. According to the context, *ālkont saṃ* should thus refer to the sinners' 'bodies', or rather to their 'bodily forms'. Although not attested in our fragment, the TA substantive expressing this idea is *arämpāt* (pl. *arämpātäntu*, alt. gender), corresponding to Skt. *rūpa-* (Carling 2009: 15a, s.v. *arämpāt*). The TB formal and semantical match, i.e., *erepate*, occurs in the passage of the *Saṃgharakṣitāvadāna* quoted above.

a1 *letäk letäk wäknantyo* 'each in a different way'

The adverb *letäk*, a hapax, has the same meaning as the related adverb *letkār*,[81] translating Skt. *pṛthak* 'widely apart, separately, differently, singly, severally, one by one (often repeated)' (MW: 645c, s.v. *pṛthak*) in A 359 a27 and A 461 a4. As in Sanskrit, the repetition expresses distributivity (Skt. *pṛthak pṛthak* ~ TA *letäk letäk*). In the present context, the phrase TA *letäk letäk wäknantyo* may be compared to Uygh. *adrok adrok körklüg* 'with many different shapes', cf. the following passage from MNB 23, folio 9 recto, lines 5 ff. (MaitrHami; Geng, Klimkeit & Laut 1998: 35):

> *yana ok sansız tümän kolti nayut* [06] *sanınča* <u>*adrok adrok körklüg*</u> *mäŋiz-* [07] *lig adın kičig tamulug-* [08] *lar katag ünin ulıyu* [09] *muŋrayu [tükäl] bilgä maitre* [10] *[burhanka] käli*
> 'Und in einer Zahl von unendlichen zehntausenden Koṭis von Nayutas [kommen(?)] die Kleinhöllenwesen <u>mit verschiedenster Gestalt</u> und verschiedensten Aussehen,[82] klagend, mit lauter Stimme, [zum vollkommen] weisen [Buddha] Maitreya ...' (transl. Geng, Klimkeit & Laut 1998: 99).

Another example with *ätözlär* 'bodies' occurs in MNB 20, folio 1 verso, lines 19 ff. (MaitrHami; Geng, Klimkeit & Laut 1998: 22):

> *bo tınlaglar* [20] *nä ayıg kılınč kılmıšlar ärki .. kim* [21] *bo muntag ažunta tugup* <u>*adrok adrok*</u> [22] <u>*ätözläri*</u> *kiši yalŋok täg yüzläri*

81 For the formation of this adverb, see Pinault (1988: 196).
82 Translation modified according to Laut (p.c.).

'Was haben diese Lebewesen wohl für schlechte Taten ausgeführt, daß sie in einer derartigen Existenz wiedergeboren wurden und daß sie verschiedenartige$_2$ Körper, (aber) den Menschen$_2$ gleiche Gesichter (aufweisen) … ?' (transl. Geng, Klimkeit & Laut 1998: 77).

a1 *ṣāmañi yap-pari(ṣkār)* '[in the shape of] a monk's barley utensil' Semantically and syntactically, we expect the *pāda* 80c to be an apposition to the 'bodily forms' referred to by *ālkont saṃ* (nom. case) in 80b. The restitution *pari(ṣkār)* — a trisyllabic word is required by the caesura — is made plausible by the new reading *(pa)r(i)ṣkāraṃ* in the following stanza (see below, s.v. a2 *(bhājantu pari)ṣkāraṃ*). On the other hand, the graphically attested sequence *ṣāmañiyap* (as edited by Sieg and Siegling) is problematic. A first hypothesis would be a scribal mistake for *ṣāmañiyāp* with long *ā*, gen. sg. of the adjective *ṣāmañi* 'of a monk', based on *ṣāmaṃ* 'monk'. This is theoretically possible, especially since we find another example of short *a* for expected long *ā* in our manuscript, i.e., A 236 b6 *käntwaṣi* 'related to tongue' for expected *käntwāṣi* (cf. A 371 b3, A 377 a2). However, a hypothetical gen. form *ṣāmañiyāp* would imply that the following (incomplete) word *pari///* is in the genitive.[83] This is excluded by the metre, for substantives beginning with *pari°* (generally borrowed from Sanskrit words beginning with the preverb *pari°*) are all at least trisyllabic in TA, therefore at least quadrisyllabic in the gen. sg.

Alternatively, one may consider a different segmentation of the sequence, i.e., *ṣāmañi yap* in two words. In this case, the adjective *ṣāmañi* could modify the noun *pariṣkār*, paralleling an expression attested in TB: PK NS 71 a3 *ṣamāññe pari(ṣkār)* 'monk's utensil' (see below, s.v. a2 *(bhājantu pari)ṣkāraṃ*). In his dictionary, Adams, probably following Thomas & Krause's glossary (1964: 224), mentions the existence of a Tocharian A noun *yap* identical to TB *yap* 'barley' ~ Skt. *yava-* 'id.' (Adams 2013: 519–520, s.v. *yap*). Peyrot (2018: 251–252) dismisses TA *yap* as a ghost form.[84] Nonetheless, the meaning 'barley' for *yap* in a com-

83 Cf. *enkälṣināp poris* 'of the fire of desire' (Krause & Thomas 1960: 92, §85).

84 For TB *yap* 'barley', see also the discussion in Pinault (2017: 128–138). Theoretically, TA *yap* could be the formal match of TB *yepe* '(cutting) weapon,

pound *yap-pari(ṣkār)* 'barley utensil, barley vessel' would perfectly fit the context. One may compare Sanskrit and Pali compounds beginning with *saktu°* / *sattu°* 'coarsely ground meal, grit, groats (esp. of barley-meal)' (MW: 1132c, s.v. *saktu*), denoting vessels: Skt. *saktudhānī-* 'a vessel of barley-meal', Skt. *saktughaṭa(-ākhyāyikā)-* '(the story of the) vessel of barley-meal' (a famous story in the *Pañcatantra*), Pa. *sattupasibbaka* 'flour sack', *sattubhasta* 'id.'.[85] Therefore, the expression *ṣāmañi yap-pariṣkār* would refer to utensils such as alms bowls, pots, cups, mortars, pestles, and so on (see Upasak 1975: 180, s.v. *mattikā-bhaṇḍa*).[86] If this analysis is correct, TA *yap* must be the loan from TB *yap* (/yə̂p/), as per Adams.[87] Interestingly, the unnoticed TA adjective *ypiṣi* (435 a3) may reflect the borrowing of TB *ypiye* 'of barley' (borrowed as **ypi*, recharacterized by the productive Tocharian A suffix *-ṣi*). Although Poucha (1955: 250, s.v. *ypeṣi*) considers *ypiṣi* to be a variant for *ypeṣi* (based on *ype* 'country'), the context favours the meaning 'of barley' rather than 'of a country': 435 a3 *ypiṣi moso e(l) elu(neyo)* 'by giving a *moso*[88] of barley as gift'.

a1 *(kāṣāri-wsāl ṣā)mañi* 'of a monk's reddish robe'

This restitution is hypothetical. According to the principle of 'karmic retaliation',[89] the shape of the sinners' bodies is expected to be related to the sins described in 81c–d (see below, s.v. a2 *(kā)swa-wsāl(u)*). In the

knife' (Adams 2013: 547, s.v. *yepe*). However, the fact that TB *yepe* was borrowed in Tocharian A as *yepe*, same meaning (Carling & Pinault forth., s.v. *yepe**), weakens this hypothesis.

85 The correspondence between TB *yap* and Skt. *saktu-* is evidenced by the equivalence, unnoticed so far, between TB *ypiye war* (PK AS 2A b1) and Skt. *saktūdaka-* 'barley water' (on the Sanskrit word, see Bisschop & Griffiths 2008: 16–17, note 49).

86 See below the mention of cups, mortars, and pots in the passage from the *Saṃgharakṣitāvadāna* quoted under 4.2.1.

87 Other examples of TB /ə̂/ (accented) borrowed as TA /a/ are: TA *ymassu* < TB *ymassu* (/ymə̂ssu/), TA *ysamo* < TB *ysamo* (/ysə̂mo/), TA *wassi* < TB *wassi* (/wə̂ssi/), TA *eṅkalsu* < TB *eṅkalsu* (/eṅkə̂lsu/), see Peyrot (2010: 139).

88 According to Pinault (p.c.), *moso* is related to *musā-* 'rise' and would mean 'subsistence, livelihood'.

89 On 'karmic retaliation' ('Vergeltungs-kausalität'), see Laut (2000: 130).

restitution proposed, the adjective *ṣāmañi* 'monastic' would modify the noun *kāṣāri-wsāl* 'reddish robe'.[90]

a1 *tosmäk tosmäk wäknaṃtyo* 'in each of these ways'

The reduplicated expression *tosmäk tosmäk* modifies the substantive in the instr. pl. *wäknaṃtyo* (see the restitution *letäk letäk wäknantyo* above) with which it agrees in gender (Hartmann 2013: 261). The repetition of the anaphoric demonstrative with emphatic particle -*(ä)k* is also attested in A 60 a1: *camäk camäk wlaluneṣi mātā(r)* 'for sure, the monster of death (will swallow) [the bodily forms] one after the other …' (transl. Carling, Pinault & Malzahn in CEToM). The repetition has distributive value: *letäk letäk wäknantyo … tosmäk tosmäk wäknaṃtyo* 'each in a different way … in each of these ways'.

a1 (*utkraṃ klopant wärpnāmāṃ*) 'enduring excruciating pains'

Hypothetical restitution on the basis of the expression *utkraṃ klopant wärpnāntär* in the description of the householders later in the text (stanza 83d, see under 4.2.2, s.v. a5 *utkraṃ klopant wärpnāntär*). An argument pointing to the restitution of a *m*-participle here is the presence of such participles in the TB version of the *Saṃgharakṣitāvadāna*, which has a similar syntax: THT 431 a3 /// *-mane <p>älwāmane kwasnāmane* (see above, s.v. a1 (*ke pa*)*t nu … neñc*).

4.1.2 Stanza 81 (~ Uygh. 53–59)

a1 (*cem ṣeñc ṣome*) 'some of these had [scil. left the house]'

~ Uygh. 53 *bolar am[arıları]* '(of) these some'. Cf. the parallel expression *ceṃ ṣeñc kātkāñ* 'those were householders' used below (stanza 84a) in the Tocharian text. The anaphoric pronoun *cem* would refer back to the relative pronoun *ke* restored in the previous stanza.

a2 (*kā*)*śyapi pättāṃñäkte märkamplaṃ* 'under the law of Buddha Kāśyapa'

90 For the postposition of the adjective in metrical context, see Knoll (1996: 77).

~ Uygh. 53–54 *[kašip burhan] šazanınta* 'under the law of Buddha Kāśyapa'. The safe restitution *(kā)śyapi* dates back to Sieg & Siegling (1921: 112, note 2). The name Kāśyapa is lost in the lacuna of the Uyghur text, at the end of the recto of folio 327.

a2 *waṣtäṣ laltuṣ ṣeñc ṣome śākyamūnis märkamplaṃ* 'some had left the house under the law of Śākyamuni'

~ Uygh. 54–55 *amarıları šakimuni burhan šazanınta toyın š(a)mnanč ärdilär* '(sind) manche von ihnen in der Disziplin des Buddha Śākyamuni Mönche und Nonnen gewesen'. The mention of Śākyamuni precludes the possibility that Śākyamuni is the narrator in the Tocharian text.

a2 *(kā)swa-wsāl(u)* '[to] beautiful clothes'

~ Uygh. 55–56 *k(ä)ntü tonları (üzä)* 'an ihren [scil. the monks and nuns'] Gewändern'. This is the first of the three items mentioned in the Uyghur text having been coveted by monks and nuns in a previous life (complement of 56–57 *aŋsız yapıšmıš bodulmıš ärdilär* 'sie hingen$_2$ sehr'): 'clothes' (Uygh. *tonlar*), 'vessel' (Uygh. *idiš*), and 'utensils' (Uygh. *tavarlar*). Wearing 'beautiful clothes' is associated with evil behaviour in PK AS 6B a6 (TB): *wästsanma krenta yäṣṣītär* 'he used to wear beautiful clothes' (about Nanda, the stepbrother of the Buddha).

a2 *(bhājantu pari)ṣkāraṃ* 'to vessel [and] utensils'

~ Uygh. 56 *idiš tavarları üzä* 'an ihrem [scil. the monks and nuns'] Geschirr und an ihrer (sonstigen) Habe'. The expression *idiš tavarlar* is again mentioned later in the Uyghur text, but referring to the shape of *householders'* infernal bodies: 69–71 *kim ymä egil karte /////g idiš tavarları osuglug [ätöz]lüg üzütlär ärsär* 'Diejenigen [ ] (Höllen)-Geister, die wie [ ], Geschirr und Habe von Laien$_2$ aussehen'. This means that in the Uyghur text, monastic belongings and householders' belongings are referred to in the same terms. For Uygh. *idiš* 'vessel', one may restore TA *bhājantu*, obl. pl. of *bhājaṃ** 'vessel', borrowed from Skt. *bhājana-* 'a recipient, receptacle, (esp.) a vessel, pot, plate, cup, etc.' (MW: 752a, s.v. *bhājana*). As for Uygh. *tavarlar*, it perfectly matches the new reading *(pa)r(i)ṣkāraṃ*, loc. sg. of *pariṣkār** 'utensil, personal belonging'. Although in the singular, the word has collective meaning. It is at the same level as the previous plural nouns, the loc. affix holding for the whole enumeration. The word *pariṣkār** is not attested elsewhere in Tocharian A, but it is attested in Tocharian B (Adams 2013: 381, s.v. *pariṣkār**): PK NS 71 a3 *(wa)t no kca ṣamāññe pari(ṣkār)* '[or] some equipment of monk', translating Skt. Pāt. 67 *anyatamānyatamaṃ vā śrāmaṇakaṃ pariṣkāram* (Ogihara 2013: 200 [text], 201 [parallel], 203 [transl.]). The Sanskrit word *pariṣkāra-* (Pa. *parikkhāra*, Tib. *yo byad*) means 'equipment, utensils, personal belongings', not necessarily those of a monk (Edgerton 1953: 331a, s.v. *pariṣkāra*). In Sanskrit as well as in Pali, next to the specific meaning '(four) standard requisite' of the monk,[91] the term is associated with a more or less variable number of small objects that a monk is authorized to possess for his personal use.[92] Note that these objects are the monk's personal property: they should not be confused with objects belonging to the Saṃgha, whose alienation constitutes a specific sin.[93] The infernal retribution concerning alienation of properties belonging to the Saṃgha, quite similar to our text

91 Sanskrit *cīvara-piṇḍapāt(r)a-śayanāsana-glānapratyayabhaiṣajya-pariṣkāra-*, lit. 'equipment consisting in robes, alms bowls, beds [and] seats, medicine against disease' (see Edgerton 1953: 331a, s.v. *pariṣkāra*).

92 According to Upasak: 'Usually eight articles are regarded as the *parikkhāras* of a bhikkhu practising penances. These are: three robes (*ticīvara*), an alms-bowl (*patta*), a razor (*vāsī*), a needle (*sūci*), a girdle (*kāyabandhana*) and a water strainer (*parissāvana*). (*Kv.* p. 184; *Abhidhānappadīpikā*, Gāthā No. 439). But ordinarily for the monks, even the small articles were also regarded as the *parikkhāra*. In the *Khuddasikkhā* [(M), pp. 90–92] some pages are devoted to the *parikkhāras* in which a good number of petty articles such as umbrella, *cīvaragaṇṭhī*, *pāsaka*, key, lighter, walking-stick, pillow etc. are mentioned as the *parikkhāras* of the monks.' (Upasak 1975: 141). For Sarvāstivādins (also in Uyghur texts according to Wilkens, p.c.), there are only six utensils: three robes (Skt. *saṃghāṭī-*, *uttarāsaṅga-*, *antarvāsa-*), an alms-bowl (Skt. *pātra-*), a water strainer, and a sitting mat (Skt. *niṣīdana-*).

93 Rule No. 29 of the *Niḥsargikā-pātayantikā* section ('offences entailing expiation with confiscation') of the *Prātimokṣasūtra* of the Sarvāstivādin goes as follows: *yaḥ punar bhikṣur jānaṃ sāṃghikaṃ lābhaṃ pariṇatam ātman(aḥ) pariṇāmayen niḥsargikā pātayantikā* 'Wenn sich ein Mönch wissentlich etwas, was in das Eigentum der Gemeinde übergegangen ist, selbst aneignet,

in form, is described in the first person in MNB 22, folio 7 recto, lines 20 ff. and verso, lines 01 ff. (MaitrSängim, Kat.-Nr. 143 ~ Taf. 73) (Tekin 1980: 185–186; see also Laut 2000: 131–132, Sünde A2):

> *amarıları* [21] *inčä tep teyürlär .. biz ymä öŋrä* [22] *toyınlar š(a)mnančlar ärdim(i)z .. saŋik* [23] *säŋräm sanlıg šu*[94] *šotse azan mančak* [24] *sunčuk kidiz töšäkda ulatı idišin* [25] *tavarın yalıŋuz äŋänip*[95] *mäniŋ* [26] *ol išlätdim adın*[96] *adın kartelar-* [27] *ka ymä ärk tartıp berür ärdim(i)z* [28] *ol tıltagın anta ölüp ulug* [29] *tamuda tugdumuz .. tamudın kurtulup* [30] *kičig tamularda tugdumuz . munta* [31] *tugup toyın bašlıg šu šotse azan* [32] *mančak tölt tösäk tagar* [01] *käviz sunčuk ešič bukač burnač* [02] *ätözlüg ärür .. tulp ätözümüztin* [03] *otın örtänür yalar .. bo ämgäka* [04] *ölü ymä umaz biz*
>
> 'Einige von ihnen sprechen folgendermaßen: 'Wir nun waren ehemals Mönche und Nonnen. Die dem Saṃgha gehörigen Kämme, Schemel,[97] Sitze, Betten, Matten,[98] Filze,[99] Kissen, also Gefäße und Güter haben wir uns persönlich angeeignet und verwendet, (wobei jeder von uns vorgab): 'Dies ist mein!'. (Außerdem) haben wir uns verschiedenen anderen Laien gegenüber Befugnisse angemaßt und ihnen (von den gestohlenen Dingen) gegeben. Deshalb starben wir dort und sind in der Großhölle wiedergeboren worden. Aus (jenen) Höllen befreit, sind wir in den Kleinhöllen wiedergeboren worden. Hier wiedergeboren, haben wir Mönchsköpfe, aber Körper in Gestalt

dann ist es ein Niḥsargikā-Pātayantikā-Vergehen.' (Simson 2000: 202 [text], 288 [transl.]).

94 SWCWSY ''Z 'RDY MCNK as per Tekin is to be read *šu šotse azan mančak* (Geng, Klimkeit & Laut 1998: 92, note 1; Laut 2000: 131–132, Sünde A2, Vergehen).

95 ''RKSNYP as per Tekin is to be read *äŋänip* (Laut 2000: 131–132, Sünde A2, Vergehen).

96 ''NDYN as per Tekin is to be read *adın* (Laut 2000: 131–132, Sünde A2, Vergehen).

97 Translation modified after HWAU (655b, s.v. *šotse*).

98 Translation modified after HWAU (631a, s.v. *sunčuk*).

99 Translation modified after HWAU (379b, s.v. *kidiz*).

von Kämmen, Schemel,[100] Sitzen, Betten, Kissen, Bettzeug, Säcken, Decken, Matten,[101] Kesseln, Töpfen und Wasserkannen$_2$. An allen unseren Körpern brennen$_2$ wir durch Feuer, können durch dieses Leid jedoch nicht sterben.' (transl. Geng, Klimkeit & Laut 1998: 92).

a2 *tatträṅkuṣ* 'attached'

~ Uygh. 56–57 *aŋsız yapıšmıš bodulmıš ärdilär* 'Sie hingen$_2$ sehr (an)'. The root *träṅk-* (TB *treṅk-*) is followed by loc., here *pariṣkāraṃ*.[102] The corresponding abstract derivative is attested in a similar infernal context: A 284[103] b7 (*kus*) *pat nu tspokäṃntwaṃ träṅkluneyā* 'or those who, because of their attachment to sensual pleasures … (those are reborn in Mahāraurava hell)' (my transl.). The same verb is used in our text (stanza 84a) in connection with householders (see under 4.2.2, s.v. a5 *wramaṃ prākär tatträṅkuṣ*). The idea is expressed with a hendiadys in the Uyghur text, *yapıšmıš bodulmıš* 'sie hingen$_2$ (an)', reinforced by the adverb *aŋsız* 'very, strongly', as if translating *prākär tatträṅkuṣ* 'excessively attached'.

a2 *kräntsonā(s wsālu pātär skam prakṣār mā märkamplā)* 'they were constantly asking for beautiful clothes and for a [new] alms bowl improperly'

~ Uygh. 57–59 *turkaru nomsuz törösüzin ton pat(ï)r tiläyür //ıgarlar ärdi* 'ständig verlangten$_2$ sie gesetzwidrig$_2$[104] nach (neuer) Kleidung und Bettelschalen'. One may restore TA *wsālu* according to Uygh. *ton* 'cloth' (cf. *kāswa-wsālu* in 81c), TA *pātär* after Uygh. *pat(ï)r* 'alms bowl', TA *skam* after Uygh. *turkaru* 'constantly', TA *prakṣār* after Uygh. *tiläyür //ıgarlar ärdi* (hendiadys) 'they were asking for',[105] TA *mā märkamplā* after Uygh.

100 Translation modified after HWAU (655b, s.v. *šotse*).
101 Translation modified after HWAU (631a, s.v. *sunčuk*).
102 On the syntax of this verbal root, see Malzahn (2010: 675) and Kölver (1965: 106–107).
103 The fragment belongs to MSN 25, see Pinault (1999: 203–204).
104 Or, 'improperly$_2$' according to Wilkens (p.c.).
105 The root TA *präk-* 'ask' is attested in the meaning 'ask for, claim': A 134 a5 /// *prakäs sām mā wsāṃ* '… erbat er (von ihr). Sie [aber] gab ihm nicht.' (transl. Schmidt, 1974: 376).

nomsuz törösüzin (hendiadys) 'improperly'.[106] The greedy attachment of monks to their 'robes' and 'bowls' is associated with the decadence of the Law in the *Saddharmapuṇḍarīkasūtra* (SaddhP 267,13–15):

> *ya imaṃ dharmaparyāyaṃ paścime kāle paścime samaye paścimāyāṃ pañcaśatyāṃ vartamānāyāṃ dhārayiṣyanti, na te bhikṣavo lubdhā bhaviṣyanti, na cīvaragṛddhā na pātragṛddhā bhaviṣyanti*
> 'those who at the end of times, in the last epoch, in the last five hundred years [of the Kalpa], will be in possession of this exposition of the Law, will not be greedy monks, eagerly longing for robes and bowls.' (my transl.).

The same theme is associated with inferior rebirth in one of the *Avadānaśataka*'s 'ghost stories', *Śreṣṭhī* 'The Merchant' (No. 48). This story shows interesting phraseological correspondences with our text (Avś I 272,10–12):

> *bhadramukha tvayaivaitad ātmavadhāya pātracīvaraṃ samudānītam yenāsyapāyeṣūpapannaḥ | sādhu mamāntike cittaṃ prasādaya asmāc ca pariṣkārāc cittaṃ virāgaya | mā haivetaḥ kālaṃ kṛtvā narakeṣūpapatsyasa iti*
> [the Buddha is berating a hungry ghost:] 'Friend, hoarding your bowl and robe like this is self-destructive! That's why you were reborn in one of the terrible realms of existence. So cultivate faith in your heart toward me! And cultivate dispassion in your heart for these monastic provisions (*asmāc pariṣkārāc*)! If not, when you die [and pass away] from here, you will be reborn in the realms of hell.' (transl. Rotman 2021: 113).

Specific rules in the *Niḥsargikā-pātayantikā* section of the *Prātimokṣa-sūtra* of the Sarvāstivādins prohibit a monk from possessing more than

106 Cf. A 374 a2–3 *pācarä lānt tā-caṃ märkampalā tā-caṃ mā märkampalā watku wätkäsmā pälkāt* 'he saw his father the king commanding sometimes according to the law, sometimes against the law'. Later in the Uyghur text (Uygh. 75), the term *törösüzin* alone translates TA *sne-plā* (see under 4.2.3, s.v. a5 *sne-plā pe(nu)*).

one robe and bowl 'as a surplus' (Skt. *atirikta-*),[107] especially by 'asking for' (Skt. *vijñāpayati*) new ones.[108]

4.2 The householders: stanzas 82–85 (sections **j–m**)

4.2.1 Stanza 82 (cf. Uygh. 12–36)

a3 *tāmäk āpaṃ* 'in that same stream'

This phrase is not reflected in the Uyghur text, but cf. Uygh. 31–32 ol örtlüg *yalınl(ı)g čad(ı)r üigüz ičintä* 'In jenem glühenden₂ Strom aus Ätzlauge'. The demonstrative pronoun *tāmäk* with emphatic particle -(*ä*)*k* means 'in that stream *precisely*, in that *very* stream'. Indeed, the householders are immersed in the same stream as the monks mentioned above. In MNB 24, this stream is visible from Mount Kukkuṭapāda ('Cockfoot') through a breach opened in the ground by Maitreya (see section *d* in the synoptic table). The TB match of TA *āp** is *āp* (Adams 2013: 46–47, s.v. *āp*). The word refers to 'running water' as opposed to 'dormant water', cf. A 45 b2 *gaṅk āpäṣ wär* 'water from the Ganges river', where it is clear that TA *āp**

107 See especially rule No. 1: *niṣṭhitacīvareṇa bhikṣuṇā uddhṛte kaṭhine daśāhaparamam atiriktaṃ cīvaraṃ dhārayitavyaṃ tata uttaraṃ dhārayen niḥsargikā pātayantikā* 'Ein Mönch, der seine Gewänder fertig hat, darf nach Aufhebung der Kaṭhina-Zeremonie höchstens zehn Tage lang ein überschüssiges Gewand behalten; wenn er es länger behält, ist es ein Niḥsargikā-Pātayantikā-Vergehen.' (Simson 2000: 184 [text], 282 [transl.]). Similarly, rules No. 21 and No. 22 prohibit the accumulation of alms bowls (see Simson, 2000: 196–197 [text], 286–287 [transl.]).

108 See rule No. 6: *yaḥ punar bhikṣur ajñātiṃ gṛhapatiṃ gṛhapatipatnīṃ vā cīvaraṃ vijñāpayed anyatra samayād abhiniṣpanne cīvare niḥsargikā pātayantikā* 'Wenn ein Mönch einen Hausherrn oder die Ehefrau eines Hausherrn, mit denen er nicht verwandt ist, um ein Gewand bittet, dann ist es – wenn nicht besondere Umstände vorliegen –, falls er das Gewand erhält, ein Niḥsargikā-Pātayantikā-Vergehen.' (Simson 2000: 185–186 [text], 282–283 [transl.]).

is the semantical match of Skt. *nadī-* 'river'. This equivalence is perfectly coherent in the context of hells, for the stream in question is that of a river too, the *kṣārodakā nadī* (Pa. *khārodakā nadī*),[109] also called Vaitaraṇī (Pa. Vetaraṇī in canonical Buddhist sources).[110] As its name suggests, the burning stream of the *kṣārodakā nadī* is made of 'alkaline solution' or 'caustic lye' (as per Zieme 2021), cf. Skt. *kṣāra-*, masc. (related to the root *kṣar-*) 'any corrosive or acrid or saline substance (esp. an alkali such as soda or potash), caustic alkali (one species of cautery)' (MW: 327a, s.v. *kṣāra*). The theme of the Caustic Lye Stream must have been of some importance, since a *sūtra* is entirely devoted to it, the *Kṣāranadīsūtra*, quoted in Asaṅga's *Mahāyānasūtrālaṃkāra* (Lévi 1911: 15, 166), and translated into Chinese in the *Saṃyuktāgama* (SĀ No. 1177, T 99 (II): 316c23–317b15).[111]

109 The identification of Uygh. *čad(ı)r ügüz* to the *kṣārodakā nadī* in MNB 24 is due to Geng, Klimkeit & Laut (1998: 109). According to the *Abhidharmakośabhāṣya* (ad AK 3.59a-c), the *kṣārodakā nadī* is the fourth *utsada* ('annex') (AKB 164,6–10): *caturtha utsado nadī vaitaraṇi pūrṇa taptasya kṣārodakasya yasyāṃ te sattvā asiśaktiprāsahastaiḥ puruṣair ubhābhyāṃ tīrābhyāṃ prativāryamāṇā ūrdhvam api gacchantaḥ svidyante pacyante adhas tiryag api gacchantaḥ svidyante pacyante | tad yathā bahūdakāyāṃ sthālyām agnāvadhiśritāyāṃ tilataṇḍulādayaḥ | sā hi mahānarakasya parikhevotpannā* 'The fourth infernal annex is the Vaitaraṇi river, full of burning caustic water, in which the beings are pushed back from both banks by men with swords, spears and javelin in their hands. Even when they swim up they are boiled and cooked, even when they swim down or across they are boiled and cooked, exactly like grains of sesame, rice, etc. in a cauldron containing a large volume of water placed over a fire. The river is like the moat of the great hell.' (my transl.).

110 On the identity between the *kṣārodakā nadī* and the Vaitaraṇī, see Van Put (2015: 243–244, s.v. 'Vaitaraṇī') and Przyluski (1923: 132).

111 The Chinese version of this sūtra explains how, by progressive meditation, the suffering sinner can manage to extricate himself from the Caustic Lye Stream, which is a metaphor for Saṃsāra.

The Uyghur phrase *čad(ı)r ügüz* is especially interesting.[112] Unlike the generic Skt. word *kṣāra-*, Uygh. *čad(ı)r* does not refer to *any* corrosive substance, but to a local alkali whose production sites are mainly localizable in Central Asia: the 'salmiac' or 'ammoniac sal', equivalent to natural ammonium chloride (Zieme 2021: 215). This rare alkaline salt is abundantly found as a mineral in the mountains north of Kuča, where it is produced by slow and continuous combustion of underground coal veins (see Kroonenberg 2011: 139–144). It was mined by local people (Tocharians?) to be sold along the Silk Roads, especially for purification of precious stones and metals, dyeing, and paper fabrication.[113] One may suppose, as does Adams (2013: 271, s.v. ˣ*cātir**), that the Uyghur word *čad(ı)r* was borrowed from Tocharian, even if it is not attested in Tocharian.[114]

a3 *ālyek nuṃ wrasañ tāloṣ klopasuṣ* '[there are] still other beings, miserable [and] suffering'

The verb 'be' is implied. Note the displacement of the adjectives *tāloṣ* and *klopasuṣ* after their syntactical head for metrical reasons (see Knoll 1996: 77). The binomial expression *tāloṣ klopasuṣ* corresponds to TB (THT 31 a2) *tallāñc läklessoñc* (Thomas 1972: 448, note 16).

112 Descriptions of hell involving a caustic lye made of salmiac (*čadır ügüz* or *čadırlıg ügüz*) are known from two Uyghur texts, both translated from Tocharian: MNB 24 and the *Daśakarmapathāvadānamālā* (Zieme 2021: 217).

113 On salmiac in Central Asia according to ancient sources, see Needham (1959: 654–655) and Needham (1980: 433–448). 'Sal ammoniac workers' (Uygh. *čadırčılar*) victims of a mine accident are mentioned in a Uyghur Jātaka fragment translated by Zieme (2021: 215). Concerning the use of salmiac: 'The [ammonium chloride] will attack, or colour, many metals, even silver, producing the chlorides; it reduces metal oxides as a flux giving a clean metallic surface suitable for tinning, silvering or gilding; it also found employment in the dyeing craft where ammonia alum was wanted as a mordant; and it has useful pharmacological properties.' (Needham 1980: 434).

114 In any case, this word is ultimately of Iranian origin, from *(a)nōš* 'immortal' + *ādar* 'fire', meaning 'immortal fire' (Zieme 2021: 216–217).

a3 *k(apśño nāṃtsuṣ) wampeṣi (ñemintwāṣi) l(e)kā cem* 'those have bodies in the shape of ornaments, of jewels'

Whereas the description of householders' infernal bodies is developed in detail along two stanzas in the Tocharian text (stanzas 82–83, corresponding to section *j* in the synoptic table), there is no such description at this point in the Uyghur text. The latter immediately goes on to the identification of the beings without describing them. However, a parallel description – unfortunately interrupted by an important lacuna – is to be found earlier in the text (Uygh. 12–36, corresponding to section *e* in the synoptic table). Moreover, the Uyghur relative clause introducing the identification of the second group of infernal beings refers to them as follows: Uygh. 69–71 *kim ymä egil karte /////g idiš tavarları osuglug [ätöz] lüg üzütlär ärsär* 'Diejenigen (Höllen)-Geister, die haben Körper wie [ ] Geschirr und Habe von Laien$_2$'.

We can deduce that in the Tocharian description, the syntactic structure with relational adjective in *-ṣi* or substantive followed by *lekā* (frozen perl. of *lek*), repeated at least three times in stanzas 82–83, means 'looking like X, in the shape of X'. This structure is syntactically and semantically comparable to the use of TB *rup* 'form' (< Skt. *rūpa-*) in the perl. associated with a relational adjective: THT 46 b6 *ñäkcye rūpsa śāmñe rūp(sa)* 'in göttlicher Gestalt, (in) menschlicher Gestalt' (Carling 2000: 224). The substantive TA *lek* originally means 'form, figure, appearance',[115] hence in the perl. 'in the shape (of)'. One may restore the already well-attested instr. sg. *k(apśño)* 'with a body', constructed with the preterit participle of 'be' with stative meaning, literally 'being provided with a body in the shape of'.[116] The restoration of *k(apśño)* is based on lines 23–31 of the Uyghur text, where the expression *amarıları … osuglug <u>ätözlüglär</u>* 'some [are] <u>with bodies</u> in the way of' repeatedly occurs.[117] The use of the name for 'body' in the instr. in this context is also paralleled by the restitu-

115 Poucha gives the meaning 'aspectus' (Poucha 1955: 271, s.v. *lek*).

116 One may note that in English, the same casual relations are expressed by means of prepositions: 'with an X in the shape of Y'.

117 Uygh. *osuglug* is a postposition based on *osug* 'way, manner', meaning 'like, in the way of', cf. Germ. *-artig* (HWAU: 516b, s.v. *osuglug*).

tion *kap(ś)i(ñño)* proposed by Itkin & al. for THT 1331.a b2 (MSN 25, infernal description, similar context): *tsoptsāṃ empely(ā)ṃ klopasutsāṃ kap(ś)i(ñño)* 'with a big terrible suffering body' (Itkin, Kuritsyna & Malyshev 2017: 74, 76). The instr. *kap(ś)i(ñño)* restored by the authors precisely corresponds to Uygh. *ätözlüg* 'Körper-, mit Körper, -körperlich, einen Körper habend' (HWAU: 128b, s.v. *ätözlüg*).[118] In order to restore the Tocharian text correctly, we can compare the expressions used in the Uyghur description (lines 23–31) to those used in the Tocharian text (stanzas 82–83):

Uygh. (lines 23–31)			
Subject	Substantive without affix	Postposition	Affix **-lIg** + pl.
amarıları	*kičig yumuz yančuk kur* 'little round bag, belt'	*osuglug*	*ätözlüglär*
amarıları	*äränčü bibru üm tärlik* 'jacket, trousers, underwear, *tärlik*'	∅	*ätözlüglär*
amarıları	*yarık ıšuk* 'armour, helmet'	*osuglug*	*ätözlüglär*
amarıları	*yer-suv bag borluk yayl(a)g kıšl(a)g kalık ısırka ävbark* 'earth, garden, wineyard, summer [and] winter palaces$_2$, houses'	*osuglug*	*ätözlüglär*

TA (stanzas 82–83)			
Subject	Adjective in **-ṣi** or bare substantive in the obl.	Frozen perl.	Instr. sg.
cem / ṣome (saṃ) / alyek (saṃ)	*wampeṣi, ñemintwāṣi, …* 'of ornaments, of jewels, …'	*lekā*	*kapśño*

118 Ch. 25, folio 11 recto, line 10 (MaitrSäng., Kat.-Nr. 169 ~ Taf. 85) (Tekin 1980: 212): *ulug bädük ätözlüg* 'in der sie riesige$_2$ Körper haben' (transl. Geng, Klimkeit & Laut, 1998: 124).

As it appears, in the Uyghur text the bodily forms are listed according to a thematic classification. The frame structure *amarıları … osuglug ätözlüglär* is repeated only when the nature of the *realia* mentioned changes: accessories, clothing, war tools, immovable property, and so on. A similar semantic grouping of terms is observed in the Tocharian text: *mokśi* and *kṣuraṣi* appear together (both designating small sharp objects), as well as *hārṣi*, *wakal-hāraṣi* and *muktihārṣi* (designating different types of necklaces, see below). In the Tocharian text, the belongings mentioned are mostly ornaments (TA *wampe*). Despite the lack of term to term parallel in the (lacunary) Uyghur description, reference is made to appropriation of 'treasures' by the laity (Uygh. 75–76 *agı bar(ı)m äd tavar* 'Schätze$_2$ und Besitztümer$_2$'), especially jewellery and ornaments (Uygh. 78–79 *törösüz kazganmıš ton ätük etig yaratıgın ätözlärin etip yaratıp* 'schmückten$_2$ sie ihre Körper mit den gesetzwidrig[119] angeeigneten Kleidern, Schuhen und Schmuckgegenständen'). According to the principle of 'karmic retaliation', one would expect some infernal punishment related to such objects. Therefore, it is possible that the Uyghur text contained a list of ornaments similar to the one found in the Tocharian text,[120] especially since the terms appearing closest to the lacuna belong to the semantic field of ornament (bag, belt).

Finally, among the Sanskrit sources which may have inspired the Tocharian text, we can mention a passage from the *Saṃgharakṣitāvadāna* which shows striking similarities with our texts, both in substance and in the expressions used. The monk Saṃgharakṣita is questioning the Buddha about the monstrous visions he witnessed (Vogel & Wille 1996: 263):

> *Tata āyuṣmān saṃgharakṣito buddhaṃ bhagavantaṃ pṛcchati || ihāhaṃ bhadanta satvān adrākṣaṃ kuḍyākārāṃ stambhākārāṃ vṛkṣākārāṃ patrākārāṃ puṣpākārāṃ phalākārāṃ rajjvākārāṃ saṃmārjanyākārāṃ khaṭvākārān* {emend to *taṭṭvākārāṇ*} *ulūkhalākārāṃ sthālyākārāṃ madhye cchinnān tantunā dhāryamāṇāṃ āgacchantaḥ kin tair bhadanta karma kṛtaṃ yasya karmaṇo vipākena evaṃvidhāḥ saṃvṛttā iti*

119 Or, 'improperly' according to Wilkens (p.c.).
120 Now lost in the 15-lines lacuna, see section *e* in the synoptic table.

'Thereupon the reverend Saṃgharakṣita asked Buddha the Exalted One: 'Here, venerable sir, I saw beings having the form of walls, having the form of pillars, having the form of trees, having the form of leaves, having the form of flowers, having the form of fruits, having the form of ropes, having the form of brooms, having the form of cups, having the form of mortars, having the form of pots, [and] coming near, cut asunder at their waist(s and) held together by string(s). Which act, venerable sir, did they do, an act by the maturation of which they come to be such ones?" (transl. Vogel & Wille 1996: 290).

The expression repeated in Skt. is X-*ākāra*, with *ākāra*-, masc. 'form, figure, shape, stature, appearance, external gesture or aspect of the body, expression of the face (as furnishing a clue to the disposition of mind)' (MW: 127b, s.v. *ākr̥*-). In the TB version of the *Saṃgharakṣitāvadāna* already mentioned (see above under 4.1.1), the expression used is *ṣamāñe erepatesa* 'in the shape of a monk'.

a3 *mahurṣi lekā ṣome* 'some in the shape of a diadem'

The term *mahurṣi* (hapax) is a -*ṣi* adjective based on TA *mahur** 'tiara, diadem' ← Skt. *makuṭa*- (see details in Pinault 2011: 157–158). The diadem is a male ornament, and it is also true of the other ornaments mentioned. The expression *ṣome (saṃ)* ... *ālyek (saṃ)* matches Uygh. *amarıları* ... *amarıları* (see the preceding restitution).

a3 *pu(skāṣi lek⫽ ālyek saṃ)* 'others in the shape of a garland'

The end of the *pāda* probably contains *ālyek saṃ*, parallel to *ṣome*, just as below *ṣome saṃ* is parallel to *ālyek saṃ*. The word beginning with *pu///* is very likely a noun or a -*ṣi* relational adjective referring to a kind of garment, accessory, ornament or jewellery. Since the 'diadem' (TA *mahur*) is mentioned just before in the text, one would expect a word meaning 'crown, garland',[121] for these two ornaments are always associated together in MSN / MNB 'hell chapters', cf. MNB 20, folio 7 recto, lines 3 ff.

121 For the semantic link between 'crown' and 'garland', one may compare Skt. *mālā*- 'a wreath, garland, crown' (MW: 813c, s.v. *mālā*). On crowns and diadems in the art of Central Asia, see Kageyama (2007).

(MaitrSäng., Kat.-Nr. 132 ~ Taf. 173) (Tekin 1980: 171) *amarı* [04] *yalınayu turur did(i)m pasak bašların-* [05] *ta urmıšlar* 'Einige haben Diademe und Kronen, die ständig brennen, auf ihre Häupter gesetzt' (transl. Geng, Klimkeit & Laut 1998: 79), or the following unidentified fragment from 'hell chapters', side B, line 21 (MaitrSäng., Kat.-Nr. 208 ~ Taf. 62) (Tekin 1980: 174) *kayusı bašım(ı)zta didim p(a)sak* 'Auf dem Kopf mancher von uns [befinden sich] Diademe und Kronen' (transl. Geng, Klimkeit & Laut 1998: 129).

A common Tocharian A noun for 'crown, garland' is *pässāk**, obl. pl. *pässākās*, related to Uygh. *psak* ~ *ps(a)k* 'crown' (HWAU: 562ab, s.v. *psak*).[122] Another Tocharian A substantive, *psuk* 'garland', is generally regarded as a doublet of *pässāk*. On the other hand, a third noun *pusäk**, pl. *puskāñ* 'sinew, muscle' (see Thomas & Krause 1964: 118, s.v. **pusäk*) should be added to the discussion, since this word clearly means 'garland' in at least two occurrences: A 70 b2 *pyāppyāṣinäs puskāsyo yetuntin tim pälkātā(r)* 'if you see the two ornamented with garlands of flowers' (transl. after Peyrot 2013: 644),[123] and A 312 b6 *mantārak (pyā)ppyāñ ñäkciñi puskāñ kāsañ wätsyāñ spa(rcw)māṃ kumṣār ptāñkät käṣṣinā kārmeṃ* 'Mandāraka-flowers, heavenly garlands, Kāśa[-grasses and] and rotating sunshades came directly towards the Buddha, the master' (transl. after CEToM). The most economical way to deal with this set of forms is to posit two lemmas: 1. *pässāk** 'garland', pl. *pässākāñ** and 2. *psuk* 'garland; sinew, muscle', pl. *puskāñ* (cf. *pkul* 'year', pl. *puklā*). In this perspective, the restoration of *pu(skāṣi)*, a relational adjective based on *psuk*, is morphologically possible and would fit the context. The *Nāṭyaśāstra* (ch. 23, v. 19) lists garlands (Skt. *mālā*) together with pearl necklaces (Skt. *vyālambamauktika hāra*) as male ornaments to be worn on the body (Ghosh 1950: 413).

---

122 As the Uyghur word, TA *pässāk** could be a borrowing from Sogd. *'ps'k* (Tremblay 2005: 425).

123 In this occurrence, *puskāsyo* corresponds to Skt. *mālā-* in the Sanskrit compound *mālabharin-* (Peyrot 2013: 644).

a4 *mokśi kṣuraṣi lek⁄⁄ ālyek saṃ* 'others in the shape of a knife, of a razor'

The word *lekā* is probably implied: *mokśi [lekā] kṣuraṣi lek⁄⁄ ālyek saṃ*. Note that *lekā* can govern either an adjective in *-ṣi* (*kṣuraṣi*) or a bare substantive in the obl. (*mokśi*). The objects in question may refer either to body care accessories or ornamental cutlery worn by rulers. The fact that the infernal beings have a body shaped like a sharp object is consistent with the sufferings described at the end of the Uyghur description (section *e* in the synoptic table): 35–36 *bıčıšu osušu ärüyü sizä ulıyu müŋräyü ämgäk ämgänürlär* 'erleiden sie Qualen [...] indem sie sich wehklagend$_2$ gegenseitig zerschneiden$_2$ und (dabei) zerschmelzen$_2$'.[124] The hendiadys used in the Uyghur text is *bıčıš-* 'sich gegenseitig (ab)schneiden', combined with *osuš-* 'einander abschneiden'.[125] The root *bıč-*, is used in MNB 'hell chapters' to describe tortures involving sharp objects such as 'axes' (Laut 2000: 137–138, Sünde A18, Strafe) or 'knives' (Laut 2000: 139, Sünde B2, Strafe; 145, Sünde E2, Strafe, etc.). The meter requires a monosyllabic word before *mokśi*, but it is difficult to make a cogent proposal.

4.2.2 *Stanza 83 (cf. Uygh. 12–36)*

a4 *hārṣi wakal-hāraṣi mu(ktihā)rṣi* '[in the shape] of a necklace, of a half-necklace, of a necklace of pearls'

All three terms contain the word *hār* 'necklace' (< Skt. *hāra-*). The first one is a derivative adjective in *-ṣi* based on this word. I propose to analyze the second term as a derivative in *-ṣi* based on an unattested substantive **wakal-hār* (in our text, the caesura occurs between the two terms of the compound), calque of Skt. *ardhahāra-* 'half-necklace'. The equivalence TA *wakal* ~ Skt. *ardha-* was already suggested with hesitation ('vielleicht') by Sieg, Siegling & Schultze (1931: 7, §9), followed by Poucha (1955: 284, s.v. *wakal*). Indeed, Skt. *hāra-* 'necklace' and *ardhahāra-* 'half-necklace' are often associated in Sanskrit literature as a *dvandva* com-

124 Differently Röhrborn (2010: 196, s.v. *ärü-*), who translates metaphorically: '(vor Schmerz) zergehen' (I thank J. Wilkens for this remark).
125 See HWAU (167a, s.v. *bıčıš-*, and 516b, s.v. *osuš-*).

pound, *hārārdhahāra-* 'necklace and half-necklace'. According to the Indian tradition, the necklace called *hāra* has 108 pearls, whereas the necklace called *ardhahāra* has 64 pearls. The third kind of necklace mentioned in the Tocharian text can be retrieved from a compound attested in the *Saddharmapuṇḍarīkasūtra*. The context is a cliché description of a jewel rain (SaddhP 197,1–2): *hārārdhahāramuktāhāramaṇiratnamahā ratnāni* 'necklaces, half-necklaces, necklaces of pearls, excellent jewels, exceptional jewels'. A slightly different lesson is preserved in a manuscript from Central Asia: *hārārddhahāramuktihāramaṇiratnāni* 'necklaces, half-necklaces, pearl necklaces, excellent jewels' (Hoernle 1916: 136 [text], 138 [transl.]). One should therefore restore the third item of the Tocharian list as *mu(ktihā)rṣi*, derivative adjective in *-ṣi* based on (attested) *muktihār* 'string of pearls' (Carling & Pinault forth., s.v. *muktihār**). Note that the Nepalese recension of *Saddharmapuṇḍarīkasūtra*, written in a more 'classical' Sanskrit, has the 'standard' form *muktāhāra-*, while the Central Asian manuscript has the 'hybrid' form *muktihāra-*, a direct source for TA *muktihār*.

a4 *wätläkṣi* '[in the shape] of a *wätläk*'

This word is a hapax of unknown meaning. We would expect the name of some ornament, such as a bracelet or a jewel. The reference grammar quotes the basis of this adjective as **wätläk* (Sieg, Siegling & Schulze 1931: 23, §44c). There is no evident segmentation of this word as a compound. According to Pinault (p.c.), this word would mean 'diamond', because in the Indian lore about gems, the diamond is sometimes named the 'splitting one', Skt. *bhidura-* 'thunderbolt, diamond' (MW: 757a, see also Finot 1896: xxiv). This term would have served as model for the formation of a Tocharian noun on the basis of a root related to *wätk-* 'separate' (see Malzahn 2010: 879–882).

a4 *kat(uṣi) pärsānt lekā* 'in the shape of a goldsmith's work, of a gemstone'

The term *katuṣi*, already attested in A 287 b4 (Carling 2009: 98a, s.v. *katuṣi**), is a derivative in *-ṣi* from *katu* 'jewellery', more precisely 'piece of goldsmith's work' (Pinault 2011: 156). As in *mokśi kṣuraṣi lekā* above, the word *lekā* is probably implied: *katuṣi [lekā] pärsānt lekā*. The noun *pärsānt* 'spotted stone, precious mineral'[126] is related to the root A *pärsā-*, B *pärs-* 'sprinkle' and to TA *ṣokyo-pärs* 'extremely variegated', translating Skt. *parama-citraka-* in A 145 b5.

a4 *kontāl lekā ṣome saṃ* 'some in the shape of an earring'

The term TA *kontāl*, a hapax, is borrowed from Skt. *kuṇḍala-* 'earring' (Carling 2009: 164a, s.v. *kontāl*).

a4 (*puk wäknantyo cem*) *letäk letäk* (*nāṃtsuṣ*) 'they have all become each one in a different way'

The context is lacunary. The same distributive expression *letäk letäk* is found in stanza 80.

a4–5 (*po*)*r*(*ṣ*)*inäs sälpiñcä śkaṃ* (*s*)*l*(*a*)*ma*(*s*)*yo* 'and they burn in flames of fire'

The restitution (*s*)*l*(*a*)*ma*(*s*)*yo* 'with flames' is due to Sieg & Siegling (1921: 112, note 5). The adjective (*po*)*r*(*ṣ*)*inäs* may be restored in the previous *pāda*, obl. pl. masc. of *porṣi*, modifying (*s*)*l*(*a*)*ma*(*s*)*yo* – although the terms belong to two different *pādas*. The flames in question are those of the Caustic Lye Stream. In the Uyghur text, the river is described as 31–32 *örtlüg yalınl*(*ı*)*g*, lit. 'fiery [and] flaming'. In the *Nimijātaka* (No. 541), the river Vetaraṇī is said to be *aggisikhūpamaṃ* 'like a flaming fire', with Pa. *aggi-sikhā* meaning 'a flame, the crest of a fire' (PED: 9b, s.v. *aggi*), lit. 'flame of fire', cf. Skt. *śikhā-* 'a pointed flame, any flame' (MW: 1070b, s.v. *śikhā*).

a5 *utkraṃ klopant wärpnāntär* 'they endure excruciating pains'

The same formulaic phrase occurs in THT 1331 a5, a passage from MSN 25 (similar context, description of infernal torments): *wrināñ lwā ś*(*w*)*eñc-äṃ tsraṃ utkraṃ ś*(*āwaṃ klopant wärpnātär*) 'water animals (= fish?) are devouring him. (He endures) cruel and torturous suffer-

126 See Carling (2009: 164ab, s.v. *kopräṅk-pärsānt*) and Carling & Pinault (forth., s.v. *pärsānt*). This word probably refers to a shimmering gemstone, possibly a 'tiger's eye' according to Wilkens (p.c.).

ing' (Itkin, Kuritsyna & Malyshev 2017: 73 [text], 76 [transl.]).[127] The corresponding expression in Uyghur, MNB 25, folio 10 recto, lines 20 ff. (MaitrHami) is: *agar ulug ämgäk täginür-* [21] *lär* 'Sie erleiden schwere, große Qual.' (Geng, Klimkeit & Laut 1998: 55 [text], 124 [transl.]). In the Pa. *Devadūtasutta* (AN 3.36), one of the earliest sources on hell, the canonical Pali expression (repeated three times) is (AN I 141,5–6): *so tattha dukkhā tibbā kharā kaṭukā vedanā vediyati* 'thus, he suffers painful, severe, intense, bitter sufferings'. This corresponds in the *Mahāvastu* (Mvu I 19,9–10) to Skt.: *te tathābhūtā adhimātraṃ duḥkhā vedanāṃ vedayanti* 'in this state they suffer agonies beyond measure' (transl. Jones 1949: 16).[128]

Interestingly, the use of the word *kaṭuka* in the Pali parallel invites us to precise the etymology of TA *utkur**. It is clear from this parallel that the meaning of the – obviously borrowed – Tocharian adjective matches that of Skt. *kaṭu(ka)*- 'pungent, acrid, sharp' (MW: 244a, s.v. *kaṭu*), Pa. *kaṭuka* 'sharp, disagreeable; (of taste) pungent, acrid (as peppers or ginger); (of words) bitter, caustic; (of pain etc.) severe, keen, keenly distressing' (DP I: 613a, s.v. *kaṭuka*). On the formal side however, it is very tempting to derive TA *utkur* via Middle Indic from Skt. *utkuṭa(ka-)* (Pa. *ukkuṭika-*) 'sitting upon the hams, squatting', as proposed by Carling (2009: 65a, s.v. *utkur*). To conciliate semantical and formal data, one may suppose a contamination of Skt. *kaṭu(ka)*- 'severe, excessive (pain)' and *utkuṭa(ka)*- 'squatting (position)'. In Sanskrit, such a contamination is attested by the existence of a variant *utkaṭuka-* (as if from *ud* 'out' + *kaṭuka-* 'sharp, disagreeable') instead of *utkuṭaka-* in the *Suśrutasaṃhitā* (MW: 175c, s.v. *utkaṭuka*). The semantic link between 'squatting' and 'sharp, disagreeable' is probably not related to ascetic exercise (pace Carling 2009: 65a,

127 On this expression, see also Schaefer (2013: 337).

128 In the description of hell of the *Lokapaññatti*, the expression frequently repeated is similar to that used in the *Devadūtasutta* (AN 3.36): *te tattha bhūtā adhimattā dukkhā tibbā kharā kaṭukā vedanā vedenti* 'les êtres qui sont là éprouvent des sensations atroces, douloureuses, intenses, âpres, amères' (Denis 1977 vol. II,1: 93 [text], vol. II,2: 90 [transl.]). For the equivalence between Skt. *vedanā-* 'feeling' and the root TA *wärpā-*, TB *wärp-*, see Pinault (1995: 30).

s.v. *utkur*). It is rather easily explained by the fact that 'squatting posture' (Skt. *utkuṭāsana-*) is characteristic of parturient women (also in iconography, see Revire 2016: 48). In this context, squatting is inevitably associated with birth-pain, hence excruciating pain in general (cf. Gr. ὀδύνη 'birth-pain' > 'excruciating pain'). In Tocharian, the expression *klopaṃ ukkur ṣäm-* 'to sit squatting in suffering' precisely occurs in a passage from the *Nandagarbhāvakrāntinirdeśa* describing childbirth (A 146 b2).

4.2.3 *Stanza 84 (~ Uygh. 71–87)*

a5 *ceṃ ṣeñc kātkāñ neṣ-cmolwaṃ* 'those were householders in previous births'

~ Uygh. 71–74 *bolar öŋrä ažunlarda ärklig eliglär bäglär buyruklar bayagutlar ärtilär* 'die waren in früheren Existenzen mächtige Könige, Befehlshaber$_2$ und Begüterte'. The use of the far deixis pronoun *ceṃ* is noteworthy. As shown by Stumpf, the demonstrative pronoun *saṃ* can denote pejorative nuance (Stumpf 1971: 142–143). In the *Koṭikarṇāvadāna*, one of the characters in the tale refers to the monstrous *preta* standing before her with this pronoun: A 341 b2 *sāṃ nāñi seyo śäṃ ṣeṣ* 'Diese da war meines Sohnes Frau.' (transl. Stumpf 1971: 143). Stumpf also comments on A 226 a5,[129] translating the occurrence as follows: 'Jene waren Haushalter in den früheren Geburten; an dem Besitz [wörtl. an der Sache] fest haftend' (Stumpf 1971: 144–145).

a5 *wramaṃ prākär tatträṅkuṣ* 'firmly attached to possession'

This passage is not reflected in the Uyghur text, but cf. Uygh. 56–57 *aŋsız yapıšmıš bodulmıš ärdilär* 'Sie hingen$_2$ sehr (an)' (about the monks, see under 4.1.2). The expression TA *prākär träṅk-* specifically refers to mundane attachment, with negative connotation, cf. A 232 b6 *kälpaṃ prākär träṅkäṣtär* 'hängt fest am Gewinn' (transl. Schmidt 1974: 107). In the *Cīvaravastu*, we find the story of a monk who was reborn first as a ser-

129 'Nicht sehr klar ist schon der Kontext zu folgendem Beispiel, in dem wohl auch eine abwertende Distanzierung zu sehen sein wird' (Stumpf 1971: 144–145).

pent inside his alms bowl, then in hell. The cause of these inferior rebirths is that he was 'excessively attached' to his alms bowl (GMs III,2 125,11–12):[130] *tasya pātraṁ śobhanam | sa tasmin atīvādhyavasitaḥ* 'he had a nice bowl; he was excessively attached to it.' The expression used in Sanskrit is composed of *atīva* 'exceedingly, very' (cf. TA *prākär*, Uygh. *aŋsız*) and *adhyavasita-*, verbal adjective of the verb *adhyavasyati* 'clings to (something deprecated), covets' (Edgerton 1953: 17a, s.v. *adhyavasyati*). The related action noun is *adhyavasāna-*, nt. 'clinging to, grasping, coveting (regularly desires or worldly things, loc. or in comp.)' (Edgerton 1953: 16b, s.v. *adhyavasāna*). One may compare TB PK AS 6B a5: *kektsenne ṣai olypotse tetreṅku* 'he [scil. Nanda] was excessively attached to his body'.

a5 *kropñā(nt ālu niṣpalntu)* 'they were amassing other people's riches' ~ Uygh. 74–76 *balık uluštakı tınl(ı)glar(ı)g ämgätip törösüzin kuna tarta agı bar(ı)m äd tavar yıgdılar kazgantılar ärdi* 'Sie quälten die Bewohner im Reich$_2$ und eigneten sich (deren) Schätze$_2$ und Besitztümer$_2$ an, indem sie sie gesetzwidrig[131] konfiszierten.' TA *niṣpalntu* is restored after the two Uyghur binomial phrases *agı bar(ı)m* 'treasures' and *äd tavar* 'possessions'.[132] The Tocharian A word *niṣpal* especially refers to the 'riches' or 'acquisitions' of a householder (Skt. *parigraha-*). In addition, the phrase *niṣpal krop-* is well attested: A 3 a3 *niṣpaltu kropitär*, YQ I.6 a7 *niṣpalntu kākropunt ṣeñc* (see also TA *akäṃtsune krop-* 'accumulate wealth'). The corresponding root TB *kraup-* is used in THT 337 b4 (Vinaya), referring to the accumulation of bowls by monks: *ṣaḍvarginta patraiṃ māka kraupiyenträ • päst taṣīyeṃträ mā paribhog yamaṣyenträ* 'the Ṣaḍvargikas accumulated many alms bowls; they were putting them aside and weren't using them.' (transl. CEToM).

130 For the translation of this story, see Schopen (2004: 113–114). The rebirth of the monk as a snake inside his bowl is probably related to the notion of *pratyekanaraka* 'individual hell' (see above under 2.1.2).

131 Or, 'improperly' according to Wilkens (p.c.).

132 The meaning of these two binomial phrases is close. It should be noted that elsewhere in the MNB, TA *niṣpal* is translated by *äd tavar* (Pinault 2020b: 323–324).

a5 (*kältsā*)*lā* 'through oppression'
~ Uygh. 74 *balık uluštakı tınl(ı)glar(ı)g ämgätip* 'Sie quälten die Bewohner im Reich$_2$'. The possibilities for °*lā* preceded by vowel are theoretically quite numerous. However, the immediate proximity of *sne-plā pe*(*nu*) (see below) makes a parallel form of perl. sg. with adverbial value very likely. It could be the perl. sg. of a substantive ending in *-l* with two syllables at most (*śol*, *ākāl*, etc.), or an adverb ending in *-ā* (*elā*, *yulā*, etc.). As noted by Pinault (p.c.), a plausible restoration would be (*kältsā*)*lā* 'through oppression', perl. sg. of **kältsāl*, unattested verbal noun based on the root *kältsā-* 'oppress'.

a5 *sne-plā pe*(*nu*) 'and also improperly'
~ Uygh. 75 *törösüzin kuna tarta* 'indem sie sie gesetzwidrig[133] konfiszierten'. The Uyghur term *törösüzin* confirms that TA *sne-plā* is the perl. sg. of *sne-pal* 'unrighteousness' (TB *snai-pele*; as per Sieg, Siegling & Schulze 1931: 240, §371c). The same Uyghur term is used in Uygh. 58 in the context of monks 'improperly' asking for a new alms bowl (see the restitution of stanza 81 under 4.1.2). One can compare the use of Skt. *asaṃmata-* 'nicht gebilligt; unautorisiert, unbeauftragt' (SWTF I: 203b, s.v. *asaṃmata*) in Vinaya texts.[134] Interesting here is the parallel drawn between violation of monastic life's rules relating to material possessions, codified in the Vinaya, and spoliation by royal and administrative authorities (laymen). The specific allusions to illegal appropriation of monastic property by kingdom's rulers in the MNB has been interpreted by scholars as pointing to the existence of latent conflicts between officials and monasteries.[135] For the idea of 'improper accumulation', one may also compare the following two *padas* from the *Petavatthu* (Pv 49): *mayaṁ bhoge saṁharimhā samena visamena ca* 'I accumulated wealth properly and improperly.'

a6 *śātoneṣiṃ trekeyo trikoṣ* 'intoxicated with the intoxication of wealth'
The Uyghur text is lacunary. The accumulation of material possessions is usually said to generate 'confusion, frenzy' (*treke*), cf. A 60 a6 *ets āmāṃ*

133 Or, 'improperly' according to Wilkens (p.c.).
134 I thank A. Huard for this suggestion.
135 See Zieme (1992: 21) and Laut (2000: 129).

treke *rapurñeyis ṣurm niṣpa(lä)ntu* 'the possessions [are] the cause of greed, of pride, of folly, of avarice' (transl. Carling, Pinault & Malzahn in CEToM). This is in line with the restitution of *niṣpalntu* in the previous *pāda* (see above, s.v. a5 *kropñā(nt ālu niṣpalntu)*). The expression *trekeyo trikoṣ* is paralleled in TB (*Udānālaṅkāra*): THT 24 b4 *cai trikoṣ traikentsa waiptār ṣeṃ* 'each in their way, they were intoxicated with intoxication' (my transl.). The corresponding Sanskrit *figura etymologica* is *X-madena mattakāḥ* 'intoxicated with the intoxication of X', as evidenced by a similar passage from the *Koṭikarṇāvadāna* about *pretas* (Divy 9,3–4): *ārogyamadena mattakā ye dhanabhogamadena mattakāḥ | dānaṃ ca na dattam aṇv api* 'We were intoxicated with the intoxication of good health, intoxicated with the intoxication of wealth and indulgence. We didn't make even the smallest offerings.' (transl. Rotman 2008: 49, slightly modified).

a6 *(tamä)nt āñc ṣakkats* 'they are fatally reborn down [in hell]'

The Uyghur text is lacunary (but see next stanza for the same idea). The restitution *(tamä)nt* is very likely. The adverb *āñc* 'down' is the semantic match of TB *ette*, same meaning. In TB, the expressions *ette ymainne täm-* 'to be reborn in an inferior existence' and *ette cmelne täm-* 'to be reborn in an inferior birth' occur in the *Karmavibhaṅga* (PK AS 7G b2, b3, b4, b6). In PK AS 7N, the same phrase refers to the three lower destinies (Skt. *durgati-*), i.e., hell, animals, and *pretas*: PK AS 7N b1 *yama(ṃ) y(o)lo (cai ette tänmas)kenträ tärya cmel(a)n(e)* '[If] (these ones) do evil, they are reborn down in the three (inferior) existences' (transl. after Pinault in CEToM). As for the adverb *ṣakkats*, note that the similar phrase *ñareyaṃ ṣakkats täm-* is attested in the same manuscript: A 229 a4 *raurāp ñareyaṃ wrasañ «:» tmäṃsantär ṣakka(ts) kupre ne mā antu ⁄⁄śśi*[136] *lotke cem : mā onmiṃ ypantär* 'beings are fatally reborn in Raurava hell if they do not turn away from it [and] if they do not show remorse.' (my transl.).

a6 *ypā(nt) ālyekäs āppärmāt* 'they were despising others'

136 Possibly *antu* with ablative meaning (= TB *entwe*, cf. TA *antu-le*, *antu-ṣ*) in sandhi with the enclitic particle *aśśi* 'then'.

The Uyghur text is lacunary. In his personal copy of *Tocharische Sprachreste*, Siegling hesitates between the restoration of 3pl. ipf. MP *ypā(nt)* and 3pl. ipf. act. *ypā(r)*. In fact, the middle form is generally used in the phrase *āppärmāt yām-* (Meunier 2013: 159–160). Meunier translates the occurrence as follows: 'ils faisaient peu de cas des autres'. Interestingly, the same expression is used in the TB *Udānālaṅkāra* (book 13) with reference to hell: THT 31 b5 *yāmtr alyeṅkäṃ appamāt yaṃ postäṃ nraintane* '[if he] mistreats the others, he will afterwards go into the hells' (transl. CEToM).

a6 *mā el eṣār mā pñi ypānt* 'they were not giving alms, they were not performing meritorious deeds (lit. merit)'

~ Uygh. 83–84 *bir tanču aš täŋinčä buši berip buyan ädgü kılınč kılmadılar* 'haben sie nicht (einmal) soviel wie einen Bissen Speise als Almosen gespendet und haben (somit) keine verdienstvollen Werke$_2$ ausgeführt.' The TA phrase *el āy-* 'give a gift' corresponds to Uygh. *buši ber-*, and TA *pñi yām-* 'perform meritorious actions' corresponds to Uygh. *buyan ädgü kılınč kıl-* (with *buyan* related to Skt. *puṇya-*, cf. TA *pñi* ← Skt. *puṇya-*). One may compare a similar expression used in one of the *Avadānaśataka*'s 'ghost stories', *Maudgalyāyanaḥ* (No. 45) (Avś I 257,3–5):

> *vayaṃ smo bhadanta mahāmaudgalyāyana rājagṛhe pañca śreṣṭhiśatāny abhūvan | te vayaṃ matsariṇaḥ kuṭukuñjakā āgṛhītapariṣkārāḥ | svayaṃ tāvad asmābhir dānapradānāni na dattāni*
> 'Bhadanta Mahāmaudgalyāyana, we were once five hundred merchants [living] in Rājagṛha. We were mean, miserly, and clung to our possessions (*āgṛhītapariṣkārāḥ*). On our own, we never gave gifts or made offerings' (transl. Rotman 2021: 94).

The absence of gift and accumulation of precious objects are naturally related: Buddhist literature abounds with examples of householders giving their precious jewellery and ornaments as offerings. In order to get a more precise idea of what kind of ornaments are mentioned in our text, consider the following example from the Uyghur *Life of Xuanzang*:

[mun]tada adın äd t(a)var ärdini[lä]r ätözdäki ton kädim yevig tizig kulgakdakı šišir biläkdäki biläzük ärdini üzäki psak boguzdakı [mu]nčuk tokırdakı ärdini bolarnı [barč]a kalısız buši birdi
'Alle seine andere Habe und seine Schätze: Kleider und Gewänder am Körper, Schmucke und Verzierungen, Achate (=Ringe) im Ohr, Armreifen und Handgelenk, Kränze aus Juwelen, Ketten am Hals und Juwelen in der Krone, dies alles gab er restlos als Almosen.' (text and transl. Zieme 1995: 233–234).

This gives a striking echo to the list of ornaments discussed above on the basis of the stanzas 82 and 83 of the Tocharian text.

4.2.4 *Stanza 85 (~ Uygh. 84–87 for a–b; c–d not reflected in the Uyghur text)*

a6 *c(a)m lyalypū yāmūräṣ (puk)* 'having committed all these deeds'
This phrase is not reflected in the Uyghur text. At the beginning of the *pāda*, the most plausible restitution is *c(a)m*, although *c(e)m* is not absolutely excluded. The phrase *c(a)m lyalypū* refers as a whole to all the above-mentioned evil deeds committed by the householders.

a6 (*tämyo antuṣ waluräṣ*) 'for that reason, having died [and passed away] from here'
Restoration after Uygh. 84–85 *ol tıltagın anta ölüp* 'Aus diesem Grunde starben sie dort'. The same Tocharian formulaic expression is preserved in A 300 b8–298 a1 (MSN 21): *täm-ṣurmaṣ antuṣ walurä(ṣ) ñ(areyaṃ tamänt)* 'for that reason, after they died [and passed away] from here, (they are reborn in he)ll'. In the Uyghur text, the same phrase *anta ölüp* 'having died there' is used in reference to the monks (without parallel in the Tocharian text): 67–69 *todunčsuz kanınčsız köŋülin anta ölüp bo kičig tamuda tugdılar* 'Unbefriedigten$_2$ Herzens starben sie dort und wurden in diesen Kleinhöllen wiedergeboren.' A Sanskrit parallel expression is to be found in the passage from the *Avadānaśataka* quoted above (Avś I

272,12):[137] *itaḥ kālaṃ kṛtvā narakeṣūpapatsyase* 'when you die [and pass away] from here, you will be reborn in the realms of hell.' (transl. Rotman 2021: 113). This parallel suggests that TA *antuṣ* ~ TB *entwe* corresponds to Skt. *itaḥ* 'hence, from here' (abl.), with local meaning.[138] According to Buddhist cosmological conceptions, one usually dies from a life to another.

a6–7 (*cem prattika-ñarentw*)*aṃ tamänt* 'they are reborn in individual hells'

~ Uygh. 85–87 *amtı bo pr(a)tikan(a)rak kičig tamuda tugmıš ärürlär* '[und] wurden jetzt in diesen Pratyekanaraka (genannten) Kleinhöllen wiedergeboren.'[139] The form *ñarentwäṣ* (without *-y-*) occurs in the same manuscript (A 238 a3).

a7 *tosäṃ klopant lkeñc* 'they see those pains'

This phrase is not reflected in the Uyghur text. In Tocharian as well as in Uyghur, the phrase 'to see sufferings' means 'to endure sufferings' (TB *läklenta läkā-*, Uygh. *ämgäk kör-*). For further examples of this phrase in TA, see A 166 a2 *tsraṃ utkraṃ klopant lkātär* 'he sees hard and painful sufferings' (transl. Carling 2009: 65a, s.v. *utkur*), or A 340 b5 *oṣeñi ñkätt oki planttär : ykonā klopant ñ(areṣṣās) lkāt* 'by night you regale yourself like a king, by day you see hellish sufferings' (transl. CEToM). In the *Kokāliyasutta* (Sn 3.10), the phrase *dukkhaṃ passati* 'he sees suffering' is used (Sn 128,666): *dukkhaṃ mando paraloke, attani passati kibbisakārī* 'The doer of wrong, the fool, sees misery for himself in the next world' (transl. Norman 2001: 88). The sentence is followed by descriptions of tortures such as impaling, swallowing of hot red iron balls, etc.

137 See under 4.1.2, s.v. a2 *kräntsonā(s wsālu pātär skam prakṣār mā märkamplā)*.

138 Uygh. *anta*, corresponding to Skt. *tatra*, has either temporal ('dann, darauf, daraufhin') or local meaning ('dort, an jenem Ort') (HWAU: 51b, s.v. *anta*), but not abl. meaning. This word may have been chosen by the Uyghur translator because of its superficial resemblance with TA *antuṣ*.

139 On the 'equivalence' between Uygh. *kičig tamular* 'little hells' and TA *prattika-ñareyntu* 'individual hells' in MNB / MSN, see the discussion under 2.1.2.

a7 *tä*(*myo*) 'therefore'

A resumptive word is likely at the beginning of the *pāda*. One could think of the neuter anaphoric pronoun *täm* followed by an absolutive, the locution *täm-ṣurmaṣ*, the adverb *tämyo*, etc.

a7 (*skenal* ...) *kātkāśśi* 'the householders should strive'

The *pāda* is difficult to restore. These words cannot belong to the infernal description, for the infernal beings are never referred to as *kātkāñ* 'householders', but as *wrasañ* 'beings, living creatures' (Uygh. *tınl*(*ı*)*glar*, *tamuluglar*, *üzütlär*, Skt. *sattva-*, *nāraka-*). The word *kātkāśśi* rather refers to 'householders' in general. The presence of the syllable *tä* at the beginning of the *pāda*, probably belonging to a conclusive word (see above, s.v. a7 *tä*(*myo*)), as well as the position of the gen. pl. (animate) at the end of the sentence, suggest a deontic expression with a gerund. One may compare: A 17 b3–4 *tämyo ptāñkte yärk skamat yal knānmāntāp* **:** *sny āñu* (*yär*)*k yatsi skenal ptāñkte tsraṣiśśi* 'therefore the veneration of the Buddha shall ever be carried out by the wise one; incessantly the energetic ones shall strive to carry out veneration of the Buddha' (transl. CEToM), A 288 a6–7 *tämyo meträkyāp kā*(*swoneyäntu*) /// (*pä*)*lskasuntāp skam skenal* 'Therefore, effort should be made constantly by a conscious person (in order to pay homage to the virtues) of Maitreya.' (transl. CEToM), and (same manuscript) A 229 b2 *tämyo pu*(*k*) *praṣtaṃ* ; *ymassu wrases skam mäskal* ; *lyalypuntwaṃ* 'Daher soll zu jeder Zeit ein Wesen in [seinem] Taten immer bedachtsam sein.' (transl. Thomas 1952: 19). An exhortation at the end of a hellish description is not surprising, cf. *Kokāliyasutta* (Sn 3.10), final stanza (Sn 131,678):

> *yāva-dukkhā nirayā idha vuttā* | *tattha pi tāvaciraṃ vasitabbaṃ* | *tasmā sucipesalasādhuguṇesu* | *vācaṃ manaṃ satataṃ parirakkhe'ti*
> 'As many as [these] miserable hells have been said [to be] here, for so long must people dwell here too. Therefore, in the midst of those who are pure, amiable, and have good qualities, one should constantly guard speech and mind.' (transl. Norman 2001: 89).

If this hypothesis is correct, the Tocharian text diverges significantly from the Uyghur text, where Maitreya's speech ends without a final exhortation.

a7 (*sparcwatsi sne-k*)*e*(*n-pä*)*lkā* 'to behave according to the absence of false view'

The <l> is no longer visible on the manuscript. However, if we trust the reading by Sieg and Siegling, possibilities are limited. The word can only be a noun or an adjective ending in °*lk* in the perl. sg., modifying the verb (lost in the preceding lacuna, hypothetically restored as *sparcwatsi*, inf. of *spärtw-* 'behave'). The most plausible solutions are: *pälk* 'view' (Carling & Pinault forth., s.v. *pälk*), and *keṃ-pälk** 'false view' (Carling 2009: 159ab, s.v. *keṃ-pälk**). The perl. can be accounted for in two ways: either without preposition, or with preposition followed by the perl., e.g., *pärne* 'out'. The context favours the first solution: *ken-pälkā*, with privative *sne*, type *sne-plā* 'improperly' (see above), *sne-knānmuneyā* 'out of ignorance' (see Pinault 1997: 452–454). The term *keṃ-pälk** occurs in the same manuscript: A 227/8 b7 *wikseñc māntlune keṃ-pälkäntwäṣ ṣñi pältsäk pāsantär* 'they expel the malice and protect their own mind from false doctrines' (transl. Carling 2009: 159ab, s.v. *keṃ-pälk**).

a7 (*ṣāmnāśśi śkaṃ puk āñmaṣ*) 'and the monks, with all their heart'

The restoration is hypothetical. The gen. pl. *ṣāmnāśśi* would be on the same syntactical level as *kātkāśśi* (see above), and *puk āñmaṣ* would modify *skenal*. We expect Maitreya's final exhortation to be addressed both to householders and monks.

a7 (*nākma*)*nt«ťä» cesmi päl*(*k*)*oräṣ* 'having seen the sins of these'

The anaphoric pronoun *cesmi* in the gen. pl. masc. refers to the infernal beings just described. Therefore, the subject of the absolutive cannot refer to these same infernal beings. It rather refers to those who are listening to Maitreya's sermon.

4.3 The followers' reaction: stanzas 86–87 (sections **n–o**)

4.3.1 *Stanza 86 (~ MNB 24, last folio, lines 12–16)*

a7 (*k$_u$ce-ne ṣāmnāñ aśyāñ śkaṃ tāṣ plāc klyoseñc tām praṣtaṃ*) 'the monks and nuns who will hear this speech at that time'

Restoration after MNB 24, last folio, lines 12 ff. (MaitrHami) *anı ešidip ärüš* [13] *[üküš kut] bulmadok toyınlar* 'Als sie dies hören, viele$_2$ Mönche, die [das Heil] noch nicht erlangt haben' (Geng, Klimkeit & Laut 1998: 40 [text], 112 [transl.]). This restitution of the missing two *pāda*s is highly hypothetical. Nevertheless, the syntactic structure of the *pāda* can be deduced from a grammatical argument: in the first *pāda* of the following stanza (87), the restitution of the relative pronoun *k$_u$ce(-ne)*[140] without particle *-ne* is possible only if the relative clause introduced by this relative pronoun is coordinated to a first relative clause where the particle *-ne* is expressed (see under 4.1.1, s.v. a1 *(ke pa)t nu … neñc*). The presence of the conjunction *pat nu* at the beginning of stanza 87 confirms the presence of two coordinated relative clauses. In addition, the restoration of the relative pronoun kuce-ne in the nom. pl. is supported by several occurrences in the same manuscript (221 b5, 227/8 b6, 229 a1, 235 a5). In the context, the category of beings most likely to be paired with the householders of stanza 87 is that of monks: *k$_u$ce pat nu kātkāñ* probably stands in opposition to *k$_u$ce-ne ṣāmnāñ* or the like, with parallelism between stanza 86 and stanza 87. This opposition would be coherent in meaning with the end of the *Anāgatavaṃsa* (v. 138–140):

> *tasmā Metteyya-buddhassa dassan'-atthāya vo idha | ubbigga-mānasā suṭṭhuṃ karotha viriyaṃ daḷhaṃ || ye keci kata-kalyāṇā appamāda-vihārino | bhikkhū bhikkhuniyo c' eva upāsakā upāsikā || mahantaṃ Buddha-sakkāraṃ uḷāraṃ abhipūjayuṃ | dakkhinti bhadra-samitiṃ tasmiṃ kāle sa-devakā*

140 Suggested by Siegling in his personal copy of *Tocharische Sprachreste*.

> 'Therefore, in order to see the Buddha Metteyya here, act rightly, energetically, firmly, with agitated mind. Those who do good things here and dwell vigilant, monks and nuns, male and female lay followers, who have performed great auspicious honour to the Buddha[s], they together with the Devas will see the auspicious assembly at that time.' (Norman 2006: 17–18 [text], 31–32 [transl.]).

Moreover, the Uyghur text shows two distinct – although parallel – 'conversion' scenes. The first one, corresponding to Uygh. 87–94, concerns beings designated as 'beings of the assembly' (Uygh. 87–88 *sansız tümän ol kuvragdakı tınl(ı)glar* 'die unzähligen$_2$ Lebewesen dieser Versammlung'). The beings in question cannot be monks, since it is said that they 'become monks' (Uygh. 92 *toyın bolurlar* 'werden Mönche'). On the other hand, the second 'conversion' – rather a 'beatification' –, located at the end of MNB 24, explicitly concerns monks. The passage in question is MNB 24, last folio, lines 12 ff. (MaitrHami):

> *anı ešidip ärüš* [13] *[üküš kut] bulmadok toyınlar kop ilig* [14] *[tutug az] lanmak köŋül<l>ärin tarkarıp* [15] *[alku] nizvanilarıg öčürüp arhant kutın* [16] *bulurlar*
> 'Als sie dies hören, entfernen viele$_2$ Mönche, die [das Heil] noch nicht erlangt haben, alle ihre Gesinnungen des 'Haftens' (*ilig*), des 'Greifens' (*tutug*) und des '[Be]gehrens' (*azlanmak*), löschen [alle] Kleśas und erlangen die Arhat-Würde.' (Geng, Klimkeit & Laut 1998: 40 [text.], 112 [transl.]).

The order of these two conversions is reversed in the Tocharian text, where the beatification of the monks (stanza 86) immediately precedes the conversion of the householders (stanza 87). In the Uyghur text, the conversion of the householders at the end of Maitreya's speech and the beatification of the monks at the end of MNB 24 are not contiguous. They are separated from each other by a passage about the consequences of greed, which is absent in the Tocharian text (sections *q*, *r*, *s* in the synoptic table).

b1 *akäntsūne tärkoräṣ* ‘having abandoned their possessions’
~ MNB 24, last folio, lines 13 ff. (MaitrHami) *kop ilig* [14] *[tutug az]lanmak köŋül<l>ärin tarkarıp* ‘[sie] entfernen alle ihre Gesinnungen des ‘Haftens’, des ‘Greifens’ und des ‘[Be]gehrens’’ (Geng, Klimkeit & Laut 1998: 40 [text], 112 [transl.]). The Tocharian text is more prosaic.

b1 *yā(m)e spal(täk ske śkaṃ cem)* ‘they will make effort and zeal’
This phrase is not reflected in the Uyghur text. The TA phrase *ske spaltäk yām-* ‘make effort [and] zeal, strive’ occurs in A 120 a6: *säm ske spaltäk yāmä(s/ṣ)* ‘he made/will make effort [and] zeal’. An exact TB match is to be found in THT 575 b6: *skeye spelke yamalle ṣai* ‘he would have made effort [and] zeal’. On the Uyghur side, TA *ske yām-* (YQ I. 7 a6, MSN 1) is translated by Uygh. *katıglan-* ‘to strive’ in MNB 1, folio 13 recto, line 25 (MaitrHami) (Geng & Klimkeit 1988: 96). In Uyghur, this verb refers to the effort of the candidate who ‘aspires’ to attain the ranks of the ‘eight noble persons’ (Skt. *aṣṭāryapudgala-*) (see Geng & Klimkeit 1988: 300–302). In TA as in TB, the same idea is expressed by the adjective TA *spaltkasu*, TB *speltkessu*. For TB, see THT 333 b2–3: *arahaṃnte ñi(ś* $nese_u$*) arahaṃnteñe perneś wat speltkessu* ‘I am an Arhat or am zealous for/aspiring to the rank of an Arhat’ (transl. Adams 2013: 789, s.v. *spelkke*), where *arahaṃnteñe perneś speltkessu* refers to the spiritual stage called in Skt. *arhatphalapratipannaka-* ‘candidate for the fruit of the Arhat’. For TA, see YQ III.9: a7 *anāgāmuneyac spaltkasuntāp* ‘[a gift given] to someone striving for the status of Anāgāmin’ (transl. Ji, Winter & Pinault 1998: 183), i.e., *anāgāmiphalapratipannaka-* ‘candidate for the fruit of the Anāgāmin’. In Sanskrit, the idea of ‘striving’ in order to attain the rank of Arhat is also expressed by the root *(ud-/vyā-)yam-* (see the passage from *Saṃgharakṣitāvadāna* quoted below).

b1 *(puk kleśās wa)wikūräṣ ārāntiśpa(rn kälpānträ)* ‘having expelled all the *kleśas*, they will attain the dignity of Arhat’
~ MNB 24, last folio, lines 15 ff. (MaitrHami) *[alku] nizvanilarıg öčürüp arhant kutın* [16] *bulurlar* ‘(sie) löschen alle Kleśas und erlangen die Arhat-Würde’ (Geng, Klimkeit & Laut 1998: 40 [text], 112 [transl.]). In Tocharian, the same formulaic expression occurs for example in A 80 a1: *kl(e)śās*

wawik ārāntiśparäṃ kälpāt 'she expelled the Kleśas [and] achieved the dignity of Arhat' (transl. CEToM). The root usually expressing the idea of 'removing *kleśas*' is *wik-* (factitive meaning). In TB, we have: PK AS 16.3 a1 *kleśanma po yaikare* 'they removed all *kleśas*'. The quadrisyllabic variant *ārāntiśparn* (for *ārāntiśparäṃ*) is required in order to fit the subcolon caesura.[141] The three-syllable remaining slot probably contains the verb. For the latter, we expect a 3pl. subjunctive form with future value, i.e., *kälpānträ*, cf. *yāme* in the same stanza and *tāke* (2×) in stanza 87. The Uyghur text has a present form instead. Similarly, at the end of MSN 25, a present form is used: A 287 + 259 a2 *tä(m kaklyuṣuräṣ sne kaś wrasañ ārāntiśpa)räṃ kälpnānträ* '(Having heard this, countless beings) obtain the (Arhat-)dignity' (transl. CEToM). The Sanskrit equivalent of the full expression occurs in several texts. One example is the *Jyotiṣkāvadāna*, of which a fragment on birch bark was recently edited by Baums:

> *(sa brāhmaṇadārakaḥ kṣatriyadārakasya kathayati) ‹|› (vaya)sya bhagavatā subhadrasya gṛhapateḥ patnī vyākṛtā ‹|› putraṃ janayiṣyati ‹|› kulam udyotayi(ṣyati divyamānu)ṣīṃ śriyaṃ pratyanubhaviṣyati mama śā(sane) pravrajya (sarvakleśaprahāṇād arhatvaṃ sākṣāt-kariṣya)tīti*
> 'The brahman boy said to the kṣatriya boy: 'Friend, the Lord has made a prophecy about the wife of the householder Subhadra: 'She will give birth to a son, he will make the family shine, enjoy semi-divine fortune, enter into my discipline and through the abandoning of all impurities realize arhatship.'' (Baums 2016: 347 [text], 349 [transl.]).

See also the following passage from the *Saṃgharakṣitāvadāna*:

> *tair udyacchamānair ghaṭamānair vyāyacchamānais sarvakleśaprahāṇād arhatvaṃ sākṣātkṛtam arhantas saṃvṛttāḥ traidhātukavītarāgāḥ* [...]

141 The existence of a metrical variant °*parn* for °*paräṃ* in the MSN is assured: A 289 a3 *puttiśparn*; A 276 a>b5 *puttiśparṇ* (written <rnä> with retroflex). In our fragment, the *akṣara* is truncated on the right, so that the *virāma* cannot be seen.

'By struggling, toiling, <and> labouring, (and) through abandonment of all depravities, they realized Arhatship <and> came to be Arhats. Freed from the passion of the triple (world) element [...]' (Vogel & Wille 1996: 263, lines 8–10 [text], 290 [transl.]).

b1–2 (*tsälpe śkaṃ cem traidhātuk saṃsā*)*rṣinās klopäntwäṣ* 'and they will be freed from the pains of the threefold Saṃsāra'

This phrase is not reflected in the Uyghur text. The redundant expression *traidhātuk saṃsār* 'threefold Saṃsāra' is attested in A 1 b6, cf. Skt. *traidhātukavītarāgāḥ* in the passage of the *Saṃgharakṣitāvadāna* quoted above. Liberation from suffering is the usual reward of the Arhat: PK AS 6A b2–3 *toṃ läklenta sa*(*ṃ*)*s*(*ārmeṃ tsälpāt*)*s*(*i*) *tākau arhānte* 'In order to be freed from those sufferings [and] from the Saṃ(sāra), I will become an Arhat.' (transl. Pinault, Malzahn & Peyrot in CEToM). The TA formulaic expression *saṃsārṣinās klopäntwäṣ tsälpā-* is well attested in the MSN: A 303 b5 *saṃsārṣinās puk klopäntwäṣ tsälpṣant källānt nervā*(*nac*) 'he who frees [beings] from all the sufferings of the Saṃsāra, he who leads to Nirvāṇa'. See also A 256 a2 (MSN 26): *metrak ptāñkät pākär nāṃtsu klopäntwäṣ tsälpṣant* 'the Buddha-god Maitreya has appeared, the liberator from sufferings' (transl. CEToM). Each *pāda* of stanza 86 describes a further step in the progression of Maitreya's followers toward the attainment of Nirvāṇa. The same progression can be observed in stanza 87 for householders.

4.3.2 Stanza 87 (~ Uygh. 87–94)

b2 (*$k_u$ce*) *pat nu kātkāñ tāke* <*ṣyak*> *kākropuṣ tām praṣtaṃ* 'as for the householders who will be gathered <together> at that time'

~ Uygh. 87–88 *sansız tümän ol kuvragdakı tınl*(*ı*)*glar* 'die unzähligen$_2$ Lebewesen dieser Versammlung'. The restitution of *$k_u$ce* is due to Siegling in his personal copy of *Tocharische Sprachreste*. The conjunction *pat nu* probably denotes an opposition between the group of monks and that of householders (see above). The subjunctive form *tāke* has future value. The phrase *tām praṣtaṃ* refers to the future time of Maitreya.[142] As Sieg and Siegling note, there is one syllable missing in the *pāda* (Sieg & Siegling 1921: 113, note 2). In his personal copy of *Tocharische Sprachreste*, Siegling suggests (with double question mark) to reintroduce the substantive *pñi* forgotten by the scribe between *tāke* and *kākropuṣ*. This would restore the rhythm 4 + 3 invariably expected at the end of a *pāda*: *tāke* ; *<pñi>* *kākropuṣ* ¦ *tām praṣtaṃ* '(who) will have gathered merit at that time'.[143] However, the phrase *pñi krop-* is not supported by the Uyghur parallel, which only refers to the gathering of Maitreya's followers. Therefore, a passive meaning for *kākropuṣ* with the monosyllabic adverb *ṣyak* 'together' would better fit, following a phrase *ṣyak krop-* which is actually attested.[144] One may compare the very beginning of MNB 20, folio 1 recto, lines 3 ff. (MaitrHami):

> *yer-* [04] *suv t[äprämišiŋä] asanke sanınča t(ä)ŋri* [05] *yal(a)ŋoklar .. üstün köktä altın yagız-* [06] *da tiši erkäk ärän išilär strayastriš* [07] *t(ä)ŋri yerintäki t(ä)ŋrilär osuglug ögrünčü-* [08] *ligin sävinčligin kukutapat tag tapa* [09] *tükäl bilgä maitre burhan tapa yıgılur-* [10] *lar .. kuvrag yıgılmıšta ken* (…)
> '[Wegen des] B[ebens] der Erde versammeln sich unzählige Götter und Menschen, oben am Himmel und unten auf der Erde, (gewöhnliche) Weiber und Männer und (hochstehende) Herren und Damen, die so beglückt$_2$ sind wie die Götter im Trāyastriṃśa-Götterland, beim Kukkuṭapāda-Berg, beim Buddha Maitreya. Nachdem sich die Gemeinde versammelt hat …' (Geng, Klimkeit & Laut 1998: 21 [text], 76 [transl.]).

The terms used in the text quoted above are the verb *yıgıl-* 'gather' (~ TA *krop-*) and the substantive *kuvrag* 'assembly' (~ TA *wartsi*).

142 For future use of *tām praṣtaṃ*, see Stumpf (1971: 37).

143 Cf. A 118 b5–6 *pñi kākro(puräṣ)*, A 250 a1 *pñi kropte*, but usually in the pl. *pñintu*.

144 Cf. A 10 a3–4 *pracres āmāś(ās mṣapantinäs) ṣyak kā(kro)puräṣ* 'having gathered his brothers, ministers (and generals)' (transl. CEToM).

b2 *cem penu* ‘they too’

This phrase is not reflected in the Uyghur text. Together with the use of the conjunction *pat nu* in *(*k_u*ce) pat nu kātkāñ*, the use of the adverb *penu* is one more clue for assuming that the opposition between the two groups runs until the end of the text, i.e., the monks on the one hand, and the householders on the other.

b2 *lyut(ār memaṣ puttiśparnac spaltkasuṣ)* ‘exceedingly zealous to obtain the rank of Buddha’

This phrase is not reflected in the Uyghur text. The restitution *lyu(tār memaṣ)* is probable. For the end of the *pāda*, one may restore the adjective *spaltkasu* (TB *speltkessu*) ‘desiring, zealous’ (in positive meaning), often used in the context of effort toward Buddhahood (see above, s.v. b1 *yā(m)e spal(täk ske śkaṃ cem)*). The expression *lyutār memaṣ spaltkasu* occurs in A 246 a3: *(ṣñi) wlesant ā(lu wle)sant yātässi naṣt lyutār memaṣ spaltkasū* ‘... die (eigenen) Dienste [und auch] die Dienste anderer auszuführen, bist du überaus [über die Maßen] eifrig.’ (rest. and transl. Thomas 1958: 164). The adjective TA *spaltkasu*, TB *speltkessu* is regularly followed by the allative.

b2–3 *(waṣt-)wṣeññe cem raryūräṣ* ‘having abandoned dwelling in a household’

~ Uygh. 88–91 *kop ilig tutug saranlanmak yapıšmak köŋüllärin kodup ıdalap* ‘geben [sie] ihre Gesinnungen des ‘Anhaftens’, des ‘Greifens’ und des ‘Geizigseins’ auf$_2$’. The TA compound *waṣt-wṣeññe**, based on *waṣt* ‘house’ and *wṣeññe* ‘dwelling’, is not attested elsewhere in TA. However, the expression finds an almost exact match in TB: PK AS 16.7 a4 *(śā)wäṣṣälñeṣṣe akālksa ta-makte wate ñiś päst lkāst ostaṣṣai wṣeñai rerīnū* ‘because of the wish concerning (living a monastic life), for a second time in such a way you looked at me having abandoned dwelling in a household’ (ed. and transl. Pinault & Malzahn in CEToM). The formation of *waṣt-wṣeññe* ‘dwelling in a household’ would parallel that of *wärt-wṣeññe* ‘dwelling in a forest’ (Carling & Pinault forth., s.v. *wärt-wṣeññe*). For the Skt. / Pali formula corresponding to the idea of ‘leaving the house’, see the next restitution.

b3 (*läñce*) *waṣtäṣ metraknac* 'they will leave the house for Maitreya'
~ Uygh. 91–92 *tükäl bilgä maitre burhan nomınta toyın bolurlar* '[sie] werden Mönche in der Lehre des vollkommen weisen Buddha Maitreya'. This is a formulaic expression, cf. A 298 b2 (MSN 21–22) *āṣānikāṃ metraknac waṣtäṣ lanturäṣ* 'having left the house for the venerable Maitreya'. It is also attested in the MAV (in the subjunctive): A 221 b4 (*tmanä*)*k metrak pättāñkte läñce waṣtäṣ märkam*(*p*)*l*(*ac*) 'thus they will leave the house for the law of the noble Buddha Maitreya' (transl. Peyrot 2013: 626). In the latter example, the sequence *läñce waṣtäṣ* ¦ *märkam*(*p*)*l*(*ac*) has the same rhythm of 4 + 3 syllables as *läñce waṣtäṣ* ¦ *metraknac* (both at the end of the *pāda*). As is well known, the expression *waṣtäṣ lä*(*n*)*t*- (TB *ostameṃ lä*(*n*)*t*-) metaphorically means 'to become a monk' (cf. *waṣtäṣ laltuṣ* in stanza 81). The corresponding Sanskrit formula is Skt. *agārād anagārikāṃ pravrajati*, Pa. *agārasmā anagāriyaṁ pabbajati* 'to go out from the house into the homeless state' (PED: 8a, s.v. *agāriya*).

b3 *ske spaltäk śkaṃ yāmūräṣ* 'and having made effort [and] zeal'
This phrase is not reflected in the Uyghur text. This is a formulaic expression (see above, s.v. b1 *yā*(*m*)*e spal*(*täk ske śkaṃ cem*)).

b3 *tā*(*ke cem poñś ārāntāñ*) 'they will all become Arhats'
~ Uygh. 93–94 *arhant kutıŋ*(*a*) *t*(*ä*)*girlär* '[sie] gelangen zur Würde eines Arhat'. The expression is the last *pāda* of stanza 87 and puts an end to MAV 22. The idea is probably similar to *ārāntiśpa*(*rn kälpānträ*) in 86d. At the end of the *pāda*, one may restore *ārāntāñ* 'Arhats' or *pättāṃñktañ* 'Buddhas' (last word of the chapter).[145]

145 Peyrot notes that 'The wish that all may become Buddhas appears to be typical for colophon-like concluding strophes' (Peyrot 2016: 322). In all the examples quoted by Peyrot (2016: 322–323), the formula is the same: TB *po* / TA *puk* + 'Buddha' in the pl. + verb 'to be' in the optative. An example from the MSN is: YQ I.10 b8 */// ·āk cor śkaṃ poñś tākimäs ptāñktañ* || '… and ….*āk* the *čor*. May we all become Buddhas!' (Ji, Winter & Pinault 1998: 64–65).

5 Lexical appendix

For convenience, I give a survey of restored forms when at least one letter is visible on the fragment (totally restored forms are omitted), newly segmented forms (marked with ⁽⁺⁾), and new words (marked with ⁺) that have been identified in the fragment A 226. Completely restored forms are omitted. For details, see the commentary.

⁽⁺⁾*ālyek saṃ* (226 a4) = Uygh. *amarıları*: 'others' (nom. pl. masc.).
ārāntiśpa(rn) (226 b1) = Uygh. *arhant kutı*: obl. sg. of *ārāntiśparäṃ* 'dignity of Arhat'.
ā(wās) (?) (226 b7): obl. sg. of *āwās* 'residence'.
kat(uṣi) (226 a4): obl. sg. masc. of *katuṣi* 'of jewellery'.
k(apśño) (226 a3) = Uygh. *ätözlüg*: instr. sg. of *kapśañi* 'body'.
(kā)śyapi (226 a2): gen. sg. of *kāśyap* 'Kāśyapa'.
⁺*(kā)swa-wsāl(u)* (226 a2) = Uygh. *tonlar*: obl. pl. of *kāswa-wsāl* 'good cloth'.
⁺*(kältsā)lā* (?) (226 a5): perl. sg. of *kältsāl*, verbal noun based on *kältsā-* 'oppress'
(k)e(n-pä)lkā (226 a7): perl. sg. of *keṃ-pälk* 'false view'.
kräntsonā(s) (226 a2): obl. pl. fem. of *kräṃtso* 'beautiful'.
kropñā(nt) (226 a5): 3pl. ipf. MP of *krop-* 'gather'.
c(a)m (226 a6): obl. sg. masc. of *säm, sām, täm* 'this'.
(tamä)nt (226 a6): 3pl. prt. MP of *täm-* 'be born'.
tā(ke) (226 b3): 3pl. act. subj. 5 of *nas-* 'be'.
tä(myo) (?) (226 a7): adv. 'therefore'.
(nākma)nt (226 a7): obl. pl. of *nākäm* 'sin'.
(pa)t nu (226 a1): conj. 'or'.
⁺*(pari)ṣkāraṃ* (226 a2) = Uygh. *tavarlar*: loc. sg. of *pariṣkār* 'utensil, vessel', cf. TB *pariṣkār* 'id.'. Borrowed from Skt. *pariṣkāra-*.
⁺*pu(skāṣi)* (?) (226 a3): obl. sg. masc. of *puskāṣi* 'of a garland'. Adjective based on *psuk* 'garland' (pl. *puskāñ*).
(po)r(ṣ)inäs (226 a4–5): obl. pl. masc. of *porṣi* 'of fire'.
pe(nu) (226 a5): adv. 'also'.

(ppāṣā)c (226 b4–5): 2pl. MP ipv. of *pās-* 'protect'.
(prattikañarentw)aṃ (226 a6–7): loc. pl. of *prattikañare* 'individual hell'.
+*(mä)rsatsi* (?) (226 b6): obl. sg. of *märsatsi* 'forgetfulness'. Substantivized inf. (present 3!) of *märs-* 'forget'.
+*mu(ktihā)rṣi* (226 a4): obl. sg. masc. of *muktihārṣi* 'of a pearl necklace'. Adjective based on *muktihār* 'pearl necklace'.
+*l(e)kā* (226 a3 and passim) ~ Uygh. *osuglug*: adv. 'looking like, in the shape (of)'. Frozen perl. of *lek* 'attitude, look', cf. *lekac* 'looking like'.
lyut(ār memaṣ) (226 b2): 'beyond measure'
+*yap-pari(ṣkār)* (226 a1): 'barley utensil'. This hybrid compound presupposes the existence of TA *yap* 'barley', probably borrowed from TB *yap* 'id.'.
yā(m)e (226 b1): 3pl. subj. 2 act. of *yām-* 'do'.
ypā(nt) (226 a6): 3pl. ipf. MP of *yām-* 'do'.
+*(waṣt-)wṣeññe* (226 b2–3): obl. sg. of *waṣt-wṣeññe* 'dwelling in a household'. Cf. TB obl. *ostaṣṣai wṣeñai.*
+*wakal-hāraṣi* (226 a4): obl. sg. masc. of *wakal-hāraṣi* 'of a half necklace'. Adjective based on the hybrid compound **wakal-hār* 'half necklace', calque of Skt. *ardhahāra- 'id.'.*
(wa)wikūräṣ (226 b1): abs. of *wik-* 'drive out'.
wätläkṣi (226 a4): obl. sg. masc. of *wätläkṣi* 'of a diamond' (?). Adjective based on *wätläk* 'diamond' (?).
(ṣa)kkatsek (226 b4): adv. 'fatally'.
(ṣā)mañi (226 a1): obl. sg. masc. of *ṣāmañi* 'of a monk'
(+)*ṣome saṃ* (226 a4) = Uygh. *amarıları*: 'some' (nom. pl. masc.).
(saṃsā)rṣinās (226 b1–2): obl. pl. fem. of *saṃsārṣi* 'of the Saṃsāra'.
spal(täk) (226 b1): obl. sg. of *spaltäk* 'zeal, effort'.
(s)l(a)ma(s)yo (226 a5): instr. pl. of *slam* 'flame'.

[RECEIVED: NOVEMBER 2021]

Appartement 1803
30 rue des Fillettes
93300 Aubervilliers
France

Abbreviations

AKB = Pradhan, Prahlad. 1975. *Abhidharmakośabhāṣyam of Vasubandhu*. 2nd ed. Patna: K.P. Jayaswal Research Institute.

AN = Hardy, Edmund and Richard Morris. 1885–1900. *The Aṅguttara-Nikāya*. London: Pali Text Society. [5 vols.]

Avś = Speijer, Jakob S. 1902–1909. *Avadānaçataka. A Century of Edifying Tales Belonging to the Hīnayāna*. St. Pétersbourg: Commissionnaires de l'Académie Impériale des Sciences. [2 vols]

Beih. II = Beiheft II, in v. Gabain 1961.

BHSD = Edgerton, Franklin. 1953. *Buddhist Hybrid Sanskrit Grammar and Dictionary*. Vol. 2: *Dictionary*. New Haven (Conn.): Yale University Press. Repr. Delhi: Motilal Banarsidass, 1970.

CeDICT = *A Comprehensive e-Dictionary of Tocharian*. projekt.ht.lu.se/cedict/.

CEToM = *A Comprehensive Edition of Tocharian Manuscripts*. www.univie.ac.at/tocharian/.

Divy = Cowell, Edward B. & Robert A. Neil. 1886. *The Divyāvadāna. A Collection of Early Buddhist Legends. Sanskrit Text in Transcription*. Cambridge: Cambridge University Press.

DP I = Cone, Margaret. 2001. *A Dictionary of Pāli*. Part I: *a–kh*. Oxford: Pali Text Society.

GMs III,2 = Dutt, Nalinaksha. 1942. *Gilgit Manuscripts*. Vol. 3, Pt. 2. Srinagar: Research Department.

HWAU = Wilkens, Jens. 2021. *Handwörterbuch des Altuigurischen. Altuigurisch – Deutsch – Türkisch*. Göttingen: Universitätsverlag Göttingen.

Mvu = Senart, Émile. 1882–1897. *Le Mahāvastu*. Paris: Imprimerie Nationale. [3 vols.]

MW = Monier-Williams, Monier. 1899. *A Sanskrit-English Dictionary*. Oxford: Clarendon Press.

PED = Rhys Davids, Thomas W. & Wilhelm Stede. 1921. *The Pali Text Society's Pali-English Dictionary*. Repr. London: Pali Text Society, 1952.

SaddhP = Vaidya, Parashurama L. 1960. *Saddharmapuṇḍarīkasūtra*. Darbhanga: The Mithila Institute of Post-Graduate Studies and Research in Sanskrit Learning.
Sn = Andersen, Dines & Helmer Smith. 1913. *Sutta-Nipāta*. Oxford: Pali Text Society. (by verse)
SWTF = Waldschmidt, Ernst & Heinz Bechert. 1973–2018. *Sanskrit-Wörterbuch der buddhistischen Texte aus den Turfan-Funden [und der kanonischen Literatur der Sarvāstivāda-Schule]*. Begonnen von Ernst Waldschmidt. Im Auftrag der Akademie der Wissenschaften in Göttingen herausgegeben von Heinz Bechert, Klaus Röhrborn & Jens-Uwe Hartmann. Göttingen: Vandenhoeck & Ruprecht. [4 vols.]
ŚS = Vaidya, Parashurama L. 1961. *Śikṣāsamuccaya of Śāntideva*. Darbhanga: The Mithila Institute of Post-Graduate Studies and Research in Sanskrit Learning.

References

Adams, Douglas Q. 2013. *A Dictionary of Tocharian B*. Revised and greatly enlarged 2nd ed. Amsterdam / New York: Rodopi. [2 vols.]
Bailey, Harold W. 1937. 'Ttaugara', *Bulletin of the School of Oriental Studies* 8 (4): 883–921.
Baums, Stefan. 2016. "A New Fragment of the Jyotiṣkāvadāna". In Jens E. Braarvig et al. (eds.), *Manuscripts in the Schøyen Collection*. Oslo: Hermes Publishing, 345–455.
Berounský, Daniel. 2012. *The Tibetan Version of the Scripture of the Ten Kings, and the Quest for Chinese Influence on the Tibetan Perception of the Afterlife. With a Comparative Description of the Paintings by Luboš Bělka*. Prague: Triton.
Bisschop, Peter & Arlo Griffiths. 2008. "The Practice Involving the Ucchuṣmas (*Atharvavedapariśiṣṭa* 36)". *Studien zur Indologie und Iranistik* 24: 1–46.
Buswell, Robert E. 1992. "The Path to Perdition: The Wholesome Roots and Their Eradication". In Robert E. Buswell & Robert M. Gimello (eds.), *Paths to Liberation. The Mārga and Its Transformations in Buddhist Thought*. Honolulu: University of Hawai'i Press, 107–134.
Carling, Gerd. 2000. *Die Funktionen der lokalen Kasus im Tocharischen*. Berlin / New York: de Gruyter.
Carling, Gerd. 2009. *Dictionary and Thesaurus of Tocharian A*. Volume 1: *a-j*. Compiled by Gerd Carling in collaboration with Georges-Jean Pinault and Werner Winter. Wiesbaden: Harrassowitz.

Carling, Gerd & Georges-Jean Pinault. forth. *Dictionary and Thesaurus of Tocharian A*. Wiesbaden: Harrassowitz.

Chamot-Rooke, Timothée. 2021. "The Tocharian Indefinite B *ksa*, A *saṃ*: Syntax and Philology". *Bulletin de la Société de linguistique de Paris* 116 (1): 203–236.

Clauson, Gerard. 1972. *An Etymological Dictionary of Pre-Thirteenth Century Turkish*. Oxford: Clarendon Press.

Demoto, Mitsuyo. 2009. "Die 128 Nebenhöllen nach dem *Saddharmasmṛtyupasthānasūtra*". In Martin Straube et al. (eds.), *Pāsādikadānaṁ. Festschrift für Bhikkhu Pasadika*. Marburg: Indica et Tibetica Verlag, 61–88.

Denis, Eugène. 1977. *La Lokapaññatti et les idées cosmologiques du bouddhisme ancien*. Lille / Paris: Atelier de Reproduction des thèses, Université de Lille III. [2 vols.]

Dhammajoti, Bhikkhu. 2015. *Sarvāstivāda Abhidharma*. 5th revised ed. Hong Kong: The Buddha-Dharma Centre of Hong Kong.

Erdal, Marcel. 1991. *Old Turkic Word Formation. A Functional Approach to the Lexicon*. Wiesbaden: Otto Harrassowitz. [2 vols.]

Erdal, Marcel. 2004. *A Grammar of Old Turkic*. Leiden / Boston: Brill.

Finot, Louis. 1896. *Les lapidaires indiens*. Paris: Librairie Émile Bouillon.

Gabain, Annemarie von. 1961. *Maitrisimit. Faksimile der alttürkischen Version eines Werkes der buddhistischen Vaibhāṣika-Schule*. II. Mit einem Geleitwort [in Beiheft II] von Richard Hartmann. Berlin [DDR]: Akademie-Verlag.

Geng, Shimin & Hans-Joachim Klimkeit. 1988. *Das Zusammentreffen mit Maitreya. Die ersten fünf Kapitel der Hami-Version der Maitrisimit*. Teil 1: *Text, Übersetzung und Kommentar. In Zusammenarbeit mit Helmut Eimer und Jens Peter Laut herausgegeben, übersetzt und kommentiert*. Wiesbaden: Harrassowitz.

Geng, Shimin, Hans-Joachim Klimkeit & Jens Peter Laut. 1998. *Eine buddhistische Apokalypse. Die Höllenkapitel (20–25) und die Schlußkapitel (26–27) der Hami-Handschrift der alttürkischen Maitrisimit. Unter Einbeziehung von Manuskriptteilen des Textes aus Säŋim und Murtuk. Einleitung, Transkription und Übersetzung*. Opladen / Wiesbaden: Westdeutscher Verlag.

Geng, Shimin, Jens Peter Laut & Georges-Jean Pinault. 2004a. "Neue Ergebnisse der *Maitrisimit*-Forschung (I)". *Zeitschrift der Deutschen Morgenländischen Gesellschaft* 154: 347–369.

Geng, Shimin, Jens Peter Laut & Georges-Jean Pinault. 2004b. "Neue Ergebnisse der *Maitrisimit*-Forschung (II): Struktur und Inhalt des 26. Kapitels". *Studies on the Inner Asian Languages* 19: 29–94.

Ghosh, Manomohan. 1950. *The Nāṭyáśāstra. A Treatise on Hindu Dramaturgy and Histrionics, Ascribed to Bharata-Muni.* Vol. I: *Chapters I-XXVII.* Calcutta: Asiatic Society of Bengal.

Goodman, Charles. 2016. *The Training Anthology of Śāntideva. A Translation of the* Śikṣā-samuccaya. New York: Oxford University Press.

Hartmann, Markus. 2013. *Das Genussystem des Tocharischen.* Hamburg: Baar-Verlag.

Hoernle, Augustus F.R. 1916. *Manuscript Remains of Buddhist Literature Found in Eastern Turkestan. Facsimiles with Transcripts, Translations and Notes.* Oxford: Clarendon Press.

Huard, Athanaric. 2020. "The End of Mahākāśyapa and the Encounter with Maitreya: Two Leaves of a Maitreya-Cycle in Archaic TB". *Tocharian and Indo-European Studies* 20: 1–82.

Itkin, Ilya B. 2002. "The Linguistic Features of Tocharian A Manuscript *Maitreyāvadānavyākaraṇa*". *Manuscripta Orientalia* 8 (3): 11–16.

Itkin, Ilya B. & Anna V. Kuritsyna. 2017. "Chapter XX of the 'Maitreyasamiti-Nāṭaka' and Its Hellish Sufferings: The Fragment THT 1308.a". *Tocharian and Indo-European Studies* 18: 63–69.

Itkin, Ilya B., Anna V. Kuritsyna & Sergey V. Malyshev. 2017. "Tocharian A Text THT 1331 and the 'Höllenkapitel' of the 'Maitrisimit Nom Bitig': Some More Remarks". *Tocharian and Indo-European Studies* 18: 71–81.

Ji, Xianlin. 1998. *Fragments of the Tocharian A Maitreyasamiti-Nāṭaka of the Xinjiang Museum, China.* In collaboration with Werner Winter and Georges Jean Pinault. Berlin / New York: de Gruyter.

Jones, John J. 1949. *The Mahāvastu.* Translated from the Buddhist Sanskrit. Volume I. London: Luzac & Co.

Kageyama, Etsuko. 2007. "The Winged Crown and the Triple-crescent Crown in the Sogdian Funerary Monuments from China: Their Relation to the Hephthalite Occupation of Central Asia". *Journal of Inner Asian Art and Archaeology* 2: 11–22.

Knoll, Gabriele. 1996. *Die Verwendungsweisen der Adjektive im Tocharischen.* Inaugural-Dissertation. Johann-Wolfgang-Goethe-Universität zu Frankfurt am Main.

Kölver, Bernhard. 1965. *Der Gebrauch der sekundären Kasus im Tocharischen.* Inaugural-Dissertation. Universität Frankfurt am Main.

Krause, Wolfgang & Thomas, Werner. 1960. *Tocharisches Elementarbuch.* Band 1: *Grammatik.* Heidelberg: Winter.

Kroonenberg, Salomon B. 2013. *Why hell stinks of sulfur. Mythology and geology of the underworld.* London: Reaktion Books.

Kumamoto, Hiroshi. 2002. "The Maitreya-samiti and Khotanese". Paper Read at the Symposium Franco-Japonais "Interactions et translations culturelles en Eurasie," jointly held by the University of Tokyo and l'École Pratique des Hautes Études, in Paris, 12–13 December.

La Vallée Poussin, Louis E. de. 1926. *L'Abhidharmakośa de Vasubandhu. Troisième chapitre*. Paris: Geuthner.

Laut, Jens Peter. 1986. *Der frühe türkische Buddhismus und seine literarischen Denkmäler*. Wiesbaden: Harrassowitz.

Laut, Jens Peter. 1996. "Höllische Fehler". In Michael Hahn, Jens-Uwe Hartmann & Roland Steiner (eds.), *Suhṛllekhāḥ. Festgabe für Helmut Eimer*. Swisttal-Odendorf: Indica et Tibetica Verlag, 121–136.

Laut, Jens Peter. 2000. "Uigurische Sünden". In Peter Zieme & Louis Bazin (eds.), *De Dunhuang à Istanbul. Hommage à James Russell Hamilton*. Turnhout: Brepols, 127–148.

Laut, Jens Peter. 2002. "Die 'begangenen' und 'angehäuften' Sünden. Ein nur scheinbar verlorenes Fragment der Murtuker Handschrift der alttürkischen *Maitrisimit*". In Wolfgang Gantke, Karl Hoheisel & Wassilios W. Klein (eds.), *Religionsbegegnung und Kulturaustausch in Asien. Studien zum Gedenken an Hans-Joachim Klimkeit*. Wiesbaden: Harrassowitz, 165–174.

Laut, Jens Peter. 2003. "Methoden und Möglichkeiten der Wiedergabe von indisch-buddhistischen Termini im Alttürkischen". In Sven Bretfeld & Jens Wilkens (eds.), *Indien und Zentralasien. Sprach- und Kulturkontakt. Vorträge des Göttinger Symposions vom 7.-10. Mai 2001*. Wiesbaden: Harrassowitz, 13–24.

Laut, Jens Peter. 2013. "Hells in Central Asian Turkic Buddhism and Early Turkic Islam". In Antonio Fabris (ed.), *Tra quattro paradisi. Esperienze, ideologie e riti reletivi alla morte tra Oriente e Occidente*. Venezia: Ca' Foscari, 18–37.

Laut, Jens Peter & Jens Wilkens. 2017. *Alttürkische Handschriften*. Teil 3. *Die Handschriftenfragmente der* Maitrisimit *aus Sängim und Murtuk in der Berliner Turfansammlung*. Stuttgart: Steiner.

Lévi, Sylvain. 1911. *Asaṅga. Mahāyāna-Sūtrālaṃkāra. Exposé de la doctrine du Grand Véhicule selon le système Yogācāra. Édité et traduit d'après un rapporté du Népal*. Tome 2: *Traduction, Introduction, Index*. Paris: Champion.

Lévi, Sylvain. 1925. 'Le Sūtra du Sage et du Fou dans la littérature de l'Asie Centrale', *Journal Asiatique* 207: 305–332.

Lévi, Sylvain. 1932. *Mahākarmavibhaṅga*. (*La Grande classification des actes*). Paris: Leroux.

Mair, Victor H. 2013. "*Maitrisimit* and the Narrative Traditions". In Yukiyo Kasai, Abdurishid Yakup & Desmond Durkin-Meisterernst (eds.), *Die Erforschung des Tocharischen und die alttürkische Maitrisimit. Symposium anlässlich des 100. Jahrestages der Entzifferung des Tocharischen (Berlin, 3. Und 4. April 2008)*. Turnhout: Brepols, 105–121.

Malzahn, Melanie. 2010. *The Tocharian Verbal System*. Leiden / Boston: Brill.

Meunier, Fanny. 2013. "Typologie des locutions en *yām-* du tokharien". *Tocharian and Indo-European Studies* 14: 123–185.

Mimaki, Katsumi. 2000. "A Preliminary Comparison of Bonpo and Buddhist Cosmology". In Yasuhiko Nagano & Samten G. Karmay (eds.), *New Horizons in Bon Studies*. Osaka: National Museum of Ethnology, 89–115.

Müller, Friedrich W.K. & Sieg, Emil. 1916. "Maitrisimit und ‚Tocharisch'". *Sitzungsberichte der Preußischen Akademie der Wissenschaften* 16: 395–417.

Nattier, Jan. 1991. *Once upon a Future Time. Studies in a Buddhist Prophecy of Decline*. Berkeley (Calif.): Asian Humanities Press.

Needham, Joseph. 1959. *Science and Civilisation in China*. Volume 3: *Mathematics and the Sciences of the Heavens and the Earth*. Cambridge: Cambridge University Press.

Needham, Joseph. 1980. *Science and Civilisation in China*. Volume 5: *Chemistry and Chemical Technology*. Part IV: *Spagyrical Discovery and Invention: Apparatus, Theories and Gifts*. Cambridge: Cambridge University Press.

Norman, Kenneth R. 2001. *The Group of Discourses (Sutta-Nipāta)*. 2nd ed. London: Pali Text Society.

Norman, Kenneth R. 2006. "The Anāgatavaṃsa Revisited". *Journal of the Pali Text Society* 28: 1–37.

Nugteren, Hans & Jens Wilkens. 2019. "A Female Mongol Headdress in Old Uyghur Secular Documents". *International Journal of Old Uyghur Studies*, 1 (2): 153–170.

Ogihara, Hirotoshi. 2013. "Tocharian Vinaya Texts in the Paris Collection". *Tocharian and Indo-European Studies* 14: 187–211.

Ogihara, Hirotoshi. 2016. "Remarks on Fragment B431 of the Berlin Turfan Collection". *Tocharian and Indo-European Studies* 17: 133–151.

Peyrot, Michaël. 2010. "Proto-Tocharian syntax and the status of Tocharian A". *Journal of Indo-European Studies* 38: 132–146.

Peyrot, Michaël. 2013. *The Tocharian Subjunctive. A Study in Syntax and Verbal Stem Formation*. Leiden / Boston: Brill.

Peyrot, Michaël. 2016. "The Sanskrit Udānavarga and the Tocharian B Udānastotra: A Window on the Relationship Between Religious and Popular Language on the Northern Silk Road". *Bulletin of the School of Oriental and African Studies* 79 (2): 305–327.

Peyrot, Michaël. 2018. "Tocharian Agricultural Terminology: Between Inheritance and Language Contact". In Guus Kroonen, James P. Mallory & Bernhard Comrie (eds.), *Talking Neolithic. Proceedings of the Workshop on Indo-European Origins Held at the Max Planck Institute for Evolutionary Anthropology (Leipzig, December 2–3, 2013)*. Washington D.C.: Institute for the Study of Man, 242–277.

Peyrot, Michaël & Ablet Semet. 2016. "A Comparative Study of the Beginning of the 11th Act of the Tocharian A *Maitreyasamitināṭaka* and the Old Uyghur *Maitrisimit*". *Acta Orientalia Academiae Scientiarum Hungaricae* 69 (4): 355–378.

Pinault, Georges-Jean. 1988. "Révision des fragments en tokharien B de la légende de Mahāprabhāsa". In Peter Kosta (ed.), *Studia Indogermanica et Slavica. Festgabe für Werner Thomas zum 65. Geburtstag*. München: Verlag Otto Sagner, 175–210.

Pinault, Georges-Jean. 1995. "The Rendering of Buddhist Terminology in Tocharian". *Journal of the Dunhuang and Turfan Studies* 1: 9–35.

Pinault, Georges-Jean. 1997. "Sur l'assemblage des phrases ("Satzgefüge") en tokharien". In Emilio Crespo Güemes & José Luis García Ramón (eds.), *Berthold Delbrück y la sintaxis indoeuropea hoy. Actas del Coloquio de la Indogermanische Gesellschaft, Madrid, 21–24 de septiembre de 1994*. Madrid / Wiesbaden: Ediciones de la UAM-Reichert, 449–500.

Pinault, Georges-Jean. 1999. "Restitution du *Maitreyasamiti-Nāṭaka* en tokharien A: Bilan provisoire et recherches complémentaires sur l'acte XXVI". *Tocharian and Indo-European Studies* 8: 189–240.

Pinault, Georges-Jean. 2008. *Chrestomathie tokharienne. Textes et grammaire*. Leuven/Paris: Peeters.

Pinault, Georges-Jean. 2011. "Let Us Now Praise Famous Gems". *Tocharian and Indo-European Studies* 12: 155–220.

Pinault, Georges-Jean. 2017. "Current Issues in Tocharian Etymology and Phonology". *Tocharian and Indo-European Studies* 18: 127–164.

Pinault, Georges-Jean. 2020a. "New Material Extracted from Revised Tocharian A Texts". Paper Read at the Workshop "Tocharian in Progress," Leiden University, 8–10 December.

Pinault, Georges-Jean. 2020b. "Tocharian Taxonomy of Wealth". In Harald Bichlmeier, Ondřej Šefčík & Roman Sukač (eds.), *Etymologus. Festschrift for Václav Blažek*. Hamburg: Baar-Verlag, 323–338.

Poucha, Pavel. 1955. *Institutiones Linguæ Tocharicæ*, Pars I: *Thesaurus Linguæ Tocharicæ Dialecti A*. Praha: Státní Pedagogické Nakladatelství.

Przyluski, Jean. 1923. *La légende de l'empereur Açoka (Açoka-Avadâna) dans les textes indiens et chinois*. Paris: Geuthner.

Revire, Nicolas. 2016. *The Enthroned Buddha in Majesty: An Iconological Study*. Thèse de doctorat. Paris 3–Sorbonne nouvelle.

Röhrborn, Klaus. 2010. *Uigurisches Wörterbuch. Sprachmaterial der vorislamischen türkischen Texte aus Zentralasien. Neubearbeitung. 1. Verben*. Band 1: *ab- – äzüglä-*. Stuttgart: Steiner.

Röhrborn, Klaus. 2017. *Uigurisches Wörterbuch. Sprachmaterial der vorislamischen türkischen Texte aus Zentralasien. Neubearbeitung. 2. Nomina – Pronomina – Partikeln*. Band 2: *aš – äžük*. Stuttgart: Steiner.

Rotman, Andy. 2008. *Divine Stories. Divyāvadāna*. Part 1. Boston: Wisdom Publications.

Rotman, Andy. 2009. *Thus Have I Seen. Visualizing Faith in Early Indian Buddhism*. Oxford / New York: Oxford University Press.

Rotman, Andy. 2017. *Divine Stories. Divyāvadāna*. Part 2. Somerville (Mass.): Wisdom Publications.

Schaefer, Christiane. 2013. "Zur Katalogisierung der tocharischen Handschriften der Berliner Turfansammlung". In Yukiyo Kasai, Abdurishid Yakup & Desmond Durkin-Meisterernst (eds.), *Die Erforschung des Tocharischen und die alttürkische Maitrisimit. Symposium anlässlich des 100. Jahrestages der Entzifferung des Tocharischen (Berlin, 3. und 4. April 2008)*. Turnhout: Brepols, 325–348.

Schmidt, Klaus T. 1974. *Die Gebrauchsweisen des Mediums im Tocharischen*. Inaugural-Dissertation. Georg-August-Universität zu Göttingen.

Schopen, Gregory. 2004. *Buddhist Monks and Business Matters. Still More Papers on Monastic Buddhism in India*. Honolulu: University of Hawai'i Press.

Sieg, Emil. 1918. "Ein einheimischer Name für Toχrï". *Sitzungsberichte der Königlich Preußischen Akademie der Wissenschaften*: 560–565.

Sieg, Emil. 1944. *Übersetzungen aus dem Tocharischen. I*. Berlin: de Gruyter.

Sieg, Emil & Wilhelm Siegling. 1921. *Tocharische Sprachreste. [Sprache A.]* 1. Band: *Die Texte*. A. *Transcription*. B. *Tafeln*. Berlin / Leipzig: de Gruyter.

Sieg, Emil, Wilhelm Siegling & Wilhelm Schulze. 1931. *Tocharische Grammatik*. Göttingen: Vandenhoeck & Ruprecht.

Simson, Georg von. 2000. *Prātimokṣasūtra der Sarvāstivādins*. Teil II: *Kritische Textausgabe, Übersetzung, Wortindex sowie Nachträge zu Teil I*. Göttingen: Vandenhoeck & Ruprecht.

Stumpf, Peter. 1971. *Der Gebrauch der Demonstrativ-Pronomina im Tocharischen*. Wiesbaden: Harrassowitz.

Takasaki, J. 1966. *A Study on the Ratnagotravibhāga (Uttaratantra): Being a Treatise on the Tathāgatagarbha Theory of Mahāyāna Buddhism.* Roma: Istituto italiano per il Medio ed Estremo Oriente.

Teiser, Stephen F. 1988. *The Ghost Festival in Medieval China.* Princeton (NJ): Princeton University Press.

Tekin, Şinasi. 1980. *Maitrisimit nom bitig. Die uigurische Übersetzung eines Werkes der buddhistischen Vaibhāṣika-Schule.* 1. Teil. *Transliteration, Übersetzung, Anmerkungen.* Berlin [DDR]: Akademie-Verlag.

Thomas, Werner. 1952. *Die tocharischen Verbaladjektive auf -l: eine syntaktische Untersuchung.* Berlin: Akademie Verlag.

Thomas, Werner. 1958. "Zum Ausdruck der Komparation beim tocharischen Adjektiv". *Zeitschrift für vergleichende Sprachforschung auf dem Gebiete der Indogermanischen Sprachen* 75: 129–169.

Thomas, Werner. 1972. 'Zweigliedrige Wortverbindungen im Tocharischen', *Orbis* 21: 429–470.

Thomas, Werner & Wolfgang Krause. 1964. *Tocharisches Elementarbuch.* Band 2: *Texte und Glossar.* Heidelberg: Winter.

Tiefenauer, Marc. 2018. *Les Enfers indiens. Histoire multiple d'un lieu commun.* Leiden: Brill.

Tremblay, Xavier. 2005. "Irano-Tocharica et Tocharo-Iranica". *Bulletin of the School of Oriental and African Studies,* 68 (3): 421–449.

Upasak, Chandrika S. 1975. *Dictionary of Early Buddhist Monastic Terms (Based on Pali Literature).* Varanasi: Bharati Prakashan.

Van Put, Ineke. 2007. "The Names of Buddhist Hells in East Asian Buddhism". *Pacific World: Journal of the Institute of Buddhist Studies,* Third Series 9: 205–229.

Van Put, Ineke. 2015. *Buddhist Hells. The Northern Tradition.* Mumbai / New Dehli: Somaiya Publications.

Vogel, Claus & Klaus Wille. 1996. "The Final Leaves of the Pravrajyāvastu Portion of the Vinayavastu Manuscript Found Near Gilgit. Part 1: Saṃgharakṣitāvadāna". In Gregory Bongard-Levin et al. (eds.), *Sanskrit-Texte aus dem buddhistischen Kanon: Neuentdeckungen und Neueditionen III.* Göttingen: Vandenhoeck & Ruprecht, 241–296.

Winter, Werner. 1992. "Tocharian". In Jadranka Gvozdanović (ed.), *Indo-European Numerals.* Berlin / New York: de Gruyter, 97–161.

Zieme, Peter. 1992. *Religion und Gesellschaft im Uigurischen Königreich von Qočo. Kolophone und Stifter des alttürkischen buddhistischen Schrifttums aus Zentralasien.* Opladen: Westdeutscher Verlag.

Zieme, Peter. 1995. "Alttürkische Halsketten und andere Schmucke". In Marcel Erdal & Semih Tezcan (eds.), *Beläk Bitig. Sprachstudien für Gerhard Doerfer zum 75. Geburtstag*. Wiesbaden: Harrassowitz, 233–246.
Zieme, Peter. 2021. "Swimming in the Caustic Lye Stream. Marginal Notes on the Old Uyghur Maitrisimit Nom Bitig". In Johannes Reckel & Merle Schatz (eds.), *Ancient Texts and Languages of Ethnic Groups along the Silk Road*. Göttingen: Universitätsverlag Göttingen, 213–220.

Nouvelles formes tokhariennes B extraites des fragments de Berlin

I. Quelques formes nominales nouvelles ou « oubliées »[1]

Ilya B. Itkin

Cet article est consacré à la discussion de quelques formes nominales tokhariennes B dont la plupart sont extraites des fragments inédits de Berlin ("THT-fragments"). Certaines de ces formes sont mentionnées dans les travaux classiques d'E. Sieg & W. Siegling, W. Krause & W. Thomas, mais elles sont « un peu oubliées » par des chercheurs contemporains. D'autres n'avaient jusqu'à présent pas encore été reconnues. Enfin, la forme *iśanaisäṃ* (THT 1534.a b5), le gén. du. de *ek* 'œil', est bien connue, mais elle est reproduite de façon inexacte (***eśanaisäṃ*) tandis que sa particularité la plus remarquable est justement son *i* initial.

0 Introduction

Les fragments tokhariens B de la Turfansammlung de Berlin non inclus dans l'édition (Sieg & Siegling 1953) et en grande majorité inédits jusqu'ici ("THT-fragments") abondent de formes importantes et intéressantes pour la grammaire et l'histoire de la langue. Le présent article (que nous espérons continuer) contient une liste assez courte de formes nominales extraites des fragments THT. L'interprétation de certaines formes est évidente, mais, puisqu'elles manquent dans (Adams 2013) et/ou (Peyrot 2008), elles ont pu rester inconnues pour les chercheurs.

1 Je voudrais remercier Sergey Malyshev, Chams Bernard et Michaël Peyrot pour des corrections et des précisions importantes.

Les mots tokhariens sont cités en translittération simplifiée standard; si le contexte n'ajoute rien à l'interprétation de la forme en question, il est omis.

La structure de l'article est la suivante:

1. Formes du vocatif.
2. Nom. pl. en *-i* du type *prere – preri.*
3. Acc. sg. f. en *-ssu-ññai.*
4. Autres formes nouvelles.
5. Formes variantes.

1 Formes du vocatif

> *arañce* 'cœur' – voc. ***arañcu***; *eṅkwe* 'homme' – voc. ***eṅkwa****; *empele* 'horrible' – voc. ***empelyu***

Dans Krause & Thomas (1960: 103) les formes *arañcu*, *eṅwa*, *empelyu* sont énumérées parmi d'autres formes du vocatif. Aucune de ces formes n'est mentionnée dans Adams (2013). Peut-être que les tokharianistes contemporains les traitent comme purement reconstruites; cependant toutes ces formes sont réellement attestées.

La forme *arañcu* n'est même pas ἅπαξ λεγόμενον, cf. || *arañc[u] ///* (IOL Toch 173 a3), *arañcu* (PK AS 16.7 a1), */// [a]rañcu* • (THT 1178 b1).

Pour le vocatif d'*eṅkwe* cf. *eṅwā k[l]ai ///* (THT 1283 a7) 'ô homme, ô femme (?)': *klai ///* est quelque forme de *klīye* 'femme', peut-être le vocatif aussi.

Quant à *empele*, cf. *[:] mā kärsnāt wesäñ pärmaṅkänta māk⸗ empelyu* **:** (THT 1573.a a3) 'tu ne détruis pas nos espérances, ô très-horrible'. Le composé *māka-empele** litt. 'très-horrible' manque aussi dans Adams (2013: 479).

2 Nom. pl. en *-i* du type *prere – preri*

plewe 'radeau' - nom. pl. ***plewi***; *were* 'odeur' - nom. pl. ***weri***; *ṣmare* 'huile, onguent' - nom. pl. ***ṣmari***

Le modèle *prere* 'flèche' – nom. pl. *preri* est très fréquent en tokharien B (Krause & Thomas 1960: 129–130). Aux formes du nom. pl. déjà connues on peut ajouter au moins trois exemples nouveaux: *plewi* (THT 1431.a a4), *weri* (THT 3120 a2), *ṣmari* (THT 1403.e a1, THT 3009 b2).

3 Acc. sg. f. en *-ssu-ññai*

Selon Krause & Thomas (1960: 156), la seule forme de l'acc. sg. f. possible pour les adjectifs en *-ssu* est *-ssuntsai*. Pourtant Sieg & Siegling (1949, II: 165) ont identifié de façon certaine *läklessuññai* comme l'acc. sg. f. de *läklessu* 'souffrant, malheureux', cf. **:** *läklessuññai lyāka tā$_u$ wertsyai trai śaiṣṣentso käṣṣi pūdñäkte* **:** (B 45 a4) 'Die leidvolle Versammlung sah der Lehrer der drei Welten, der Buddha' (ibid.: 66). Cette forme vraiment "bien oubliée" n'est point isolée; on peut y ajouter encore deux exemples:

- *(ke)kts(e)ñ källoym skwassuññai* **:** (PK AS 17H b4) 'que j'obtiendrai un corps heureux!'; *skwassuññai* est l'acc. sg. f. de *skwassu* 'heureux'
- */// w· ssu ññai – ///* (THT 3566 b3); la conjecture la plus plausible est *(ñem klā)w(i)ssuññai*, l'acc. sg. f. de *ñem-klāwissu* 'renommé'.

Il est à noter que la variante *-ssuntsai* n'est ni plus fréquente, ni plus "standard". Elle est limitée à un seul lexème (le même *läklessu*) et par un seul ouvrage, l'*Udānālaṅkāra*, cf. *läklessuntsai* (B 1 a2), *lä[kl]es(su)[ntsai]* (B 15 a4) = *(lä)kl(e)ssunts[ai]* (B 17 a5).

Une distribution quelconque (chronologique, contextuelle, etc.) entre *-ssuññai* et *-ssuntsai* est difficile à établir: sur la ligne B 1 a2 on trouve une locution très proche de B 45 a4, */// läklessuntsai lyāka werts[yai] ///* '...Er sah die betrübte Versammlung...' (Sieg & Siegling 1949, II: 3). Les fragments B 1 et B 45 appartiennent au même manuscrit, l'*Udānālaṅkāra A*.

4 Autres formes nouvelles

kressu* '± digne'

Cf. *mā kressoñc* (THT 1296+1399.hh+1612 a5; Ogihara 2014: 247–248). Partant de la lecture *mākressoñc*, Ogihara (ibid.: 248) indique justement qu'il s'agit du nom. pl. m. de quelque adjectif avec le suffixe *-ssu*, mais le laisse sans interprétation. Nous jugeons nécessaire de revenir à la division de mots proposée par Tamai (2007): *mā kressoñc*. L'adjectif *kressu** peut être dérivé du nom *kare* 'dignité, rang, classe'; cette hypothèse s'accorde bien avec le fait que le suffixe *-ssu* se construit avec *nomina abstracta*.

ispetse '± voisin'

Cf. *ispetse* (THT 1313+1314 b2). Le dérivé d'*isäpe*, *ysape* 'près'.

*lymiye** 'lèvre' – acc. sg. ***lyami****

Cf. *ñormeṃ l[y]ämisā* (THT 1313+1314 b7) 'dessous sur la lèvre'. C'est la première attestation (au perlatif) du singulier du mot 'lèvre' connu par le duel *lymine*. On a donc ici le modèle analogue à *yṣiye* 'nuit' ~ acc. sg. *yaṣi*. Pour l'interprétation du passage entier cf. Itkin (2021).

kantwo 'langue' – acc. pl. ***kaṃtwaṃ***

L'acc. pl. du mot *kantwo* est présenté dans Adams (2013: 147) de façon suivante: « kantwaṃ (K-T) ». Il semble que la référence "(K-T)" renvoie ici à (Thomas 1964: 179), où le perlatif *kantwaṃtsa* est mentionné. Bien sûr, cette forme, suivie d'un point d'exclamation, n'est pas reconstruite, mais sa source reste inconnue pour le moment. En même temps, l'acc. pl. se découvre tel quel dans un des fragments THT, cf.: */// taksanan=me kaṃtwaṃ koynam[e](ṃ) ///* (THT 1363.e b4) litt. 'il détruit / ils détruisent notre / votre / leur ..., les langues de (notre / votre / leur) bouche...’. Le pronom enclitique du pluriel =*me* assure qu’il s’agit de plusieurs personnes; il est intéressant qu’avec cela le mot *koyṃ** ‘bouche’ est au singulier néanmoins.

keṃts ‘oie’

Cf. *keṃts* (THT 1396.f a2). Ce mot, pour lequel cf. spécialement (Adams 2011: 34–37; Huard 2020a: 32–34; Huard 2020b), continue i.-e. **ǵʰans*[2]; il est connu par le gen. pl. *kentsantso* (PK NS 506 a3) ~ *keṃtsaṃts* (THT 1399.r b2) ~ *kentsänts* (THT 1859 a3). La forme *keṃts* est sans contexte, de sorte qu’elle pourrait représenter quelque lexème homonymique, mais l’identification proposée ici est appuyée un peu par la ligne suivante, THT 1396.f a3, où on trouve le mot *lymanta* ‘étangs’.

arwārñe ‘± empressement’

Cf. *a[rw]ārñe* (THT 1443 a1; il est possible que le même mot soit attesté aussi sur les lignes b5 et b6). Ce mot doit être dérivé d’*arwāre* ‘prêt’.

*last** (ou *lasto*?) ‘tige (?)’ – nom.-acc. pl. ***lästuwa***

Cf. */// lṣi lästuwa ya ///* (THT 1443 a2) ‘des tiges (?) de ...*l*’.

L’acception de ce mot est litigieuse: ‘stalk (= skr. *gaṇḍa-*)’ (Ogihara 2009: 447) ou ‘root-bark (?)’ (Adams 2013: 593 sans mention de la supposition d’Ogihara). La forme du nom.-acc. sg. est aussi discutable: sa seule attestation est *[ka]ravīräṣṣe las[t]o* (B 497 b7) ‘tige (?) du laurier-rose’, mais Adams (l.c.) note que « [p]erhaps the final *-o* is not part of the word, but rather an exemple of *bewegliches -o* ». En effet, le pluriel *lästuwa* et l’adjectif dérivé *lästäṣ(e)* (IOL Toch 106 a2) témoignent, semble-t-il, en

2 En slave commun, le descendant d’i.-e. **ǵʰans* est **gǫsь* (cf. russe *гусь*, etc.) avec *g-* au lieu de ***z-* attendu. Contestant à bon droit l’idée populaire que le mot slave est un emprunt au germanique, Adams (2011: 35, n. 7) suppose que « the lack of palatalization is <...> the result of some internal factor ». Mais cet « internal factor » est bien connu: c’est la loi de dissimilation des spirantes établie par Antoine Meillet, cf. (Meillet 1924: 24).

faveur de *last**. Si c'est vraiment ça, il est possible que la corrélation entre le *-st* final et le pluriel en *-uwa* ne soit pas fortuite en tokharien B, cf. l'observation de Krause & Thomas (1960: 102): « Die Bildungen auf B *-t* flektieren, soweit bezeugt, nach Kl. I: B *ost* [A *waṣt*], B *tarst** (Pl. *tarstwa*) <...> ».

Selon l'attestation à B 497 b7, *last** est masculin ou alternant (Adams l.c.; Hartmann 2013: 349). À juger par */// lṣi*, ce mot est notamment masculin, tandis que *tarst** '± arrière-pensée' est féminin au pluriel, cf. *ṣkas toṃ tarstwasa* (B 33 b3) 'par ces six arrière-pensées'. Le mot *ost* 'maison' (nom.-acc. pl. *ostūwa*) est masculin au singulier, cf., par exemple, *c[e]w ostne* (B 42 b7) 'dans cette maison'. Thomas (1964: 177) traite *ost* comme alternant, mais des exemples pertinents pour le pluriel nous sont inconnus. Dans Adams (2013: 134) le genre de ce mot n'est pas désigné du tout.

Pour quelques hypothèses étymologiques à propos de *last** voir maintenant (Blažek 2019).

eñcuwo 'fer' – acc. sg. ***eñcuwa***

Cf. *eñcuwa pilke wat* (THT 1543.d b2[3]) 'le fer ou le cuivre'. La forme *eñcuwa* est bien attendue: cf. *luwo* 'animal' – acc. sg. *luwa* (nom.-acc. pl. *lwāsa*) d'un côté et *kantwo* 'langue' – acc. sg. *kantwa* (nom. pl. *kantwañ**, acc. pl. *kaṃtwaṃ* (voir plus haut)) de l'autre[4]. Puisque des formes du pluriel d'*eñcuwo* (si elles existent) sont inconnues, on ne peut pas faire un choix.

3 Peyrot (2008: 60) mentionne cette attestation sans indiquer la forme grammaticale concrète.

4 M. Peyrot (communication personnelle) a attiré notre attention sur cette dernière possibilité.

5 Formes variantes

cmelaṣṣe 'se rapportant à la (re)naissance' – acc. sg. f. ***cimelaṣṣai***

Cf. *///* – *cimelaṣṣai (ne)rvāṃṣṣai ytāri* **:** – *///* (THT 1687.a a1) 'la route de naissance et du nirvāṇa'. La forme *cimelaṣṣai* est le résultat du changement de *ä* inaccentué et "invisible" à *i* devant ou après une consonne palatale (Peyrot 2008: 57–58), cf., par exemple, *ñikañceṃ* acc. sg. m. de *ñkañce* 'd'argent'. Nous n'avons pas réussi à trouver d'autres exemples du thème *cimel-*.

śikwaśko 'épine-vinette'

Cf. *śikwaśko* (THT 1391 b2). Encore une variante à côté de *śkwaśko (saepe)*, *śwaśko* (PK AS 3B a3, W-7 b3), *śkwäśko* (IOL Toch 881 b2, PK AS 9B a4) et *śkwiśko* (B 500, 6[5]; Itkin 2004: 164 d'après Sieg & Siegling 1953: 311, n. 12); seule la forme *śkwaśko* est enregistrée dans (Adams 2013: 700).

L'orthographe *śikwaśko* reflète le même effet *ä* "invisible" → *i* qui est présent dans *cimelaṣṣai*.

ek 'œil' – gén. du. ***iśanaisäṃ***

Cf. *iśanaisäṃ* (THT 1534.a b5). Cet exemple n'est ni inconnu ni négligé, mais son sort est étrange. Il s'agit évidemment de quelque forme du mot *ek* 'œil'. Pour cette raison peut-être, Tamai (2007) et Peyrot (2008: 121, n. 199) donnent *eśanaisäṃ*, mais la lecture *e-* est exclue. De plus, Peyrot (l.c.) note: « The case of *eśanaisäṃ* THT1534.a b5 is unclear ». C'est bien cela du point de vue syntaxique car la ligne est fort endommagée, mais du point de vue morphologique la forme contenant *-aisä-* ne peut pas être autre chose que le gén. du.

Le changement *ñ#* → *ṃ#* est attesté plusieurs fois, y compris pour la désinence du génitif (Peyrot 2008: 78–84, 120–121). Par contre, l'*i* initial est remarquable, et il n'est sans doute pas une simple erreur. La transition *#e-* → *#i-* devant une consonne palatale était jusqu'ici limitée à un seul

5 Plus précisément, B 500–502, 9, voir CEToM.

lexème, *eñcuwo* ~ *iñcuwo* 'fer' (ibid.: 60)[6]. Probablement le thème du du. et du pl. du mot 'œil', *eś*-, n'a pas pu se transformer en *iś*- car le thème du sg. était *ek*-. Néanmoins, la forme *iśanaisäṃ* montre que cette transition pouvait sporadiquement se réaliser, même au dépens d'une alternance irrégulière du vocalisme radical.

[RECEIVED: OCTOBER 2021]

Institute of Oriental Studies of the RAS
National Research University Higher School of Economics
Rozhdestvenka Street 12
107031 Moscow, Russia
ilya.borisovich.itkin@gmail.com

Références bibliographiques

Adams, Douglas Q. 2011. "Three additions to the Tocharian B aviary". *Tocharian and Indo-European Studies* 12: 33–43.

Adams, Douglas Q. 2013. *A dictionary of Tocharian B. Revised and greatly enlarged.* 2nd ed. Amsterdam / New York: Rodopi.

Blažek, Václav. 2019. "Tocharian B *lasto* in Balto-Slavic perspective". *Journal of Indo-European Studies* 47: 213–222.

Hartmann, Markus. 2013. *Das Genussystem des Tocharischen*. Hamburg: Baar.

Huard, Athanaric. 2020a. "The end of Mahākāśyapa and the encounter with Maitreya – Two Leaves of a Maitreya-Cycle in Archaic TB". *Tocharian and Indo-European Studies* 20: 1–82.

Huard, Athanaric. 2020b. "On Tocharian B *kents** and the origin of PIE **ĝʰans*-". In Romain Garnier (ed.), *Loanwords and Substrata. Proceedings of the Collo-*

6 Avec cela, Peyrot (ibid.: 171–172) traite les paires *ākteke* ~ *āktike* 'merveilleux, étonnant; étonné', *ente* ~ *inte* 'où, quand' et aussi *eprer* ~ *iprer* 'ciel, air', qu'il mentionne seulement (ibid.: 60, n. 54), séparément d'*eñcuwo* ~ *iñcuwo*. Cela se comprend car pour *ākteke*, etc. l'influence des consonnes palatales est exclue. Si tous ces mots, auquels on peut ajouter *ewe* ~ *iwe** 'peau', cf. (Adams 2013: 70), appartiennent vraiment à un seul groupe où *e* est primaire et le mécanisme du changement est identique, il est à noter qu'on trouve toujours encore un *e* en syllabe suivante, c'est pourquoi il est possible qu'il s'agit tout simplement de la dissimilation *e* … *e* → *i* … *e*.

quium held in Limoges (5th – 7th June, 2018). Innsbruck: Institut für Sprachen und Lite-raturen der Universität Innsbruck, 215–262.

Itkin, Ilya B. 2004. Compte-rendu de: Adams, Douglas Q. A dictionary of Tocharian B. Amsterdam / Atlanta: Rodopi, 1999. *Voprosy Jazykoznanija* 4: 159–165.

Itkin, Ilya B. 2021. Compte-rendu de: Kim, Ronald I. The Dual in Tocharian. From Typology to *Auslautgesetz*. Münchener Studien zur Sprachwissenschaft, Beiheft 26. Verlag J. H. Roll Dettelbach, 2018. *Kratylos* 66: 124–148.

Krause, Wolfgang & Werner Thomas. 1960. *Tocharisches Elementarbuch. Band I. Grammatik*. Heidelberg: Winter.

Meillet, Antoine. 1924. *Le slave commun*. Paris: Champion.

Ogihara, Hirotoshi. 2009. *Researches about Vinaya-texts in Tocharian A and B [Recherches sur le Vinaya en tokharien A et B]*. PhD, Paris: École Pratique des Hautes Études.

Ogihara, Hirotoshi. 2014. "Fragments of The "Chujia Gongde Jing" in Tocharian B". *Tokyo University Linguistic Papers* 35: 233–261 (en japonais).

Peyrot, Michaël. 2008. *Variation and change in Tocharian B*. Amsterdam / New York: Rodopi.

Sieg, Emil & Wilhelm Siegling. 1949. *Tocharische Sprachreste, Sprache B, Heft 1. Die Udānālaṅkāra-Fragmente. [I] Text, [II] Übersetzung und Glossar*. Göttingen: Vandenhoeck & Ruprecht.

Sieg, Emil & Wilhelm Siegling. 1953. *Tocharische Sprachreste, Sprache B, Heft 2. Fragmente Nr. 71–633*. Edited by Werner Thomas. Göttingen: Vandenhoeck & Ruprecht.

Tamai, Tatsushi. 2007. *A preliminary edition of unpublished texts from the Berlin Turfan Collection*. Thesaurus indogermanischer Text- und Sprachmaterialien (TITUS): Tocharian manuscripts from the Berlin Turfan collection. http://titus.fkidg1.uni-frankfurt.de/texte/tocharic/tht.htm.

Thomas, Werner. 1964. *Tocharisches Elementarbuch. Band II. Texte und Glossar*. Heidelberg: Winter.

In too deep: the tale of Vyāsa and Kāśisundarī in Tocharian A

A new reading of THT 743 and 744 (A 110–111)[1]

Véronique M. Kremmer

This is the story of how the mythical sage Vyāsa gets "ditched". The hitherto untranslated Tocharian A fragments 110 and 111 (THT 743 and 744) contain the story of an ill-fated love affair between Vyāsa and a courtesan named Kāśisundarī, which ends with Vyāsa digging a ditch for his beloved and receiving a blow to the head. The text is established through the comparison with the only known parallel text of this narrative: a commentary on Udbhaṭasiddhasvāmin's *Viśeṣastava*, of which only the Tibetan translation survives. This paper presents a new edition of the Tocharian fragments, a translation, and a linguistic and philological commentary.

1 Introduction

This paper proposes, for the first time, a translation of the Tocharian A fragments 110 and 111 (THT 743 and 744) from the Berlin Turfan Collection. This new edition and translation have been made possible because of the recent discovery that the story told within them closely matches a

1 The research for this article was conducted under the HisTochText project. This project has received funding from the European Research Council (ERC) under the European Union's Horizon 2020 research and innovation program (grant agreement No. 788205). I would like to thank an anonymous reviewer for their careful reading of the text and for their insightful comments and suggestions, as well as express my gratitude to Dr. Martin Straube (Philipps-Universität Marburg) for his useful comments on the figure of Kāśisundarī. All remaining errors are my own.

Tibetan parallel text, found in the *Viśeṣastavaṭīkā*, which could be used to restore some of the missing parts. The story is that of the mythical sage Vyāsa's ill-fated love affair with a courtesan called Kāśisundarī or "beautiful maiden of Kāśī". The events of the story take place in Vārāṇasī (henceforth Kāśī), under the reign of a certain king Brahmadatta. Fearing a foreign invasion, Brahmadatta makes all citizens dig ten-cubit ditches to defend the city. Vyāsa, having just taken up quarters with the prostitute, with whom he has madly fallen in love, offers himself up to the task against all expectations. The story ends with the prostitute kicking Vyāsa in the head, a scene which is alluded to a few times in Buddhist *kāvya*.

The new interpretation of fragments A 110 and 111 helps to establish the relationship between the larger manuscript they belong to and previous works of Buddhist literature. Moreover, thanks to the discovery of this connection, it has been possible to ascertain the meaning and etymology of a few hapaxes in the fragments.

2 Material description

The fragments A 110 and 111 are part of a larger manuscript comprising fragments A 89 to 143, which was discovered in the so-called Stadthöhle at Šorčuq. The leaves of paper, according to Sieg and Siegling (1921: 51), are 12.5 cm high and 49 cm wide, with a string hole situated about 12 cm from the left edge. The string hole, about four to five akṣaras wide, is located at the level of lines a3 to a4. Each side contains six lines of originally about 42 akṣaras. The manuscript was badly damaged by fire, so that only about one third of each sheet remains intact. In the case of fragments 110 and 111, only the right third of the leaf is preserved (about 16 akṣaras per line), and some akṣaras, especially at the edges, are illegible. Photographs of the manuscripts, which have been used to suggest tentative restorations of the text wherever possible for the purposes of this new edition and translation, are available on the websites of the CEToM project[2] and the International Dunhuang Project.[3]

3 Narrative context

The manuscript A 89–143, or at least part of it, has been given the provisional title of *Nandacarita*[4] by Sieg & Siegling (1921: 51), since it features Nanda, the Buddha's handsome half-brother, alongside his wife Sundarī. It also preserves certain chapter titles reminiscent of the epic *Saundarananda* by Aśvaghoṣa (2nd century CE), such as *nandapravrājaṃ* (A 127 a2), which directly corresponds to the name of canto 5 of the *Saundarananda* (*nandapravrājana* or "Initiation of Nanda"). The first few fragments of this series (A 89ff, according to Sieg & Siegling, *loc. cit.*) seem to match the contents of cantos 6 (*bhāryāvilāpa*) and 7 (*nandavilāpa*) of Aśvaghoṣa's epic. Unlike the *Saundarananda*, which is a *kāvya* work, composed entirely in verse, this Tocharian manuscript is a *campū* composition, alternating prose and verse.[5] The identification of fragments 110 and 111 provides important elements towards the understanding of the narrative structure of the Tocharian *Nandacarita* and its relationship to Aśvaghoṣa's *Saundarananda*, of which it seems to be a dramatic adaptation. Indeed, the encounter between Vyāsa and a prostitute in Kāśī is also alluded to in Aśvaghoṣa's epic, although only briefly and without any details about the circumstances leading to the events:

Saundarananda VII.30
dvaipāyano dharmaparāyaṇaś ca

2 https://www.univie.ac.at/tocharian/?A 110 and https://www.univie.ac.at/tocharian/?A 111
3 http://idp.bbaw.de/idp.a4d
4 It has been brought to my attention by Georges-Jean Pinault (p.c.) that this title can now be emended to *Saundaracarita-nāṭak*, based on the attestations in A 171 a4 *saundar·* and A 127 a2 *-ritanāṭkaṃ*. See also Carling & Pinault (forth.) *s.v. Saundaracarita-nāṭak*.
5 On this mixed genre, see Pinault (2008: 407).

reme samaṃ kāśiṣu veśyavadhvā |
yayā hato bhūc calanūpureṇa
pādena vidyullatayeva meghaḥ ||
And Dvaipāyana who was devoted to religion,
dallied with a harlot in Kāśī
Who struck him with her foot with its jingling anklet,
as a cloud is struck by lightning.[6]

This verse is part of a long monologue by the main character Nanda, who has just left his wife to follow the teaching of his half-brother, the Buddha. In an attempt to convince himself not to go back to her, he evokes a list of gods and sages who have gone astray through women, showing that even those who are deeply devoted to the *dharma* are unable to resist temptation. Vyāsa, who is here referred to by his patronymic name Dvaipāyana, is mentioned alongside the likes of Sūrya, Agni, Vasiṣṭha and his own father Parāśara.

The verse from the *Saundarananda* is not the only allusion to this episode by Aśvaghoṣa, suggesting that the narrative was well known at least by Aśvaghoṣa and his disciples, around the 2nd century CE. A cryptic reference to an episode where Vyāsa suffers a kick to the head by a prostitute is also found in the *Buddhacarita*, in a series of strophes recited by a certain Udāyin, son of a *purohita*, in response to love-stricken women being rejected by the Buddha when he was still a young prince. Udāyin instructs the women to double their efforts of seduction, insisting on the power that they may hold over men if applied properly, and recalling examples of great sages who have failed to resist temptation.

Buddhacarita IV.16
purā hi kāśisundaryā veśavadhvā mahān ṛṣiḥ |
tāḍito bhūt padā vyāso durdharṣo devatair api ||
Of old time, for instance, the great seer, Vyāsa, whom even the gods could hardly contend with,

6 Text and translation after Johnston (1928: 46 and 1932: 38)

was kicked with her foot by the harlot, Kāśisundarī.[7]

In these works of Buddhist *kāvya*, Vyāsa is always brought up as a negative example, alongside other examples of sages and gods who were led astray by heedless passion and subsequently humiliated. For a long time, the story behind this anecdote remained unidentified.[8] In order to satisfactorily explain this reference, especially the motif of Vyāsa being kicked in the head, attempts have been made to connect it to existing narrative material in the *Mahābhārata*. In this epic, which Vyāsa himself is famously said to have compiled, the mythical sage also appears as a secondary character. Thus, Sullivan (1990: 290f) identifies the "beautiful maiden of Kāśī" as the princess Ambikā, widow to Vyāsa's half-brother Vicitravīrya, who, having already given birth to the blind Dhṛtarāṣṭra, refused to have intercourse with the frightening seer a second time. She, according to Sullivan (*loc. cit.*) would have been considered a prostitute (*veśavadhū*) because she had initially agreed to sleep with a man other than her husband. Hiltebeitel (2006: 246) on the other hand, speculates that the term *Kāśisundarī* might have referred not to Ambikā herself, but to the *śūdra* servant-woman whom she adorns with her own jewels and sends to the bedchamber in her own stead to fool Vyāsa.

However, it now becomes increasingly clear that the references by Aśvaghoṣa allude to an entirely different folktale involving Vyāsa, and that Kāśisundarī is a literary figure in her own right. This tale once probably enjoyed a certain popularity, but nowadays only survives in a Tibetan version and in the two Tocharian A fragments 110 and 111.

7 Text and translation after Johnston (1935: 32 and 1936: 46). Compare the translation by Olivelle (2009: 93): 'Long ago Kashi-sundari, the prostitute, kicked with her foot Vyāsa, the great seer, whom even the gods found hard to assail.'

8 Johnston (1936: 46 n. 16): 'The story is unidentified and it is uncertain if Kāśisundarī is a proper name or not.'

4 The Tibetan parallel

The Tibetan version of the story, which made possible the identification of the Tocharian fragments, is part of Prajñāvarman's *Viśeṣastavaṭīkā* (*VSṬ*), an eight- or ninth-century commentary (*ṭīkā*) to Udbhaṭasiddhasvāmin's *Viśeṣastava* (*VS*). The *Viśeṣastava* or *Praise of the Superiority* (*of the Buddha*) is a 76 or 77-stanza apologetic hymn by a Brahmin convert which highlights the Buddha's qualities compared to the non-Buddhists or *tīrthikas*. The original Sanskrit versions of Udbhaṭasiddhasvāmin's work and Prajñāvarman's commentary have been lost. Much like Aśvaghoṣa, Udbhaṭasiddhasvāmin alludes to Vyāsa's affair with a "beautiful maiden of Kāśī" (Tib. *ka śi mdzes dga' mo*) in a passage enumerating several negative examples, against which the Buddha's moral superiority is highlighted. The Tibetan text and its translation run as follows:[9]

Viśeṣastava 31–32

| ka śi mdzes *dga'* mo la ni |
| rgyas pa yoṅs chags rnam par 'gyur |
| khyod khab bźugs na'aṅ phuṅ khrol ba'i |
| *don* gyis dbaṅ po rmoṅs ma gyur | <31>
| rgyas pa 'dod gduṅs g.yen spyu ba |
| bud med kyi ni rdog pas bsnun |
| khyod ni khyim par bźugs pa na'aṅ |
| phyir źiṅ 'khrugs par gyur pa *med* | <32>
Vyāsa, through desire for Kāśisundarīnandā
has been confused;
(but your) senses - even when you (still) lived in the house -
were not blinded by evil things.
Vyāsa, lovesick and confused
was hit by the foot of a woman;
but you - even when you (still) lived in the house -
were not blinded by evil things.

9 Text from Schneider (1993: 60–61), English translation based on his German translation.

The commentary to these stanzas in the *VSṬ* finally explains the circumstances leading up to Vyāsa being kicked in the head by his lover. The story is split up into two parts by the commentator, as explanations to stanzas 31 and 32 respectively. The first part describes the initial meeting and scene of seduction between Vyāsa and the courtesan Kāśisundarī, leading to their eventual love affair. It also highlights Vyāsa's exceptional massage skills. The second part of the story has a somewhat unconventional premise: king Brahmadatta orders every citizen of Kāśī to dig within a single day a trench to defend the city from an attack by an unidentified foreign people. As Kāśisundarī refuses to do her share of the work, Vyāsa, although old and feeble, offers to do it in her stead. Blindly devoted to the task, he refuses to stop digging even as Brahmadatta calls off the workers at dusk, because he obeys none but his lover. Kāśisundarī eventually appears at the scene to talk reason into Vyāsa, and as she leaps off her chariot, kicks him in the head, since he is still sitting in the ditch. It is not clear whether this kick is accidental or not. At the end of the story, Vyāsa agrees to get out of the trench.

Because of the importance of the Tibetan text for the restoration of the Tocharian fragments 110 and 111, the relevant parts of the German translation by Schneider (1993: 154ff) are being reproduced here:[10]

> <31>
> Zu der (Strophe), die mit den folgenden (Worten) beginnt: "Nach der Kāśīsundarīnandā", wird folgendes überliefert:
>
> Nicht lange nachdem der Krieg der Bhāratas vorüber war, war Vyāsa wegen des Leids und Elends seiner Verwandten in seiner geistigen Verfassung ganz niedergeschlagen. Auf seinen Wanderungen kam er nach Benares. Mitten auf der Straße sah er, wie eine vornehme Hetäre namens Kāśīsundarīnandā an ihrer (Haus-)Tür von einer großen Menschenmenge umringt war. (Sein) Herz fühlte sich zu dem Spektakel hingezogen, und darum ging er zu ihnen und fragte, wessen Haus (das) sei. Da erfuhr er von ihren körperlichen und anderen Vor-

10 Out of concern for the length of the present paper, some non-narrative, exegetical parts of the commentary have been cut.

zügen; das nahm (seinen) Sinn gefangen, und er blieb (dort). Da teilte ein Diener der Kāśīsundarīnandā mit, daß an der Tür ein Seher warte. Nun aber hieß sie ihn aus Furcht vor (seinem) Fluch persönlich mit gastlichem Empfang, Waschen der Füße und weiteren Ehrerbietungen willkommen, bat ihn herein, ließ (ihn) einen Sitz an einem abgesonderten Platz einnehmen, und wusch (ihm) selbst die Füße.
Vyāsa lachte. Das faßte sie als Zeichen (seiner Zuneigung) auf, erkannte, daß sie eine Gelegenheit gefunden hatte, und sprach aus großer Freude: „Lacht Ihr ohne Grund?" Er antwortete: „Man hört zwar, daß Ihr Euch in allen Künsten auskennt; (doch) Ihr versteht es nicht, Hände und Füße zu massieren!"
Sie sprach: „Wenn Ihr Euch darin auskennt, so streckt (Eure) Hände aus und zeigt (es mir)!"
Da gab er ihr (seine) Hände.
Dann ließ er sie, die doch schon von so vielen, vorzüglichen Liebhabern berührt worden war, eine solche Berührung verspüren, wie sie sie zuvor noch nicht erlebt hatte.
Und dabei ist dann (in ihm) das Verlangen, d.h. die Liebesleidenschaft erwacht, sich mit ihr sehr lange Zeit über vergnügen zu wollen. [...]

<32>
In der (Strophe), die mit den folgenden (Worten) beginnt: „Der liebeskranke, verwirrte Vyāsa", (heißt Vyāsa) „liebeskrank", weil (er) von Liebe krank geworden, d.h. gepeinigt worden ist; damit ist gemeint, daß (ihn) die Liebesleidenschaft verwundet hat.
[...] Das aber (erzählt man) folgendermaßen:
Der Seher Vyāsa war dabei, mit Kāśīsundarīnandā unbeschwert die Liebesfreuden auszukosten. Als nun einmal Brahmadatta, der König in der Stadt Benares, in Furcht vor einem feindlichen Angriff geriet, befahl er selbst den Jünglingen – und erst recht (allen) anderen – an einem einzigen Tage einen zehn mal zehn Ellen (messenden) Festungsgraben auszuheben. Da erging der Befehl auch an die Kāśīsundarīnandā. Doch obwohl sie mit großem Entgelt um Lohnarbeiter warb, fand sie keine und geriet in Sorge.

Vyāsa sprach: „Warum bist du traurig? Gib (mir) einen Spaten und einen Eimer! Ich will den Festungsgraben ausheben!" Und als er nun gegangen war und gegraben hatte, neigte sich die Sonne nach Westen, ohne daß der Festungsgraben fertiggestellt war. Vyāsa erkannte, daß die Abendzeit (bereits) hereingebrochen war, und blieb an eben diesem Ort, ohne umzukehren.

Als sie an den Zeichen der Wasseruhr und dergleichen erkannt hatten, daß der Tag vergangen und die Zeit der Nacht hereingebrochen war, wurden der König und die Minister mitsamt den Bürgern innerlich sehr unruhig, Als diese Gruppe sich zu gehen anschickte, erblickte ein anderer Brahmane, der innerlich über das Ausheben des Festungsgrabens beunruhigt war, den Vyāsa, und nach einiger Zeit erkannte (er) ihn.

Als der König dies von ihm vernommen hatte, gingen er und die Minister mitsamt den Leuten aus der Stadt zu ihm (d.h. zu Vyāsa), fielen zu (seinen) Füßen nieder und baten (ihn) um Verzeihung. (Doch) er schaute weg und fuhr zu graben fort.

Da aber fürchtete sich jener (König) vor (Vyāsas) Fluch, und als er in Erfahrung gebracht hatte, daß jener Kāśīsundarīnandās Teilstück ausgrub, sandte er ihr diese Nachricht: „Da (du) diesen vorzüglichen Festungsgraben auszuheben geheißen hast, hole (ihn auch nun wieder) heraus!". Doch obschon sie (ganze) drei Male ein Mädchen, (ihre) Dienerin (nämlich), aussandte, wollte er nicht herauskommen.

Da bestieg sie selbst das Gefährt, kam, sprang von ihm herab und traf (Vyāsas) Kopf mit (ihrem) Fuß, der mit Fußringen geschmückt war. „Weil ich betrübt war, habe ich (dir) ganze drei Mal eine Nachricht gesandt; warum kommst du (trotzdem) nicht heraus?"

Vyāsa freute sich in seinem Herzen und sprach: „Für eine so große Liebe(sbekundung) bin (ich dir) sehr dankbar!"[11] Mit diesen Worten kam er heraus.

11 In an earlier translation of the Tibetan text, Zwilling (1978: 68f) reads *bar tu* instead of *rab tu* and translates: 'It is because up until this I was very much in love'.

According to Schneider (1993: 35f) and to my own research on this topic, there are no other known parallels of this story. The story of a certain princess Sundarī of Kāśī, daughter of Brahmadatta, told in the *Avadānaśataka* (8.6), appears to be entirely unrelated.[12] The isolated nature of this story reinforces the theory that this might be a purely Buddhist narrative, especially given the abundance of stories involving Vyāsa elsewhere in Indian literature. Indeed, the unusual motif of the digging recalls a particular *pātayantika*-offense listed in the *Vinayavibhaṅga* of the Sarvāstivādins: there, digging (*khanana-*) is listed as a forbidden activity for a Buddhist monk.[13] One may even conceive that this type of manual labor was considered inappropriate for any sage or religious person, including of Brahmanic profession. The standard equivalent of the Skt. verb √*khan^i^*- is TA *räpā-* (TB *rāpā-*) 'dig', which occurs several times in our text.

Even though this narrative explains the circumstances of the head-kick, none of the previous allusions to it (*Saundarananda* VII.30, *Buddhacarita* IV.16, and *Viśeṣastava* 31–32) mention Vyāsa digging or even sitting on the ground when it occurs. Thus, the narrative could have been adapted, from a popular folktale for instance, and retroactively fitted onto the circumstances described in the verses.

Given the fragmentary nature of the Tocharian texts, we must rely on this Tibetan version to understand the context of the story and translate the extant Tocharian parts, as well as propose tentative restorations. However, we are most likely not dealing with a translation into Tocharian of Prajñāvarman's text, which is certainly of a later date, but with two different adaptations of the same source material, now lost. This is especially

12 Schneider (1993: 155, fn. 2). A manuscript preserved on microfilm which is mentioned by Schneider (*loc. cit.*) and which he did not have access to, has since been digitalized by the Nepalese-German Manuscript Cataloguing Project (NGMCP) and identified as also relating the same story from the *Avadānaśataka*. The transcription and manuscript details can be found here: http://catalogue-old.ngmcp.uni-hamburg.de/mediawiki/index.php/B_24-43_Kāśīsundaryavadāna (last retrieved in October 2021)

13 *yaḥ punar bhikṣuḥ pṛthivīṃ khanyāt khānayed vā pātayantikā* 'If a monk digs the soil, or orders to dig the soil, he is guilty of a *pātayantika*-offense' (Rosen 1959: 200, fn. 3). See also von Simson (2000: 228, 298).

evident in the metrical interludes, which the Tibetan prose commentary lacks. As usual in Tocharian, the content of the three metrical interludes (110 a3–5, 111 a3–5, 111 b5–6) elaborates on the narrative, mostly introducing direct speech or additional descriptions. This makes the restoration of the Tocharian text in these metrical passages more difficult.

5 Edition and translation of the fragments A 110 and 111

Based on these recent findings, I propose a new edition and translation of the fragments A 110 and 111. For this new edition, I relied on photographs of the manuscripts provided by the International Dunhuang Project and the CEToM project. I took over the restorations already proposed by Sieg & Siegling (1921), including one in Siegling's personal copy which was recorded on the CEToM website. Based on the Tibetan parallel and on the now newly understood context of this narrative, I also propose several new restorations, especially at the edges of the text. For the reasoning behind each proposed restoration, I refer to the next section of this paper, where I also offer a brief philological and linguistic commentary of the text.

A 110 (THT 743)
recto
a1 */// māk śomināsyo worpus ñäkci ap[t](sarr oki)* – –
a2 */// (kä)lpāt-äṃ pkäṃntäk āsānā lyalymā[t-äṃ]* – – – –
a3 */// (ṣu)[rma]ṣ säm riṣak pläśluneyo kakuru* **:** *śralu-*
a4 *-(ne)*[14] */// (sä)[lp]ts(y o)ky osāt eṅkälyo* **:** *līt säm mäsratsune-*
a5 *(-yäṣ) /// ṃ opäśśuneyo cami riṣakyāp yärk*
a6 */// ś· vyāse träṅkäṣ puk ṣāñäntuyo ka* •

a1 ... a [woman] (like a) divine (Apsaras) surrounded by many girls ...
a2 she (re)ceived him and made him sit separately on a seat ...

14 Probably *śraluneyo* or *śraluneyäṣ*, see commentary below.

a3 (because of ...) this sage has become feeble through ascetism. Separ(ation) ...
a4 ... he started to burn with passion. This one moved away from shyness ...
a5 With (all sorts of) skillfulness (she paid) honor to this sage ...
a6 Vyāsa says (openly?): "With every skill, Ka(śisundarī)..."

verso

b1 */// naṣ t(e) nu cam ṣāñaṃ o{p}äśśune*[15] || *vyāse trä-*
b2 *-(ṅkäṣ) /// marmas tsitā-ṃ sarkā penu säm ñä-*
b3 *-(kci aptsar) /// [ts](ī)tālune mā kälpos ṣeṣ mäṃtne wyāses tsa-*
b4 *-(ränyo) /// (ylā)r penu säm riṣak ṣeṣ marmas tsinātsi nu opäśśi ṣeṣ*
b5 */// (ca)[m] ypeyaṃ brahmadattes lānt ālakäñcaṃ (yäsluntäṣ pra-)*
b6 *(-ski tāk) /// (ypeṣinäṣ wra)saśśi konaṃ śäk pokes yärśār yṣaṃ (rpātsi wotäk) –*

b1 "But which is the expertise in that skill?" Vyāsa sa(ys) ...
b2 He touched her vital body points. In turn, she, the di(vine Apsaras-like woman) ...
b3 She had not (ever) received a touch such as (by) Vyāsa's (hands).
b4 Although this sage was (feeble), he was, however, skilled in touching the vital points ...
b5 In this country, to the king Brahmadatta (arose the fear) of some other (enemy).
b6 (He ordered) the inhabitants (of the country to dig) within a (single) day a ditch [measuring] ten cubits around.

A 111 (THT 744)
recto

a1 */// tämyo yutkos lmos ṣeṣ tmäṣ vyāse śla poto (n)[mä](smāṃ tränkäṣ):*
a2 */// ñc yo wātsakäl essi putäk näṣ nāśye pāk yṣaṃ*
a3 *(rāpam) /// (wo)täk säm täm kāmat yṣaṃ rpātsi kälk* • || *ṣeraśi-ni-*

15 Following the conventions of the CEToM Project (https://www.univie.ac.at/tocharian/?edition), curly brackets indicate corrected misspellings. The manuscript reads *omäśśune*.

a4 -(*ṣkramāntaṃ*) /// (*mäccā*)*kyāṃ tkaṃ rāp skānt yṣanaṃ skeyasyo* **:** *puk wrasañ ā-*
a5 (*-rar wlessi*) /// *ypeṣiñi wrasañ kñāññānt riṣakäṃ*
a6 /// (*ākā*)*l* (*kākä*)*tku mar säm wasäṃ ypeyis śāp tāṣ kä*

a1 Because of this, she was worried and remained seated. Then, Vyāsa b(owing with respect, says):
a2 "... Give command to give (me) a (spade) and a basket! I shall (dig) the lady's share of the ditch."
a3 She ordered [to give him these implements]. He carried this and went to dig the ditch. In [the tune] *ṣeraśi-ni*(*ṣkramāntaṃ*):
a4 He dug the earth (itself). They scratched in the trench with efforts. All beings
a5 (stopped working). [...] The inhabitants of the country recognized the sage.
a6 (The wish ar)ose (to the people): "He should not put a curse on our land!"

verso
b1 /// (*r*)*iyäṣ läc vyāse riṣaknac yeṣ śl⸗ āmā*(*śās*)
b2 /// - *mäskatār mā āṣāṃ naṣt tāṃ wle*(*s*) (*wlessi*)
b3 /// - *cwā mā penu lek kälk ṣät akmalyo rāpäkk ats*
b4 /// *penu lānt praskañi śpālmeṃ klaṅkā lmoräṣ*
b5 /// (*yāmäṣt u*)*mpar brāhmaṃ tu $k_u$yalte mā yat lānt watku* **:**
b6 /// (*na*)*śśi tkaṃ rārpu* **:** *taṃne pe träṅkmāṃ mā säm pre kälk ra*(*ryu*)

b1 He [the king] went out of the city. He was going to the sage Vyāsa with his ministers.
b2 "You are [a Brahmin / sage?]. You are not worthy of [doing] this wor(k)."
b3 ... by you." He also did not go away. He kept digging indeed face down.
b4 Also, she, being afraid of the king, having mounted a splendid vehicle ...
b5 "You (have done) an evil deed, Brahmin, because you did not execute the king's command."

b6 "It is for your sake that this ground has been dug!" Speaking also in this way, this one [sage] did not come out, (having given up [his tools]) (?).

6 Philological and linguistic commentary

A 110 (THT 743)

a1 *ñäkci ap[t](sarr oki)* 'like a divine Apsaras' can be restored on the grounds of comparison with similar passages 68 a4 *ñäkcy⫽ aptsarr oki* and 59 a4 *aptsarr oki $k_u$lewāsaṃ* 'like a (divine?) Apsaras among women'. For the phraseology, see also Pāli *devaccharā-* 'celestial nymph' (*PED*: 9), with a regular development of the cluster [*ps*] to [*cch*] (Von Hinüber 2001: 185, §238). The Tocharian text does not preserve the word for 'prostitute' or 'courtesan'; compare in the Tibetan version, *smad 'tshoṅ ma'i gtso mo*[16] 'noble / chief prostitute'. For the last two akṣaras of the line, one may consider restoring *$k_u$li* 'woman' or even *kräntso $k_u$li* 'a beautiful woman'.

a2 *pkäṃntäk āsānā lyalymāt-äṃ* 'she made him sit separately on a seat': this part of the hospitality ritual offered by Kāśisundarī is strikingly similar in the Tibetan text: '(sie) ließ (ihn) einen Sitz an einem abgesonderten Platz einnehmen'.[17]

16 Throughout this paper, the Tibetan passages are quoted from Schneider (1993).

17 Similar practices of hospitality, including the details of the guest being seated separately (on the seat of the householder) and being offered a foot wash and massage, are described in different *Jātakas*, e.g., in the *Mahā-assāroha-jātaka* (no. 302). Here, a king in distress is well hosted by a citizen who does not know his true identity:
Rājānaṃ gehaṃ netvā attano pīṭhake nisīdāpetvā "ehi bhadde, sahāyassa pāde dhovā" 'ti
'He led the king to his home and made him sit down on his own seat and said: "Come on, my dear wife, wash my friend's feet".
The king later returns the favor towards his loyal subject with a similar ritual, where his chief consort also performs a foot massage on the guest:

a3 Here, we have the first of three metrical interludes (A 110 a3 until the beginning of a5). The metrical scheme is probably 4 × 14 (7|7 or 4¦3|4¦3). Indeed, the lines that remain more or less intact are generally compatible with a seven-syllable scheme, sometimes divided into four-syllable and three-syllable subcola (σ σ σ σ ¦ σ σ σ), e.g., *pläśluneyo* ¦ *kakuru, sälptsy oky osāt* ¦ *eṅkälyo* and *līt säm mäsratsuneyäṣ*[18].

a3 (*ṣu*)*[rma]ṣ* 'because': the akṣara <rma> at the left edge of the manuscript can be read with some difficulty. The restoration of *ṣurmaṣ* is tentative. If the metrical scheme is really based on seven-syllable cola, one would expect a two-syllable word preceding (*ṣu*)*[rma]ṣ*.

a3 *śralu*(*ne*) 'separation' is probably in a secondary case (e.g., instr.sg. *śraluneyo* 'through separation', or abl.sg. *śraluneyäṣ* 'from separation'), which would also fit the hypothetical metrical scheme as it would fill a four-syllable subcolon. This verse may allude to the fact that Vyāsa has been separated from his relatives after the events of the *Mahābhārata*, as mentioned at the beginning of the Tibetan version: 'Nicht lange nach-

---

Rājāsane nisīdāpetvā aggamahesiṃ pakkosāpetvā "bhadde, sahāyassa me pāde dhovā" 'ti āha. Sā tassa pāde dhovi. Rājā suvaṇṇabhiṃkārena udakam āsiñci. Devī pāde dhovitvā gandhatelena makkhesi.
"He (= the king) made him sit on the royal throne, summoned his chief consort and said: "My dear wife, wash my friend's feet." And she washed his feet. The king sprinkled water from a golden vessel on them. The queen, after having washed his feet, anointed them with a scented oil.' (ed. Fausbøll, my translation)

18 Based on an alternative reading of the dot at the beginning of line a5 as a punctuation mark indicating the end of a colon, an anonymous reviewer has suggested that the metrical interlude extends to the end of this line. The 5-syllabe structure of *opäśśuneyo* would then rather point to a metrical schema of 4 × 25 (5¦5¦4¦4¦4¦3). The same reviewer then suggests reading *līt säm mäsratsune* as 'this shyness fell away'. However, this sequence would still be a syllable to long to fit in a 5-syllable colon, unless *mäsratsune* is a misspelling for *mäsrats*$_{u}$*ne*. Finally, the dot at the beginning of line a5 appears as a single dot slightly above the line, whereas the metrical punctuation marks in this manuscript consist of two dots traced together using a single stroke and sit lower on the line (cf., e.g., line A 110 a4).

dem der Krieg der Bhāratas vorüber war, war Vyāsa wegen des Leids und Elends seiner Verwandten in seiner geistigen Verfassung ganz niedergeschlagen'.

a4 *(sä)[lp]ts(y o)ky osāt eṅkälyo* 'he started to burn from passion' was cogently restored by Siegling in his personal copy of Sieg & Siegling (1921: 62).[19] The restoration is supported by the context, as well as by similar expressions, e.g.: 186ext [= A 186 + THT 1143 + A 202] /// *(ṣa)[kk a]ts eṅkälyo kapśañi sälpālyī [ṣe]ṣ-äṃ* (leaf) 'His body would have certainly burnt down from passion' (Itkin 2019: 21).[20]

a4 *līt säm mäsratsune(yäṣ)* 'he fell off from his shyness; he let go of his shyness'. The abl.sg. can be restored through comparison with other occurrences of the verb *litā-* 'fall off from, abandon' with the ablative, e.g.: A 344 b3 *ñäktañ (s)$_u$ku(n)tw(äṣ) litanträ* 'the gods are letting go of their happinesses', A 65 a5 *säm krañcäṃ wäknäṣ lāletu* '[he has] strayed from the good way'.

a5 *-ṃ*: probably an oblique ending of an adjective agreeing with *opäśśuneyo* (instr. sg.) 'skill'. Alternatively, it could be the end of an adverb, which would be *wkäṃ-wkäṃ* or *puk-wkäṃ* 'in every way',[21] fitting in this context. Yet another alternative would be to interpret this dot as the upper portion of a punctuation mark separating cola, even though this is less likely in my opinion (see fn. 18).

a6 *-ś·*: this may represent a word ending in *-śe* or *-śi*, maybe the adverb *pākraśi* 'evidently'. A genitive plural ending in *-śśi* here is to be excluded, because only a single <ś> can be read.

a6 *ka ·*: an emendation of <ka> to *kaṃ* 'tune' has been proposed (see the edition given in CEToM), to be translated as 'Vyāsa tells a tune with all artistic devices'.[22] However, there is clearly no *anusvāra* in the manu-

19 Cf. https://www.univie.ac.at/tocharian/?m-a110, retrieved 7 Oct. 2021.

20 I thank an anonymous reviewer for bringing to my attention the very cogent restoration of this passage in Itkin (2019).

21 Reference in Poucha (1955: 306).

22 https://www.univie.ac.at/tocharian/?m-a110 (retrieved Oct. 18, 2021)

script. The sign after <ka> looks like a punctuation mark, a single dot. In my opinion, *träṅkäṣ* introduces direct speech. The line likely corresponds to the Tibetan passage which translates to '***Er antwortete***: „Man hört zwar, daß Ihr Euch ***in allen Künsten*** auskennt; (doch) Ihr versteht es nicht, Hände und Füße zu massieren!"' (emphasis mine). However, this does not really explain the sequence *ka* •. A possible interpretation would be an abbreviation of the proper name *Kāśisundarī*,[23] which is not otherwise attested in the Tocharian text.

b1 *naṣ t(e) nu cam ṣāñaṃ o{m/p}äśśune* 'But which is the expertise in that skill?': This question is probably uttered by Kāśisundarī in response to Vyāsa's boasting about his massage skills (cf. in the *VSṬ*: 'Wenn Ihr Euch darin auskennt, so streckt (Eure) Hände aus und zeigt (es mir)!')

b1 *omäśśune* is a scribal error for *opäśśune* (a.) 'skill, know-how'. For the association of *ṣāñ* 'art, skill' and *opäśśi* 'skillful' cf. A 245 b1 *ysomo ṣāñäntwaṃ opäśśi* 'skilled in all the arts'.

b2 *marmas tsitā-ṃ* 'he touched her vital body parts': this most certainly refers to the massage given by Vyāsa to his lover. TA *marmañ* (nom.pl.), *marmas* (obl.pl.), TB *marmanma* (nom./obl.pl.) represent independent borrowings from Sanskrit *márman-* 'mortal spot' (*SSS*: 53, n.3). This noun is synchronically associated with the root √*mar-* / √*mr̥-* 'die'.[24] In most occurrences, the Tocharian terms designate the blood vessels or veins of the human body (see *DoT*: 474–475).

In the Vedic tradition, the term *márman-* designates vulnerable spots in the body, the pressing or hurting of which inevitably leads to death

23 This interpretation hinges on whether *Kāśisundarī* is a proper name that would be loaned into Tocharian, or a honorific title that would rather be translated, as it is in Tibetan (*ka śi mdzes dga' mo* 'beautiful maiden of Kāśi'). Of course, even in translated rather than transcribed form, the name might still start with the syllable <ka>, as the name of the city would probably not change.

24 According to *EWAia* (vol 2: 329) *márman-* must be, for lack of parallel formations, a derivative of Indo-Aryan date, and the underlying root might be PIE **meld-* 'become soft' (LIV2: 431).

(Filliozat 1949: 133). Case in point: in the *R̥gveda*, Indra famously kills Vr̥tra by striking his *márman*:

R̥V VIII.100, 7cd
ní ṣīṃ vr̥trásya mármaṇi vájram índro apīpatat
'Indra has let fly his mace down onto Vr̥tra's mortal place' (transl. Jamison & Brereton 2014: 1210)

Attempts to interpret the 107 canonical *marman* points as therapeutical points equivalent to the *moxa* points from Chinese acupuncture have been rebuked due to the lack of evidence for such claims in Āyurvedic literature, where the *marman* points are only ever described as points that should best be avoided (Wujastyk 2009: 204f). Traditional techniques for healing injured *marman* spots through massage with oils are described in Dravidian texts and were, as it seems, still in use in the 20th century in Kerala, particularly among athletes and martial artists (Roşu 1981: 427; Roşu & Jobard 1987).

In the present context, Vyāsa touches Kāśisundarī's *marmas* and displays a certain skill while doing so (see A 110 b4: *marmas tsinātsi nu opäśśi ṣeṣ* 'he was skilled in touching the vital points'), leading to their eventual implied love affair. The touching of the *marmas* is supposed to be an act of healing, or at least a relaxing or seductive massage. Unfortunately for our purposes, there is no mention of the *marman*, or even of the exact massage techniques used by Vyāsa, in the Tibetan text.

b3 *ñä(kci aptsar) vel sim.*: cf. A 110 a1. A feminine noun is expected after the demonstrative *sām* (b2).

b4 *(ylā)r*, adj. 'old, feeble, frail, decrepit' (TB *ylāre*).[25] Although there are certainly other possibilities for the restoration of an adjective ending in *-r*, I propose to restore *ylār* because Vyāsa is repeatedly described as old (cf. 110 a3: *pläśluneyo kakuru* '(has) become feeble through ascetism'). Additionally, a contrastive adjective is expected in this concessive clause introduced by *penu*, cf., e.g., A 125ext [= A 125 + THT 1425 fgm. e + A 117]

25 See *DoT*: 562 and Poucha (1955: 251); German 'gebrechlich' according to *TEB* II: 132 and 229.

b3–4: *räskär penu sāṃtäk tāṣ wraskentu nu cämpam[o] wikässi tāṣ* 'Even though the medicine will be bitter, it will be able to eliminate illnesses' (Itkin 2020: 221, 227).

b5 *(ca)[m] ypeyaṃ* 'in this country': this presumably refers to Kāśī, where the story is set.

b5 *brahmadattes lānt ālakäñcaṃ (yäsluntäṣ praski tāk)* 'to king Brahmadatta arose the fear of some other enemy': this clause corresponds to the following line in the parallel text: 'Als nun einmal **Brahmadatta, der König** in der Stadt Benares, **in Furcht vor einem feindlichen Angriff** geriet...' (emphasis mine). The restoration of *yäsluntäṣ* 'enemy', abl. sg. of *yäslu* 'enemy' is fairly certain[26] and paralleled in Tibetan by the genitive expression *phas kyi rgol ba'i* 'of an enemy / opponent'. The expression *praski tāk* is supported by *brahmadattes lānt* being in the genitive, as well as by similar expressions, e.g., although in a negative context: A 1 a3–4 *wrasa(śśi) tsraṣiśśi mā praski naṣ* 'the energetic ones do not know fear'.

b6 (*rpātsi wotäk*) 'he ordered to dig': this has been restored according to the Tibetan parallel (cf. 'Brahmadatta, der König (...) **befahl** (...) [einen] Festungsgraben **auszuheben**', emphasis mine)

b6 *śäk pokes yärśār yṣaṃ* 'a ditch measuring ten cubits around' corresponds exactly to the Tibetan *'obs khru bcu bcu* 'einen zehn mal zehn Ellen (messenden) Festungsgraben'. The use of the oblique case in the form

26 Another possible option would be a genitive. Verbs of fearing normally take complements in the ablative or, mostly in TB, in the perlative (*TEB* I: 88–89, §80.3). However, when the object of fear is [+HUMAN], it is usually expressed in the genitive (*TEB* I: 89, §74.6, Meunier 2015: 234, see also the discussion about *praskañi* below). As for the abstract *praski* 'fear', it seems as though it may govern a complement in the ablative (A 295 *omäskuney(ä)ṣ praski* 'fear of evil') or the perlative (A 44 a4 *āsluneyā praski* 'fear of dying of thirst'). I have not found instances where a [+HUMAN] object of fear was expressed. Since the entire clause in A 111 b5 is reconstructed on the basis of the Tibetan text, the case of *yäslu* (or whichever other noun *ālakäñcaṃ* is the epithet of) may not be determined in the end.

pokes 'arms; cubits'[27] seems to coincide with the type labelled by Carling as 'extensional' (see the definition and other examples in Carling 2000: 7, 37).

111 (THT 744)

a1 *śla poto (n)[mä](smāṃ)* 'bowing with respect': the participle *nmäsmāṃ* is restored from the context, there is no corresponding passage in the Tibetan text.

a2 *-ñc yo wātsakäl* 'hoe and basket'[28]: there is no doubt that this syntagm designates the digging equipment requested by Vyāsa, consisting of two complementary utensils. The meaning is ascertained by the Tibetan parallel: *tog tse daṅ skon pa* 'hoe and basket'.[29] An Indic equivalent would be Pāli *kuddālapiṭaka-* 'a spade and a basket' (*PED*: 221, 457; Cone 2001: 709).

The second member *wātsakäl* probably means 'basket', 'bucket' or more generally 'receptacle'. It is then to be connected with TB *watsālo** '[a type of] pot' or 'waterskin' (*DoT*: 635), attested in THT 91 a1, a passage of the *Araṇemijātaka* where the eponymous hero appears as a gardener: *(ā)ntsesa watsālai premane war āṣtsiś yakne yamaṣäṃ* 'Carrying a waterskin (?) over his (s)houlder, he [= Araṇemi] behaves like a water bearer.' (transl. from CEToM). The translation 'waterskin' is visibly influenced by a previous etymological interpretation going back to Van Windekens

27 The specialized use of TA *poke*, TB **pokai* 'arm' as a unit of measure is not very frequent, but it seems to have been widespread enough for Khotanese to borrow the word, presumably from TB, as *puka*, with the specialized meaning 'cubit' (see Bailey 1979: 242b, Tremblay 2005: 444).

28 The identification of this fragment confirms the segmentation of the text recently proposed by Itkin and Malyshev (2021: 70) as *-ñc yo wātsakäl*, excluding the reading of a previously proposed verb form **yowā* from a verb A *yäw- / yow-* 'to enter'.

29 *skon pa* was translated as 'Eimer' ('bucket') by Schneider (1993: 159) but its actual meaning is 'basket' (Jäschke 1881: 17), as pointed out by Schneider himself (*loc.cit.*, fn. 1).

(1988: 101), who interprets the TB term as a derivative of Skt. *vatsa-* 'calf, young of any animal, offspring', comparing Gk. *βοείη* 'ox-hide; ox-hide shield' and *ἀσκός* 'skin, hide; wineskin' for the semantic development of 'zoonym' to 'skin' to 'object made of skin'. This interpretation fails to convince because it does not explain the presumed derivational suffix, and because *vatsa-* and its derivatives do not generally designate leather or objects made of leather. More probably, TA *wātsakäl* and TB *watsālo** are independent borrowings from a Middle Indic language, with a hypercorrection that resulted in a 'false Sanskritization' of the forms. A likely candidate for the source form is Skt. *vakṣaskāra-* 'basket', itself probably a hypercorrective Sanskritization of Middle Indo-Aryan (MIA) *vakkhāra-* (m.) 'granary' (Turner 1966: 652, No. 11189), based on a folk etymology which presumes a verbal governing compound meaning 'that which is borne on the chest (*vakṣas-*)'. The sound change /ts/ > /(c)ch/ is well attested in Middle Indic, to the point where <ts> and <cch> may actually represent the same sound in some Middle Indic languages (Von Hinüber 2001: 185, §237). Given that /kṣ/ is also regularly reflected by /(c)ch/ in Middle Indic (besides the more frequent /(k)kh/), it is not hard to imagine a back-formation to /ts/ from /kṣ/ or /kkh/. As for the commutation of /r/ and /l/, it is a well-attested phenomenon across multiple Indo-Aryan languages which, for the purposes of this paper, I am not going into detail about.

I interpret *yo* as the postposed enclitic conjunction 'and', corresponding to the Tibetan *daṅ* (postp.) 'with, and', instead of the instrumental morpheme. This leaves us with a word ending in *-ñc*, presumably meaning 'spade' or 'hoe'. The restoration of the original form of this word is more difficult.

There is only a handful of TA nouns ending in the consonant cluster *-ñc*:[30] *wiskāñc* (m.) 'swamp, mud', *āriñc* (m.) 'heart' (TB *arañce*), *nkiñc* 'silver' (cf. TB *ñkante*, adj. *ñikañce*) and *weṣkiñc** 'body part; intestines?',

30 This list excludes the animate nouns suffixed with the productive feminine suffix *-āñc*, e.g., *ārāntāñc* 'female Arhat', *pretāñc* 'female ghost', *brāmnāñc* 'female Brahmin', which are irrelevant here, as one would not expect an instrument noun to take on this suffix.

*āsäñc** 'buttocks', as well as the adjectives *ākiñc* 'remote' (from *āk* (a.) 'end') and *ṣuliñc* 'mountainous' (from *ṣul* (m.) 'mountain'). Besides the adjectives in *-iñc* (< **-äñc*, see *SSS*: 17, §32), they do not point to a particularly productive pattern of derivation with a suffix in *-ñc*. If the noun meaning 'spade' and ending in *-ñc* is a native Tocharian word or an early borrowing, the cluster [*ñc*] could go back to **-nT-*$_{[+\text{PAL.}]}$, where *T* represents any dental.[31] In case of a loanword, Tocharian *-ñc* could go back to a Sanskrit or Prakrit cluster *-ṇḍ-* as in TB *śuñc*, a variant of TA and TB *śuṇḍ* 'elephant's trunk' from Skt. *śuṇḍa-* (m.) '*id.*'. Then, one may consider restoring **khañc*, as a loan from **khant* or **khaṇṭ* < **khanit* or **khaṇit*[32] (with syncope), itself from a Middle Indic equivalent of Skt. *khanitra-* (n.) 'instrument for digging, spade, shovel', cf. Pāli *khanittī-* (f.) (*PED*: 232), Nepāli *khanti*, Oriyā *khaṇatā*, °*-tī*, *khaṇantā*, °*-tī*, Marāthī *khaṇtẽ*, etc. (see Turner 1966: 200b, No. 3814).

a2 *nāśye*, gen.sg. of *nāśi* 'lady', refers to Kāśisundarī. Either Vyāsa is addressing her using the third person as a kind of honorific, or he is speaking to her servants.[33]

a2 *pāk* may be interpreted as an obl.sg. of *pāk* (a.) 'part, share', a predicate of the direct object *yṣaṃ* 'ditch', meaning the share of the work al-

31 It might even be possible that auslauting /nt/ was palatalized by the following *yo*, based on one attestation of *wäñcyo* 'wind' from *want* (A 191 a6, see Hilmarsson (1987a: 66f) for the root vocalism). There, we also have an enumeration (*wäñcyo ysār sakuyo* corresponding to TB *yente sekwe yasar*; *SSS*: 51, fn. 3) and thus *yo* may be interpreted as the conjunctive particle and not the instrumental suffix.

32 Note that the verbal root had variant forms with a retroflex nasal, e.g., *khaṇati* besides *khanati*, etc. See Turner (1966: 200a, No. 3811).

33 Indeed, it seems as though Kāśisundarī does little herself, i.e., with her own hands: throughout the story, a recurring motif is her avoidance of any effort and delegation of labor to her staff, starting with Kāśisundarī's refusal to dig the trench, prompting her to search for a willing laborer. The Tibetan text also tells us that in order to convince Vyāsa to stop digging, she initially sent out a servant girl to the trenches three times, before riding herself to the spot in order to resolve the issue.

lotted to Kāśisundarī. A similar expression occurs in the *VSṬ*, albeit at a different point in the story, when king Brahmadatta learns that Vyāsa is digging Kāśisundarī's part of the ditch: *ka śi mdzes dga' mo'i skal ba* 'Kāśisundarīnandās Teilstück' and *khyed kyi skal ba'i 'obs* 'deinen Anteil am Festungsgraben' (Schneider 1993: 158f)[34]. The Tocharian *pāk* would correspond to Tibetan *skal ba* and translate Sanskrit *bhāga-* (m.) 'share, portion'.

Alternatively, *pāk* could act as a postposition governing the genitive *nāśye* 'lady': this syntagm would then be translated as 'for the sake of the lady'. This reading has also recently been proposed by Itkin and Malyshev (2021: 70, fn. 33), with a similar use of *pāk* being observed in A 313 b6: *ṣomāp ṣomāp pāk* 'for the sake of every single (being)', see also TB *pakāna* (postp. governing a genitive) 'for the sake of', although the etymology of the latter form is dubious, and its appurtenance to the paradigm of TA *pāk*, TB *pāke* is most uncertain.

a3 (*rāpam*) 'I shall dig', 1sg. subj. V of *räpā-* 'dig', was restored according to the Tibetan parallel ('Ich **will** den Festungsgraben **ausheben**!', emphasis mine).

a3 (*wo*)*täk* 'she ordered', 3sg. prt. II act. of *wätkā-* 'order': out of the multiple possibilities for an ending *-täk*, this seems the most plausible based on the context, especially in light of the imperative *putäk* (111 a2). There is no parallel in the Tibetan text.

a4 *ṣeraśi-niṣkramāntaṃ*: lines 111 a4–5, and presumably the beginning of a6, contain a versified interlude in a meter of 4 × 25 (5|5|8|7 or 5¦5¦4¦4¦4¦3). Not a single pāda is preserved in entirety, but a colon of 7 (4¦3) syllables can be found in a4 (*skānt yṣanaṃ ¦ skeyasyo*), and a colon of 5 in a5 (*kñāññānt riṣakäṃ*).

34 Concerning *skal ba'i 'obs*, Schneider (1993: 159, fn. 5) points out that the two members of the compound in the original Sanskrit text (presumably **parikhābhāga-* 'share of the ditch') must have been translated the wrong way around, as *skal ba'i 'obs* means 'ditch of the share'.

a4 *(mäccā)kyāṃ tkaṃ* (obl.sg.f.) 'the earth itself': the ending *-kyāṃ* clearly points to the obl.sg.f. of an adjective in *-k* that agrees with *tkaṃ* 'earth'. Alternatives to *mäccākyāṃ* would be *āläkyāṃ* (obl. sg. f.) 'another' (in the sense of 'belonging to someone else', i.e. Kāśisundarī) or even *snākyāṃ* (obl. sg. f.) 'alone'.[35]

a4 *skānt yṣanaṃ skeyasyo* 'they scratched zealously in the ditch': previously *skānt* has been translated as 'they followed'. The root *säkā-*, which is attested in another text (A 51 b5 and b6), was interpreted as meaning 'follow' and, as a matter of course, reflecting PIE **sek*^{w}- 'follow'[36] (see however some hesitation in Malzahn 2010: 937). Now, there is evidence to suggest that this verb means 'scratch'.[37] Even though there is no clause directly corresponding to this one in the Tibetan text, as this is a slightly more elaborate metrical interlude, the context is straightforward. The subject of *skānt* are most likely the other inhabitants of Kāśī who share the same predicament as Vyāsa and are trying to finish digging their trenches before dusk. While Vyāsa, equipped with a spade and bucket (*-ñc yo wātsakäl*, see 111 a2), can properly dig the ground (*tkaṃ rāp*), the other citizens might not be as fortunate and must resort to their hands or other methods using lighter utensils, requiring more efforts (*skeyasyo*). The meaning 'scratch' is also supported by at least one other occurrence in A 51 b6, where the direct object is *krāṃ* '(inner) skin' (Van Windekens 1976: 420): *tmäṣ krāṃ penu säknāmāṃ* 'thus even scratching the skin'. The story is that of a lion (*śiśäk*) hunting and flaying a deer or some other wild animal (*mṛgamätträk*).[38] If this interpretation is correct, the underlying root would be **sekH-* 'separate; cut' (*LIV*^{2}: 524). The *seṭ*-character of the root was established by Rix (1999: 525f) on the grounds of the Latin

35 For the inflection of this type of adjectives, see *SSS*: 192–193.

36 The same meaning is suggested by Carling & Pinault (forth.), s.v. *säkā-*. The new findings presented in this paper confirm the results achieved by them after an independent study of the relevant passages.

37 For the meaning of TA *krāṃ* 'inner skin' as contrasting with *yats* (TB *yetse*) 'outer skin', I refer to a paper given by Georges-Jean Pinault on 9 Dec 2020 at the "Tocharian in Progress" workshop hosted by Leiden University.

38 Following *SSS*: 16, §39.

perfect *secuī* < **seca-u̯ai*. The A-character of the Tocharian root *säkā-* thus provides further evidence and support to this claim.

a4 *puk wrasañ ā(rar wlessi)* 'all beings stopped working': the restoration is a conjecture based on the Tibetan text. As the day comes to an end, the citizens stop doing their work and return home, except for Vyāsa, who keeps digging frantically. This eventually leads to Vyāsa being singled out and confronted by the king himself.

a5 *ypeṣiñi wrasañ kñāññānt riṣakäṃ* 'the inhabitants of the country recognized the sage': the text differs slightly from the Tibetan parallel, because there, a single Brahmin initially recognizes Vyāsa.

a5 *(ākā)l (kākä)tku* 'the wish arose':[39] the akṣara <l> can be read with some difficulty. This restoration is based upon other occurrences of this expression, e.g., A 24 b2: *ākāl kātka-ṃ puttiśparnac ṣokyo wärṣṣälts* 'a very strong wish for the Buddha rank arose in him'.

a5 *kä-*: there are many possible restorations for this word, one of them being *käṣṣi* (nom.sg.) 'teacher, guru', referring to Vyāsa. In this case, *säm* would have to be interpreted as a demonstrative adjective rather than a pronoun.

b1 *śl⁄ āmā(śās)* 'together with the ministers': cf. in the Tibetan text 'er [= der König] und die Minister (= Tib. *blon po*)'

b2 This line most likely contains direct speech. Someone, maybe king Brahmadatta himself, is addressing Vyāsa who is still in the ditch, refusing to stop digging. There is no directly corresponding passage in the Tibetan text.

39 An anonymous reviewer suggested to read the akṣara before <ma> as <tku>, not <nku>. The line could then be restored as *l[o n](a)nku* '(he?) vanished far away'. Although this is an interesting alternative suggestion, it finds no support in the Tibetan parallel text.

b2 *mäskatār* 'you are', 2sg. prs. III MP. of *mäskā-* 'be, become', stands at the end of a clause. The predicative expression may be restored as *brā(h)maṃ* 'Brahmin' or *riṣäk* 'sage', assuming this refers to Vyāsa.

b2 *mā āṣāṃ naṣt tāṃ wle(s) (wlessi)* 'you are not worthy of doing this work': the restoration of *wles* 'work (n.)' is certain from the context, besides agreeing with the feminine demonstrative *tāṃ* (obl.sg.). The construction *āṣāṃ naṣ-* calls for an infinitive, and *wlessi* 'work (vb.)' often selects *wles* as an internal cognate direct object (cf., e.g., A 258 a4: *puttiśparṣinās wlesant wlesmāṃ*, A 313 a6: *wles wlessi*), making this restoration relatively certain.

b3 *cwā*, perl.sg. of the 2nd person pronoun *tu*: if this interpretation is correct, *cwā* may be the last word in a clause of direct speech addressed to Vyāsa by the king and his ministers. Of course, it could be the ending of a different word, but I have yet to find any other plausible alternative.

b4 *praskañi* (nom.sg.f.) 'fearful': this adjective was already translated as 'furchtsam' by the *TEB* I (146, §218.2),[40] evidently because it is related to *praski* (a.) 'fear' and the verb *pärskā-* 'be afraid'. Meunier (2015: 234), following the *TEB* I (89, §74.6), describes *pärskā-* as governing an objective genitive if the object of fear is [+HUMAN]. This contrasts with the ablative if the object of fear is [−HUMAN]. Under this light, the syntagm *lānt praskañi*, previously translated as 'of the fearful king' (Carling 2000: 237), with *praskañi* as an epithet of *lānt* (gen.sg. of *wäl*), may now be translated as 'in fear of the king', where *praskañi* is a nom. sg. f. referring to Kāśisundarī and *lānt* the genitive governed by it. Indeed, at this point in the narrative, king Brahmadatta has been repeatedly urging Kāśisundarī to forcibly remove Vyāsa from the ditch. The authority of the king is alluded to again in the next line (*lānt watku* 'the king's command').

The form *praskañi* is to be analyzed as the feminine of an adjective in TA *-i* (TB *-iye*), whose suffix triggers the palatalization of the preceding final consonant of the base stem, cf. TA *ñäkci* 'divine' (TB *ñäkciye*), f. *ñäkci* (TB *ñäkc(i)ya*), based on TA *ñkät* (TB *ñakte*) 'god' (*TEB* I: 145, §

40 Following *SSS*: 16, §39.

216). At face value, TA *praskañi*, if one postulates the masculine form being homonymous with the feminine, contains the suffix TA *-ñi* (TB *-ññe*) also found in *yokañi* 'thirsty' and *oñi* < **oṅkäñi* 'human' (TB *eṅkwaññe* 'male') (Hilmarsson 1987b: 85). This adjective *praskañi* is, as mentioned, cognate with the verbal root TA/TB *pärsk(ā)-* 'be afraid' and *praski* (m. in the singular, f. plural *praskintu*) 'fear', TB *prosko* / *proskiye* (f.) 'id.' but it might not necessarily be derived from the latter. For these abstracts to the root *pärsk(ā)-*, Hilmarsson has set up the following Common Tocharian pre-forms, all derived from *o*-grade of the present stem suffixed in *-sḱ-*:

(1) a feminine abstract in *-eh₂*, **præsko* < **proḱ-sḱ-eh₂*
(2) a neuter substantive (or substantivized adjective) **præskiyæ* < **proḱ-sḱ-i̯o-*

The abstract in **-eh₂* would survive in TB *prosko*, having undergone *o*-Umlaut. The neuter substantive yielded TA *praski* and TB *proskiye*, with the latter reflecting the influence of *prosko*, whose vocalism, gender, and inflection it must have adopted.[41] The adjective *praskañi*, however, can just as well be explained as a derivative of a putative **-on*-stem action noun, whose nominative **proḱ-sḱ-ōn* would have yielded Common Tocharian **præsko* and TB *prosko*. If both TA *praskañi* and TB *prosko* point to and can be derived from an underlying **-on*-stem, there is no need to reconstruct an additional abstract noun **proḱ-sḱ-eh₂*. The rest of Hilmarsson's scenario concerning the derivation of TB *proskiye* and TA *praski* would remain unchanged.

b4 *klaṅkā*, perl. sg. of *klaṅk* 'chariot' (?) or 'vehicle' in general: like for its match TB *kleṅke*, it is not clear whether this term designates a riding animal or some sort of a chariot (Skt. *yāna-*). The corresponding Tibetan term *bźon pa* 'riding-beast, carriage, vehicle' shows the same semantic ambiguity (Jäschke 1881: 484). For the use of the perlative case in this context, as well as an earlier translation of this line, cf. Carling (2000: 237). In the *VSṬ*, this clause corresponds, *mutatis mutandis*, to: *de nas de*

41 Hilmarsson (1989: 124; 1986: 29, 123, 193, 239, 326); differently *DoT*: 455, *s.v.* *prosko* / *proskiye*.

raṅ ñid bźon pa la źon te 'Da **bestieg sie** selbst das **Gefährt**...'. This would imply that Kāśisundarī drives the vehicle alone, without any accompanying servant, contrasting with her earlier attitude.

b5 Lines A 111 b5 and b6 contain the last of three metrical interludes. The metrical scheme seems to start with a colon of five syllables (b6, *taṃne pe träṅkmāṃ*) and end with a colon of seven (4¦3) syllables (b5, *$k_u$yalte mā yat* ¦ *lānt watku*): The most likely option for this configuration would be 4 × 12 (5¦4¦3).

b5 (*yāmäṣt*) 'you did', 2sg. prt. act. of *yām-* 'do': the expression *umpar yām-* 'do evil' is attested elsewhere, e.g., YQ II.7 b2 *maśkaṃ yas umpar yac* 'do henceforth no evil deeds!' and A262 b8, YQ N.5 b1 *umpar* (*yā*) *mluneyā* 'by doing evil' (perl.sg. of the abstract). However, the restoration of this verb is not supported by the meter, under the assumption that it does follow the structure 5¦4¦3. Indeed, *yāmäṣt umpar* ¦ *brāhmaṃ tu* would yield a colon of seven syllables (4¦3) instead of the expected 5, before the sequence *$k_u$yalte mā yat* ¦ *lānt watku* (4¦3).

b5 The word *umpar* has been taken as an adjective, albeit morphologically isolated (*TEB* I: 147, §221), but mostly occurs in substantivized form as an abstract meaning 'evil'. Pinault & Carling (2009, forth., *s.v.*) interpret *umpar* as a substantive, the corresponding adjective being restored as **umparäñ*, since all clearly inflected adjectival forms contain a suffixal nasal. If one accepts this split, one should expect *umpar* in 111 b5 to be preceded by a 2Sg. verb form of *yām-* 'do', the subject being *tu*. However, if this verb form is not metrically licit, *umpar* would need to be interpreted as a nom/voc.sg.masc. adjective form agreeing with *brāhmaṃ*. The phrase *[u]mpar brāhmaṃ tu* would then mean "You evil Brahmin!".

b5 *brāhmaṃ* 'Brahmin' is best interpreted as a vocative here, since Kāśisundarī is speaking.

b6 (*na*)*śśi* = *naṣ-ci*, 3sg. prs. act. of *nas-* 'to be' and enclitic 2sg. pronoun *ci* 'is ... for you': the part. prt. *rārpu*, from the verb *räpā-* 'dig', combines with the copula in the present to form a complex verb form corresponding to a present perfect. The use of this contraction is paralleled in the *Maitreyasamitināṭaka* (see Ji *et al.* 1998: 236). The clause *(na)śśi tkaṃ rārpu*, to be translated as 'It is for your sake that this ground has been dug!' seems to be Vyāsa's reply to Kāśisundarī's scolding in the previous line. This restoration is in my opinion more likely than a genitive plural ending in *-śśi*, as there are no phraseological parallels for a syntagm $X_{[GEN]}$ *tkaṃ* 'the earth of X'. Alternatively, the form ending in *-śśi* could be the adverb *aśśi* 'thus', which may be combined with an interrogative pronoun, e.g., *k$_u$yall aśśi* 'why then?'[42].

b6 *ra(ryu)* 'having given up', Part. Prt. nom.sg.m. of *ri-* 'leave, abandon; surrender': this restoration is speculative, purely based on the context. Even though Vyāsa may not be ready to leave the ditch yet (*mā säm pre kälk* 'he did not come out'), this might be the point in the story where he puts down his digging tools. No diacritical mark may be securely read on the akṣara <*ra*>, and the rest of the folio is either blank, or the last akṣara is illegible on the photograph. Other restorations would certainly be possible, such as *ra(rku)* 'having covered' or *ra(rätku)* 'having (a)risen', again referring to Vyāsa.

At first glance, the ending of the story in Tocharian remains enigmatic.[43] Due to the damaged state of the fragments, the crucial scene of the head-kick is absent from the text, but it may have occurred in the next leaf. The participle *träṅkmāṃ* and the pronoun *säm* most likely refer to Vyāsa himself. But the fact that he 'does not come out' (*mā säm pre kälk*) does not really make sense: the story can only come to a satisfying conclusion if Vyāsa finally comes to his senses and leaves the ditch, like in the

42 However, this restoration would leave us with a subcolon of six syllables (*k$_u$yall aśśi tkaṃ rārpu*), which would be surprising, considering that the previous pāda ends in with a subcolon of seven (4¦3) syllables (b5, *k$_u$yalte mā yat lānt watku*).

43 Although slightly clearer and not incomplete, the meaning of the conclusion of the Tibetan version of the story also remains elusive, as evidenced by the differences in translation of the final line of dialogue delivered by Kāśisundarī in the translations of Zwilling (1978) and Schneider (1993).

Tibetan version (*źes smras nas laṅs par gyur to* 'Mit diesen Worten kam er heraus.').

Finally, even though the Tocharian text lacks this scene, I briefly want to touch upon the significance of the blow to the head that Vyāsa receives. As mentioned, it is not clear from the few allusions to it whether the kick is accidental or not. Kāśisundarī jumps off the chariot while Vyāsa is kneeling in the ditch: one can imagine her accidentally landing on Vyāsa's head, but in my opinion, this is not very likely. Interestingly, in two of the descriptions, special mention is made of Kāśisundarī's adorned ankle (*Saundarananda* VII.30: *calanupureṇa pādena*, and in the *VSṬ*: *rkaṅ gdub daṅ bcas pa'i rkaṅ pas*). The jingling ankle bracelets appear to be a characteristic attribute signaling the status of Kāśisundarī as a prostitute.[44]

According to canonical erotic Indian literature, lovers may sometimes hit one another as a form of seductive foreplay. However, those hits are usually dealt with the hand and not the foot (Schmidt 1922: 283). In the present context, one would rather deem this gesture as the mark of the humiliation of the Brahmin and of the ingratitude of the prostitute, his lover. This woman does not show any pity for the sage: instead of thanking him for his immense service, she even blames him for not having obeyed the king, and finally hurts him as he is still in the ditch. This last cruel point can at least be inferred from the end of the fragment A 111.

Nevertheless, the motif of the kick by the prostitute's ankleted foot certainly has some erotic implications. Although the story of Vyāsa and Kāśisundarī has no direct parallels outside of the Tibetan narrative in the *VSṬ*, the one may surmise that the motif of a Brahmin being kicked in the head by a prostitute was drawn from popular folk tales or drama.

44 For a description of these identifying attributes, see for instance the *Sāhityadarpaṇa* 116/117, quoted and translated by Schmidt (1922: 224), emphasis mine: 'Wenn eine anständige Frau einen Liebesbesuch macht, kriecht sie in sich zusammen, läßt ihre Schmucksachen verstummen und verhüllt sich in ihren Schleier. Wenn eine **Hetäre** aber einen Liebesbesuch macht, trägt sie bunte, glänzende Gewänder; **die Fußreifen erklingen bei der Bewegung**, und ihr Gesicht strahlt vor Freude.'

As it happens, this motif also occurs as the main plot device in a satirical monologue play (*bhāṇa*) from the 5th century C.E., the *Pādatāḍitaka* by Śyāmilaka[45]. Here, during their lovemaking, the Brahmin Tauṇḍikoki Viṣṇunāga suffers a head kick from a prostitute called Madanasenikā, making him the laughing stock of the whole Brahmin assembly (*pīṭhikā*).[46] The ensuing humiliation prompts him to seek redemption for this insult, invoking the assembly to devise a suitable punishment. However, not all Brahmins react in the expected manner to the news of this unfortunate incident. Some would, indeed, see it as an honor 'to be favoured with a kick from [a] lotus-like foot' (Schokker 1976: 34). The head of the court, Bhaṭṭijīmuta, finally pronounces the following judgment, which is in reality a punishment for the plaintiff:

Pādatāḍitaka 147:

(a) *tasyā madālasavighūrṇitalocanāyāḥ*
(b) *śroṇyarpitaikakarasaṁhatamekhalāyāḥ*
(c) *sālaktakena caraṇena sanūpureṇa*
(d) *paśyatv ayaṁ śirasi mām anugṛhyamāṇam iti*

'He must see me, my head favoured by her lacquered foot covered with ankle ornaments, while her eyes are languid and rolling with love and she clasps her girdle with one hand lying in her lap.' (text Schokker 1966: 138–139, transl. Schokker 1976: 45–46)

---

45 For a critical edition and translation of the Sanskrit text, see Schokker 1966 and 1976.

46 Note that Śyāmilaka also draws attention to the prostitute's jingling anklets (*nūpura-*), and that the description of the kick bears some resemblance to those of Aśvaghoṣa cited above:
(a) *praṇayakalahodyatena*
srastāṁśukadarḍitorumūlena
(b) *jitam eva madakalāyā*
nūpuramukhareṇa pādena (8)
'While she gives expression to the soft sounds of love, her foot, which gingles with ankle ornaments, has won a victory after it has been raised up in the love battle and while the furthest part of her thigh is revealed by the garment sliding from it.' (text Schokker 1966: 67, translation Schokker 1976: 2)

This tongue-in-cheek court ruling illustrates the ambiguous nature of the gesture as being an act of humiliation on the one hand, and on the other, a possible source of sexual arousal.

7 Concluding remarks

In this paper I have proposed a new reading of fragments 110 and 111, thanks to my recent discovery of a Tibetan parallel text in Prajñāvarman's *Viśeṣastavaṭīkā*. All the restorations that I proposed above remain open to future discussion. They would have been impossible without the Tibetan version of the story, even though it is not always parallel in the strict sense. The identification and translation of A 110 and 111 is a small but nevertheless significative step towards the restoration of the dramatic adaptation of Aśvaghoṣa's *Saundarananda* into Tocharian A. It is now evident that the Tocharian work elaborates on the original *Saundarananda*, and that the story of Vyāsa and Kāśisundarī, probably an old popular folktale, is a narrative digression inserted into the main story, inspired by the condensed allusion to it in the original Sanskrit text. It is also probable that the Tocharian text itself draws from a lost or yet undiscovered Sanskrit narrative, which also served as the source for the Tibetan translation in Prajñāvarman's commentary. Future research on the fragments A 89 to A 143, which have been identified to constitute this so-called *Nandacarita* (or *Saundaracaritanāṭaka*), is needed to piece together as many parts as possible of this lost work. To achieve this, it is necessary to translate these fragments, in the hopes of discovering further connections to works of Buddhist literature, thus slowly completing our (still rather fragmentary) picture of the literary landscape of the Tarim Basin.

[RECEIVED: NOVEMBER 2021]

10 rue des Volontaires
75015 Paris, France
veronique.kremmer@ephe.psl.eu

References

Bailey, Harold W. 1979. *Dictionary of Khotan Saka*. Cambridge: Cambridge University Press.

Carling, Gerd. 2000. *Die Funktionen der lokalen Kasus im Tocharischen*. Berlin / New York: Mouton de Gruyter.

Carling, Gerd, Georges-Jean Pinault & Werner Winter (ed.). 2009. *Dictionary and Thesaurus of Tocharian A*. Volume 1: *A–J*. Wiesbaden: Harrassowitz.

Carling, Gerd, Georges-Jean Pinault (ed.). forth. *Dictionary and Thesaurus of Tocharian A*. Wiesbaden: Harrassowitz.

CEToM = *A Comprehensive Edition of Tocharian Manuscripts*. https://www.univie.ac.at/tocharian/ last retrieved on 24 August 2021.

Cone, Margaret. 2001. *A Dictionary of Pāli. Part I. a–kh*. Oxford: The Pali Text Society.

DoT = Adams, Douglas T. 2013. *A Dictionary of Tocharian B: revised and greatly enlarged*. Amsterdam / New York: Rodopi.

EWAia = Mayrhofer, Manfred. 1986–2001. *Etymologisches Wörterbuch des Altindoarischen*. 3 vols. Heidelberg: Winter.

Fausbøll, V. (ed.). 1877–1896. *The Jātaka Together With its Commentary Being Tales of the Anterior Births of Gotama Buddha*. vol. III. London: Trübner and Co.

Filliozat, Jean. 1949. *La doctrine classique de la médecine indienne. Ses origines et ses parallèles grecs*. Paris: Imprimerie nationale.

Hilmarsson, Jörundur. 1986. *Studies in Tocharian phonology, morphology and etymology, with special focus on the o-vocalism*. Reykjavík.

Hilmarsson, Jörundur. 1987a. "Reflexes of I.-E. *$suH_2\eta$to- /-ōn-* "sunny" in Germanic and Tocharian". *Die Sprache. Zeitschrift für Sprachwissenschaft* 33: 56–78.

Hilmarsson, Jörundur. 1987b. "On the history and distribution of suffixal *-y-/-iy-* in Tocharian". *Die Sprache. Zeitschrift für Sprachwissenschaft* 33: 79–93.

Hilmarsson, Jörundur. 1989. "Rounding and exceptions from rounding in East Tocharian". *Indogermanische Forschungen* 94: 101–134.

Hiltebeitel, Alf. 2006. "Aśvaghoṣa's "Buddhacarita": The first known close and critical reading of the brahmanical Sanskrit epics". *Journal of Indian Philosophy* 34: 229–286.

IDP = International Dunhuang Project. idp.bbaw.de last retrieved on 18 October 2021.

Itkin, Ilya B. 2019. *Ukazatel′ slovoform k neopublikovannym toxarskim A tekstam iz sobranija Berlinskoj biblioteki.* Moskva: Rossijskaja Akademija Nauk, Institut Vostokovedenija.

Itkin, Ilya B. 2020. "Budda uveščevaet Nandu (toxarskij tekst A 125 + THT 1425 fgm. e + A 117)". *Problemy Obščej i Vostokovednoj Lingvistiki (Trudy Instituta Vostokovedenija RAN)*, vol. 27: 220–228.

Itkin, Ilya B. 2020. "Budda uveščevaet Nandu (toxarskij tekst A 125 + THT 1425 fgm. e + A 117)". , vol. 27: 220-228.

Itkin, Ilya B., Malyshev, Sergey V. 2021. "Notae Tocharicae: *apälkāts, pärsā(n)ts, letse* et autres addenda et corrigenda – 4". *Voprosy Jazykoznanija* 2021/3: 47–75.

Ji, Xianlin, Winter, Werner, Pinault, Georges-Jean. 1998. *Fragments of Tocharian A Maitreyasamiti-Nāṭaka of the Xinjiang Museum, China.* Berlin / New York: Mouton de Gruyter.

Jamison, Stephanie W., Brereton, Joel P. 2014. *The Rigveda. The earliest religious poetry of India.* 3 vols. New York: Oxford University Press.

Jäschke, Heinrich A. 1881. *A Tibetan-English Dictionary. With special reference to the prevailing dialects, to which is added An English-Tibetan Vocabulary.* Reprint by Munshiram Manoharlal Publishers Pvt. Ltd., New Delhi.

Johnston, E.H. 1928. *The Saundarananda of Aśvaghoṣa. Critically edited with notes.* London: Humphrey Milford for the University of the Panjab, Lahore.

Johnston, E.H. 1932. *The Saundarananda or Nanda the Fair.* Translated from the original Sanskrit. London: Humphrey Milford for the University of the Panjab, Lahore.

Johnston, E.H. 1935. *The Buddhacarita: or, Acts of the Buddha. Part I: Sanskrit text.* Calcutta: Baptist Mission Press for the University of the Panjab, Lahore.

Johnston, E.H. 1936. *The Buddhacarita: or, Acts of the Buddha. Part II: Cantos I to XIV translated from the original Sanskrit supplemented by the Tibetan version.* Calcutta: Baptist Mission Press for the University of the Panjab, Lahore.

*LIV*² = Rix, Helmut (ed.). 2001. *Lexikon der Indogermanischen Verben. Die Wurzeln und ihre Primärstammbildungen.* Zweite, erweiterte und verbesserte Auflage bearbeitet von Martin Kümmel und Helmut Rix. Wiesbaden: Reichert.

Malzahn, Melanie. 2010. *The Tocharian Verbal System.* Leiden / Boston: Brill.

Meunier, Fanny. 2015. *Recherches sur le génitif en tokharien.* Linguistique. École pratique des hautes études - EPHE PARIS. PhD thesis.

MW = Monier-Williams, Sir Monier. 1899. *A Sanskrit-English Dictionary.* Oxford: Clarendon Press.

Olivelle, Patrick. 2009. *Life of the Buddha by Aśvaghoṣa.* New York: New York University Press & JJC Foundation (The Clay Sanskrit Library).

PED = Rhys Davids, T.W., Stede William. 1921-1925. *The Pali Text Society's Pali-English dictionary.* London: Luzac.

Peyrot, Michaël. 2018. "A Comparison of the Tocharian A and B Metrical Traditions". In Olav Hackstein & Dieter Gunkel (eds.), *Language and Meter.* Leiden: Brill, 319–345.

Pinault, Georges-Jean. 2008. *Chrestomathie Tokharienne. Textes et Grammaire.* Leuven / Paris: Peeters.

Poucha, Pavel. 1955. *Thesaurus Linguae Tocharicae Dialecti A.* Praha: Státní Pedagogické Nakladatelství.

Rix, Helmut. 1999. "Schwach charakterisierte lateinische Präsensstämme zu Seṭ-Wurzeln mit Vollstufe I.". *Compositiones Indogermanicae in Memoriam Jochem Schindler.* Praha: Enigma Corporation, 515-535.

Rosen, Valentina. 1959. *Der Vinayavibhaṅga zum Bhikṣuprātimokṣa der Sarvāstivādins. Sanskritfragmente nebst einer Analyse der chinesischen Übersetzung.* Berlin: Akademie-Verlag.

Roşu, Arion. 1981. "Les marman et les arts martiaux indiens". *Journal Asiatique* 269: 417–451.

Roşu, Arion, Jobard, Myriam. 1987. "Arts de santé et techniques de massage en Inde". *Annales de Kinésithérapie* 14 /3: 87–91.

Schmidt, Richard. 1922. *Beiträge zur Indischen Erotik. Das Liebesleben des Sanskritvolkes, nach den Quellen dargestellt.* 3rd ed. (1922). Berlin: Hermann Barsdorf Verlag.

Schneider, Johannes. 1993. *Der Lobpreis der Vorzüglichkeit des Buddha.* Bonn: Indica et Tibetica Verlag.

Schokker, Godard H. 1966. *The Pādatāḍitaka of Śyāmilaka. Part 1. A Text-Critical Edition.* Dordrecht / Boston: D. Reidel Publishing Company.

Schokker, Godard H. 1976. *The Pādatāḍitaka of Śyāmilaka. Part 2. A Translation by G. H. Schokker and P. J. Worsley. With a Complete Word-Index of the Four Ancient Sanskrit Bhanas.* Dordrecht / Boston: D. Reidel Publishing Company.

Sieg, Emil & Wilhelm Siegling. 1921. *Tocharische Sprachreste. I. Band.* Berlin / Leipzig: Walter De Gruyter & Co.

Simson, Georg von. 2000. *Prātimokṣasūtra der Sarvāstivādins*. Teil II: *Kritische Textausgabe, Übersetzung, Wortindex sowie Nachträge zu Teil I*. Sanskrittexte aus den Turfanfunden XI. Göttingen: Vandenhoeck & Ruprecht.

Sullivan, Bruce M. 1990. "A Note on Kāśisundarī and Kṛṣṇa Dvaipāyana Vyāsa". *Annals of the Bhandarkar Oriental Research Institute*, vol. 71/1: 290–292.

SSS = Sieg, Emil, Siegling, Wilhelm. 1931. *Tocharische Grammatik*. Im Autrage der Preußischen Akademie der Wissenschaften bearbeitet in Gemeinschaft mit Wilhelm Schulze. Göttingen: Vandenhoeck & Ruprecht.

TEB I = Thomas, Werner, Krause, Wolfgang. 1960. *Tocharisches Elementarbuch. I: Grammatik*. Heidelberg: Winter.

TEB II = Thomas, Werner, Krause, Wolfgang. 1964. *Tocharisches Elementarbuch. II: Texte und Glossar*. Heidelberg: Winter.

Tremblay, Xavier. 2005. "Irano-Tocharica et Tocharo-Iranica". *Bulletin of the School of Oriental and African Studies* 68: 421–449.

Turner, Ralph Lilley, Sir. 1966. *A comparative dictionary of the Indo-Aryan languages. Vol. I: Text*. London: Oxford University Press.

Van Windekens, Albert J. 1976. *Le tokharien confronté avec les autres langues indo-européennes*. Vol. I: *La phonétique et le vocabulaire*. Louvain: Centre International de Dialectologie Générale.

Van Windekens, Albert J. 1988. "Réflexions sur l'origine de quelques termes tokhariens." *Indogermanische Forschungen* 93: 96–101.

Von Hinüber, Oskar. 2001. *Das ältere Mittelindisch im Überblick. 2. erweiterte Auflage*. Wien: Verlag der Österreichischen Akademie der Wissenschaften.

Wujastyk, Dominik. 2009. "Interpreting the Image of the Human Body in Premodern India." *International Journal of Hindu Studies* 13: 189–228.

Zwilling, Leonard. 1978. "The Story of Vyāsa and Kāśīsundarī". *Journal of the International Association of Buddhist Studies* 1: 65–70.

Tocharian A leaf A 429 in light of its parallels in the Kṣudrakavastu[1]

Sergey V. Malyshev

In the present article I compare the content of Tocharian A leaf A 429 with the parallel text from the Tibetan and Chinese Kṣudrakavastu of the Mūlasarvāstivāda-vinaya. This analysis, among other things, allows shedding light on the meaning of two Toch. A dis legomena: *kāṅkuk* and *kāw-*.

The lost leaves A 429–433 of the Berlin Collection contain a story about Mālikā (named Somā at birth), a slave-girl of Śākya Mahānāman, and her marriage to king Prasenajit. As was already observed in Sieg & Siegling (1921: 235), this Tocharian text, whose title and author are yet unknown, has a very close parallel in the Kṣudrakavastu section of the Mūlasarvāstivāda-vinaya, originally compiled in Sanskrit. In particular, Sieg and Siegling quote such works as Schiefner (1849/1851: 270) and Rockhill (1884: 74 ff.), where this portion of the Kṣudrakavastu is retold.

The original Sanskrit text of the Kṣudrakavastu is lost. The work has only survived in a 9th century Tibetan translation by Vidyākaraprabha, Dharmaśrībhadra and dPal 'Byor and an 8th century Chinese translation by Yijing. Besides, there survives — only in a Tibetan translation by Śrībuddhaśānti and dGe-ba'i Blo Gros — a commentary on it, called Āgamakṣudrakavyākhyāna, written by *Śīlapālita (Tshul Khrims bsKyangs in Tibetan).

In this article, I would like to review an episode of the Tocharian text found on leaf A 429 — or, more precisely, lines A 429 a2 – 431 a2 — in the light of its parallel in the Kṣudrakavastu. Judging by the content, leaf A

1 The author would like to express his sincere gratitude to Ilya Itkin, Michaël Peyrot and the anonymous reviewer for valuable suggestions on the text of the article.

429 immediately follows leaf A 430 and immediately precedes leaf A 431 (this was already clear to Siegling, cf. his note 'gehört hinter 430!' in his personal copy of Sieg & Siegling 1921 on p. 235 next to 'No. 429').

The preceding episode tells about Mālikā giving alms to the Buddha and making a wish to be released from slavery thanks to the merit gained by that good deed, cf. the Tocharian text in line A 429 a1 /// *·oneyäṣ tālorñyäṣ tākim cā* /// '…may I be (freed) from … [and] misery…'

Since the episode I will analyze is completely absent in Schiefner and Rockhill's retellings, I will have to work directly with the Tibetan and Chinese texts. As the Tibetan translations of the Mūlasarvāstivāda-vinaya are much more literal than the Chinese ones, I shall present below my translation of the Tibetan text (Derge 'dul-ba Tha 75 b4–76 a1[2]):

> Now, her father had a friend who was a Brahmin and a soothsayer. He saw her and asked, 'Daughter, where did you come from?'
>
> 'From the same village.'
>
> 'At whose place do you live?'
>
> She said, 'Upon an unfortunate series of events, I became a slave-girl of Śākya Mahānāman.'
>
> 'Where is your father?'
>
> 'He is dead.'
>
> 'Where are your mother and brother?'
>
> 'I don't know where they are.'
>
> 'Somā, it is not befitting for you to be a slave-girl. Hold out your hand, I shall have a look.'
>
> She held out her hand. He had a look and spoke in verses:
>
> 'She whose palms have a sign of an iron wheel, even if born in a family of slaves, shall be declared a king's wife.
>
> She who has a broad face and whose voice is like that of a king of geese, even if born in a family of slaves, shall be declared a king's wife.
>
> She whose soles have a city with *cog* and arches, even if born in a family of slaves, shall be declared a king's wife.

2 The corresponding Chinese text is found in T 1451, 234c1–13.

> Go, and don't be upset. You shall not be a slave-girl, but a king's wife.'

The text then goes on to tell about Mālikā's lucky encounter with king Prasenajit, which leads to the fulfillment of the Brahmin's prophecy.

Let us try to locate the fragmentary Tocharian lines in this story.

The words *(mahā)nāmes warpiśkeyac ysi osāt okā[k] ///* '…went (lit. started to go) to Mahānāman's garden, until…' in line A 429 a2 probably refer to the Brahmin, because, according to the story, Mālikā was already there.

Line a3 contains the first series of questions of the Brahmin: */// s t[ā]k(a)ṣt tā pat ysi onus naṣt tā ///* '…were you? And where have you gone (lit. have you started to go)? (And) where…?' Note that the questions here are coordinated with a word meaning 'or' (*pat*) rather than 'and', which is common in Sanskrit as well, cf. *kathaṃ padbhyām iha prāptau kimarthaṃ kasya* ***vā*** *mune* 'Oh sage, how did they get here by foot, and for what purpose, and whose [sons are they]?' (Rāmāyaṇa's Balakāṇḍa, verse 47.4 = 49.19).

In lines a4–5, we have Mālikā telling her life story:

a4

> */// (pä)k[l]yoṣ u[p]ādhy(ā) riyäṣ kakmus tākā tm· ///*
> 'Listen, teacher. I have come from the city…'

a5

> */// (mahā)nāme (krä)tolāñcāṃ y[ā]msāt-(ñ)i ///*
> '…Mahānāman made me [his] slave-girl.'

The word *krätolāñc** is not found outside this manuscript. Carling (2009: 172) claims that it means 'adopted girl', but in the Kṣudrakavastu Mālikā is said to be a slave or a servant (*mngag gzhug byed pa* 'home slave (?)' or *bran mo* 'female slave' in Tibetan, *bì* 婢 'female servant' in Chinese).

In line a6, the Brahmin asks Mālikā about her relatives: */// (m)ā[c]ar kuc [p]ā(ca)r – [c]e ///* '…(what about your) mother, what [about your] father…'

In line a7, judging by the female word *ñuk* 'I', we have again Mālikā speaking: */// ñuk krätol[ā](ñc) ///* '...I, slave-girl...'

Lines a8 and b1 are lost. Then we have a short line b2, reading:

/// sam-ci tm-äk ///
'"...I... you." Right afterwards...'

/// sam-ci is most likely a first person singular form of a present or subjunctive of some verb, with a second person singular suffix pronoun *-ci*. The number of eligible verb forms is quite large. In the context of the story, one might suggest, for example, *(āksi)sam-ci* 'I shall instruct you' or *(e)sam-ci* 'I shall give you (e.g., a prophecy)', being the words of the Brahmin.[3]

Line b3 reads */// s ṣ(o)treyäntu täm pälkorä(ṣ) ///* '...signs. Having seen that...' It undoubtedly describes the Brahmin's inspection of Mālikā's signs.

Next, in lines b4–8 come three stanzas in the tune *Maitraṃ*, of the structure 5/4/3. Here I present them with division into pādas and cola:

|| *maitraṃ* ||
kāṅkuk yo cākrä ¦ *pässā(k)* – – ¦ – – – (:)
– – – – – ¦ – – – – ¦ – – – (:)
– – – – – ¦ – – – – ¦ *(ta)tmus tāṣ* ·
ṣakk ats sny-ālak-wkäṃ ¦ *sām* – – – ¦ – – – (: *1*)
– – – – – ¦ – – – – ¦ – – – (:)
– – – – – ¦ *(wä)ll oki śkaṃ* ¦ *nusmāṃ tāṣ* ·
wkän penu sā – ¦ – – – – ¦ – – – (:)
– – – – – ¦ – – – – ¦ – – – (: 2)
– – – – – ¦ *(śa)l-penaṃ msāṣ* ¦ *lkāl tāṣ-äṃ* :

3 For the usage of present referring to future events in the first person cf. Malyshev (2017: 120–121, fn. 10) with examples like *(nä)ṣ śolā sisāṃ rāmes mā esam* (A 10 b5) 'I shall never give Sitā to Rāma'. This usage is very common in Sanskrit as well, cf. the following dialogue from the Kathopaniṣad, 1.4–5:
— *tata kasmai māṃ dāsyasīti* 'Father, to whom will you give (future) me?'
— *mṛtyave tvā dadāmīti* 'I shall give (present) you to Death'.

ri śla kāwas – ¦ – – – – ¦ – – – (:)
– – – – – ¦ – – – – ¦ – – – (:)
– – – – – ¦ – – *lānt śäṃ* ¦ *mäskatär* : 3 ||

Note that at two occasions pādas are separated with a single dot (·) instead of the usual two dots (:).

Counting the missing syllables allows us to roughly estimate the length of the lines of this manuscript to be about 35 syllables.

In spite of the large lacunae, we can see that the verse is very similar to that found in the Kṣudrakavastu; both consist of three stanzas.

In the Kṣudrakavastu version, each stanza has a 'refrain' as its third and fourth pādas: 'even if born in a family of slaves, shall be declared a king's wife' (in Tibetan, */bran gyi rigs su skyes gyur kyang / /rgyal po'i btsun mor bzhes par 'gyur/*). It is not impossible that the same is the case with the Tocharian verse; at least there are no overlaps to disprove it. If we put the remaining parts of the third and fourth pādas of each stanza together, the 'refrain' will look as follows:

wkän penu sā – ¦ – – – – ¦ *(ta)tmus tāṣ* :
ṣakk ats sny-ālak-wkäṃ ¦ *sām* – *lānt śäṃ* ¦ *mäskatär* :
'Even if… is born… will surely, undoubtedly (lit. 'without another way') become a king's wife.'

The resulting text is quite coherent and only has six missing syllables, apart from the obvious restoration *(ta)tmus*. After *wkän penu* and/or before *lānt śäṃ* we might restore, without any certainty, *sām* k_u*li* 'this woman'.

The translation of the rare phrase *wkän penu* as 'even if' is suggested by the context and the Tibetan parallel; however, 'even though' could be a more accurate rendition, if we look at a pāda in line A 93 a3, expressing Nanda's regret of becoming a monk:

näṣ nu pracar käṣyāp ¦ *watkurā wkäṃ penu* ¦ *wärpo ṣā(mnune* :)
'Even though I have accepted monkhood by the order of [my] brother-teacher'

Compare the likely source of this pāda from Aśvaghoṣa's Saundarananda (7.17):

> *ahaṃ* ***gṛhītvāpi hi bhikṣuliṅgaṃ*** *bhrātṛṣiṇā dvir guruṇānuśiṣṭaḥ /*
> *sarvāsv avasthāsu labhe na śāntiṃ priyāviyogād iva cakravākaḥ //*
> 'For, **though I have accepted the mendicant's badge** and am taught by One Who as my brother and spiritual guide is my Guru in two senses, in no circumstances, like a sheldrake separated from its mate, can I obtain peace.' (Johnston 1932: 38)

Besides these two occurrences, I can only cite */// śāsnis kāryap wkäṃ pe[nu] ///* in line A 329 a2 without context. If this fragment is in verse too, we might assume that *wkäṃ penu* is a chiefly poetic extension of *penu*.

The form *mäskatär* is usually regarded as a present here (cf. Poucha 1955: 227). But given the meaning of the sentence, we would rather expect a subjunctive ('will become'), although it is believed that no subjunctive forms of the verb *mäsk-* 'to become' are known. A class 3 middle subjunctive form *mäskatär*, coinciding with the present, next to an active preterit form *mäskäs* goes against the general rules of Tocharian A grammar (requiring the same voice for subjunctive and preterit bases), but that is exactly what we see with another irregular verb *wäl-* 'to die' with its middle subjunctive *wlatär* and active preterit *wläs*. However, in order to definitely prove that *mäskatär* can serve as a subjunctive, we would need to find somewhere a verbal noun **mäskalune*. See also Peyrot (2013: 232, 237), who claims that the verb *mäsk-*, while having no subjunctive, 'carries an element of future in its lexical meaning'.

Dealing with the rest of the verse requires engaging with more material than just the Tibetan translation. Besides the Chinese translation and the commentary text Āgamakṣudrakavyākhyāna, we will also have to employ parallels in the extant Sanskrit sources.

The stanzas cited by the learned Brahmin belong to the genre called *Samudra*, or the science of reading the signs of the human body. A number of texts belonging to this genre were edited in Zysk (2016). The stanzas of our Brahmin have parallels in many of those texts, the closest being chapter 64 of the Garuḍapurāṇa, chapter 2 of Utpala's Samudra, as well as the Śārdūlakarṇāvadāna (part of the Divyāvadāna, a Mūlasarvāstivādin text, just like the Kṣudrakavastu).

The first stanza in the Tibetan translation (without the refrain) looks as follows:

> *gang gi lag pa'i mthil dag la/ /lcags kyi 'khor lo'i mtshan yod pa/*
> 'She whose palms have a sign of an iron wheel'

The Chinese text and the Āgamakṣudrakavyākhyāna disagree with it, and it is their text that proves to be closer to the Tocharian version. In Chinese, we have:

> 若人於手中有鬘鉤輪相 (*ruò rén yú shǒu zhōng yǒu mán gōu lún xiāng*)
> 'If a person's hand has signs of a garland, a hook and a wheel'

The Āgamakṣudrakavyākhyāna reads (Derge Tangyur Dzu 32 b1–2):

> */lag pa'i mthil te lag pa'i dkyil na lcags kyu'i rnam pa dang / 'khor lo'i rnam pa dang / phreng ba'i rnam pa lta bu'i ri mo gang la yod pa de'i phyir na rgyal por 'gyur te/ bdag po nyid du 'dzin par byed do/*
> 'As for the words 'palm of a hand', whoever has depictions resembling a hook, resembling a wheel and resembling a garland in the middle of their hand, because of that they will become a king, will have sovereignty.'

Where the Tibetan Kṣudrakavastu has an iron wheel, both the Chinese translation and the Āgamakṣudrakavyākhyāna have a hook, a garland and a wheel. To explain the discrepancy, we might assume that *lcags kyi 'khor lo'i mtshan* 'sign of an iron wheel' in the Tibetan Kṣudrakavastu is a corruption of **lcags kyu 'khor lo'i mtshan* 'signs of a hook [and] a wheel' and that the word for a garland (*phreng ba*) was omitted for some unclear reason.[4]

4 Cf. a similar case in a verse from the Jyotiṣkāvadāna, also part of the Kṣudrakavastu, where the compound *lavaṇajalādrirājadhairyāḥ* 'whose calmness is like that of the Sea and the King of Mountains' is translated as *ri rab ltar brtan pa* 'whose calmness is like that of the King of Mountains' (Tha

Now, in Tocharian, the first pāda reads:

kāṅkuk yo cākrä ¦ pässā(k) – – ¦ – – – (:)
'A *kāṅkuk*, a wheel and a garland…'

Apart from this text, the word *kāṅkuk* is only found one more time, in a verse describing the signs on the Buddha's body (A 24 b1):

vājär kāṅkuk ¦ śrivās parnont ¦ ṣotreyäntu
'The brilliant signs of a *vajra*, a *kāṅkuk* and a *śrīvatsa*'

Carling (2009: 109) takes *kāṅkuk* as a borrowing from Sanskrit *kaṅguka* 'a kind of Panic seed' or *kāṅguka* 'a kind of corn'. However, both words are extremely rare and neither of them is found in the extensive Samudra literature (unlike, for example, *vajra* and *śrīvatsa* from the verse above).

As 'wheel' and 'garland' are found in the Tocharian version of the Brahmin's prophecy as well as in the Kṣudrakavastu version, it would be natural to deduce that *kāṅkuk* means 'hook' and corresponds to Chinese *gōu* 鉤 and Tibetan *lcags kyu* 'hook'. However, this is not one hundred percent secure, because the Tocharian text is not the translation of the Kṣudrakavastu story, but is only inspired by it (or by their common source). Nevertheless, I think that given the very high level of similarity between the two versions, the meaning 'hook' for *kāṅkuk* is more likely correct than not. Another good reason for that is that a hook is quite appropriate next to a *vajra* and a *śrīvatsa* mentioned in A 24 b1, because all three are found in lists of symbols on the Buddha's body given in Skilling (1996).[5] For example, *vajra*, *śrīvatsa* and *aṅkuśa* are all includ-

15b), with a word for 'Sea' lacking. Had we not known the original Sanskrit text, extant in the Divyāvadāna (Cowell & Neil 1886: 267), we would also have to rely on the Āgamakṣudrakavyākhyāna (*lan tshwa'i chu ni rgya mtsho'o* 'The "salt-watered one (*lavaṇajala*)" is the Sea', Dzu 12b) and the Chinese translation (如大海内妙山王 *rú dà hǎi nèi miào shān wáng* 'like in the great Sea [or] the marvelous King of Mountains', T 1451, 211c25).

5 It should be noted, as suggested by the anonymous reviewer, that *aṅkuśa* as a royal symbol should be understood as 'elephant goad' rather than just a 'hook'. There is a picture of this object as an auspicious symbol on the feet of the Buddha in Karunarante (1976, plate 1, fig. 3, symbol c).

ed in a list of signs on the palms of the Buddha's hands found in the Pratimāmānalakṣaṇa of Maharṣi Ātreya (Skilling 1996: 22).

As Ilya Itkin has pointed out to me, line a2 of the Toch. B fragment THT 2981f reads _/// – kaṃkūk[e] – ///_ and therefore might contain the cognate of Toch. A _kāṅkuk_. One might think that the spelling with an anusvāra before _k_ suggests a non-native origin of this word, but see such examples as _raṃktsi_ 'to climb' (B 238 b3), _eṃksate_ 'took' (THT 1108 a2), _eṃkäl_ 'passion' (THT 1105 a4), etc. for _raṅktsi, eṅksate, eṅkäl_ with native Toch. B words.

As for its etymology, Proto-Tocharian *_kāṅkuke_ might descend from PIE *_k̂ankūko-_, a diminutive from *_k̂ankū-_, from which Middle Welsh _cainc_ 'branch, bough, antler' (< *_kankī-_ < *_kankū-_), pl. _cangau_ is thought to descend (Morris Jones 1913: 200), from Pokorny's root *_k̂ank-_ 'branch'.[6] Cf. also Sanskrit _śaṅkú_ 'peg, nail, spike' with a short _u_ and a thematic stem seen in Russian _suk_ 'bough' < Proto-Slavic *_sǫkъ_ < *_k̂anko-_. Proto-Tocharian *_kāṅkuke_ would therefore be analogous to such diminutives as Sanskrit _śaṅkuka_ 'small peg or nail' and Russian _sučók_ 'little bough'. For PIE *_a_, *_ū_ becoming Proto-Tocharian *_ā_, *_u_ see Burlak (2000: 118); examples are Toch. A _śpāl*_ = Greek _κεφαλή_ 'head', Toch. B _pruk-_ = Russian _prýgat'_ 'jump'. Diminutives from _ū_ stems are rare in Indo-European languages, but compare Latin _sūcula_ from _sūs_ 'pig'. I am aware that the traditional PIE reconstruction that I adhere to goes against more recent works that doubt the existence of *_a_, *_ū_ in the proto-language.

The anonymous reviewer suggests that _kāṅkuk_ could be an Indian or Iranian loanword, e.g. from a word related to Persian _changak_ 'a hook for an elephant', and compares it to Toch. A _pātruk_ 'skull', which, according to Malzahn (2014: 92), comes from Sanskrit _pātraka_ 'bowl' via suffix alternation.

Because of the differences in the vowels, _kāṅkuk_ is not likely to be related to Lithuanian _kéngė_ 'hook, knob' from *_keng-_ 'hook, grappling hook, handle' and Old Norse _kengr_ 'bay, bend, hook' from *_geng_^{h}_-_ 'to wind; to weave' (only found in Germanic and Slavic).

6 I used the digital version of Pokorny's dictionary found at https://indo-european.info/pokorny-etymological-dictionary/index.htm.

The corresponding verses from the Samudra literature are as follows:

Garuḍapurāṇa, 64.6:

aṅkuśaṃ *kuṇḍalaṃ* ***cakraṃ*** *yasyāḥ pāṇitale bhavet /*
putraṃ prasūyate nārī narendraṃ labhate patim //
'A woman whose palm has **a hook**, an earring and **a wheel** will give birth to a son and will marry a king.'

Utpala's Samudra, 2.19–20:

yasyāḥ pāṇitale ***cakraṃ*** *kacchapo vā dhvajo 'pi vā /*
śrīvatsaṃ kamalaṃ śaṅkham āsanaṃ cāmaraṃ tathā //
aṅkuśaś *caiva* ***mālā*** *ca yasyā haste tu dṛśyate /*
ekaṃ sā janayet putraṃ rājānaṃ pṛthivīpatim //
'She on whose palm are seen a **wheel**, or a turtle, or a banner, a *śrīvatsa*, a *kamala* lotus, a conch, a throne, as well as a chowry, **a hook and a garland** will give birth to one son, [who will become] a king, a lord of the earth.'

Śārdūlakarṇāvadāna, 919:

yasyāḥ pāṇitale vyaktaḥ kacchapaḥ svastiko dhvajaḥ /
aṅkuśaṃ *kuṇḍalaṃ* ***mālā*** *dṛśyante supratiṣṭhitāḥ /*
ekaṃ sā janayet putraṃ taṃ ca rājānam ādiśet //
'She on whose palm are clearly seen a turtle, a *svastika*, a banner, **a hook**, an earring or a **garland** will give birth to one son, and he will be foretold to become a king.'

The second stanza is much less complicated, as Tocharian (*wä*)*ll oki śkaṃ nusmāṃ tāṣ* 'And (who) cries like the king (of geese)' corresponds well to Tibetan *ngang pa'i rgyal po'i gdangs 'dra ba* 'whose voice is like that of a king of geese'.

The third stanza in Tibetan reads (again, without the refrain):

/gang gi rkang pa'i mthil dag la/ /grong khyer cog dang rta babs bcas/
'She whose soles have a city with *cog* and arches'

The Chinese translation is:

若人於手中有城樓閣相 (*ruò rén yú shǒu zhōng yǒu chéng lóu gé xiāng*)
'If a person's hand (sic) has a sign of a city with *lóugé*'

The Āgamakṣudrakavyākhyāna reads (Derge Tangyur Dzu 32 b2–3):

/gang gi rkang mthil la grong khyer dang rtsig pa'i rnam pa lta bu'i ri mo yod pa'o/ /rta babs ni rtsa ba'i sgo las phyi rol gyi rtsig pa ma gtogs par shing gnyis bsgrengs pa la shing gcig gis steng nas bkab pa sgo'i rnam pa lta bu yin te/ 'di'i ming gzhan ni sgo dang po zhes bya ba yin no/
'On the sole of whose foot there is a depiction resembling a city and walls. As for the word 'arch' (*toraṇa*), it resembles a kind of a gate on two vertical wooden [beams] covered from above with one wooden [beam], not including the wall outside the principal gate (*mūladvāra*).[7] Another word for it is 'the first gate' (*sgo dang po*).'

Sanskrit parallels are as follows:

Garuḍapurāṇa, 64.9:
yasyāḥ pāṇitale rekhā prākāras toraṇaṃ bhavet /
api dāsakule jātā rājñītvam upagacchati //
'She whose palm has a line [shaped like] a wall or an arch, even if born in a family of slaves, will become a queen.'

Utpala's Samudra, 2.21:
yasyāḥ pāṇitale dṛśyaḥ koṣṭhāgāraḥ satoraṇaḥ /
api dāsakule jātā sā rājamahiṣī bhavet //
'She on whose palm a treasury with an arch is seen, even if born in a family of slaves, will become a queen.'

Śārdūlakarṇāvadāna, 920:
yasyāḥ pāṇau pradṛśyeta koṣṭhāgāraṃ satoraṇam /
api dāsakule jātā rājapatnī bhaviṣyati //
'She on whose hand a treasury with an arch is seen, even if born in a family of slaves, will become a queen.'

7 The commentary seems to indicate that an arch (*toraṇa*) is a structure separate from the city gates.

First of all, the Sanskrit parallels for this stanza give us an idea of what our 'refrain' could have looked like in its original Sanskrit form. Its first pāda in all three texts reads *api dāsakule jātā* 'even if born in a family of slaves', whereas the second one shows some variation. Note that this condition does not technically suit Mālikā, because she was not a slave by birth, but became enslaved after her father died in debt.

The surviving text of the first half of the third stanza in Tocharian reads */// (śa)l-penaṃ msāṣ lkāl tāṣ-äṃ : ri śla kāwas ///* 'a city with *kāwas* is seen below, on the soles of her feet'. *kāwas* is the obl. pl. of a noun, of which the nominative singular is difficult to infer. Tocharian A does not allow word-final *w*, and we have such words as *pärko* 'profit', where the final *w* is dropped (it is seen in other forms, such as nom. pl. *pärkowäntu*), therefore we might expect the nom. sg. form of *kāwas* to be *kā**. As Ilya Itkin and Michaël Peyrot have suggested, the nom. sg. form could also be **ko*, and we are then dealing with the same alternation as in *śot* 'you live' ~ *śāweñc* 'they live'. It would thus be homonymous with *ko* 'mouth' (and possibly *ko** 'cow'). The anonymous reviewer suggests *kāp**, cf. nom. sg. *svabhāp* 'own nature' next to nom. pl. *svabhāwäntu* (from Sanskrit *svabhāva*); in this case, it must be a loanwoard.

There is just one more occurrence of this word, namely in line A 459 a3 of a bilingual Sanskrit–Tocharian A manuscript No. 457–459,[8] which reads:

/// – ṭī • kāwaṣi keṣti waṣt • pā ///

At the beginning of this line, Carling (2009: 160) restores *(ku)ṭī* 'hut, cottage, house, hall, shop', and the surviving part of the first akṣara does not

8 I was unable to identify the original Sanskrit text of this manuscript. Leaf A 457 looks a lot like a section on medicines of some Vinaya akin to the Bhaiṣajyavastu of the Mūlasarvāstivāda-vinaya. Judging by the words *catasra kalpikā vasā* (A 457 b1) 'four allowable fats' (glossed as *śtwar ka[pp]i ///*, with *kappi** 'allowable' lacking in Toch. A dictionaries), it might belong to the Sarvāstivāda school, because the Vinaya of Ten Recitations (十誦律), associated with the Sarvāstivādins, allows exactly four kinds of fat, unlike the Mūlasarvāstivāda-vinaya, which allows five (see a comparative table of allowable fats in different Vinayas in Wut 2019: 100–101).

exclude such reading. *kāwaṣi* is an adjective derived from our word *kāw-*; *keṣti* is a hapax legomenon (probably also an adjective), and *waṣt* means 'house'.

The Kṣudrakavastu parallel does not allow determining the meaning of *kāw-* with certainty, mostly because of the disagreement between the versions. The Tibetan translation says that the city has *cog* (see below for the meaning) and *rta babs* (arches[9]); the Chinese text only mentions *lóugé* 樓閣 (see below for the meaning); the Āgamakṣudrakavyākhyāna has *rtsig pa* (walls) and *rta babs* (arches), and so does the parallel verse from the Garuḍapurāṇa (*prākāra* and *toraṇa*, respectively), while Utpala's Samudra and the Śārdūlakarṇāvadāna only mention *toraṇa* (arches).

Chinese *lóugé* 樓閣 has a wide range of meanings. Hirakawa (1997: 669) gives the following Sanskrit terms translated by it: *prāsāda* 'lofty building', *kūṭāgāra* 'apartment on the top of a house', *harmya* and *hārmya* 'palace'; *kūṭa* 'summit', *khoḍaka-śirṣa* 'coping or cornice' (see below), *toraṇa* 'arch', *vimāna* 'mansion', *harmyatala* 'flat roof or upper room of a palace'. So it can signify virtually any lofty building or structure.

Since all versions, maybe excluding Yijing's translation, mention arches, it is reasonable to suggest that *toraṇa* was also present in the original Sanskrit text. There was clearly something else as well, which the team working on the Tibetan translation of the Kṣudrakavastu rendered as *cog*, and the translators of the Āgamakṣudrakavyākhyāna as *rtsig pa* 'walls'.

Roerich (1986, vol. 3, p. 58) translates *lcog* (a spelling variant of *cog*) as 'pinnacle, turret (on a house-top)'. But according to the Mahāvyutpatti (entry 5529), *lcog* is used to translate the Sanskrit *khoṭakaḥ* (with variants *koḍhakaḥ*, *khoḍakaḥ*), which denotes, according to BHSD: 206b, 'some part or appendage of a wall or rampart', probably 'coping' or 'cornice'. And indeed, in the Avadāna of Māndhātṛ found in the Vinayavastu, *cog* is

9 Hereinafter I use plurals when referring to the accessories of a city, but the actual number in each case is impossible to determine because neither Tibetan nor Chinese express number regularly, and Sanskrit bahuvrīhi-compounds like *satoraṇa* 'with arch(es)' are likewise ambiguous.

used to translate what in the Sanskrit manuscripts of the Divyāvadāna[10] is spelled as *ṣoḍakā* and is probably a mistake for *khoḍakā*. The Divyāvadāna reads (see Cowell & Neil 1886: 220):

> *teṣu prākāreṣu caturvidhāḥ ṣoḍakā māpitāḥ suvarṇamayā rūpyamayā vaiḍūryamayāḥ sphaṭikamayāḥ /*
> 'they [= ramparts] are fitted with four kinds of coping: gold, silver, beryl, and crystal.' (translation by Rotman 2008: 220)

The Tibetan text reads (Derge 'dul-ba Kha 117a):

> */ra ba de rnams la cog rnam pa bzhi po gser las byas pa dang / dngul las byas pa dang / bai DUr+ya las byas pa dang / shel las byas pa dag btags so/*
> 'These walls had quadruple cornices of gold, silver, beryl, and crystal' (translation by Schiefner & Ralston 1906: 14)

The meaning 'coping' or 'cornice' rather than 'tower, turret' for *khoṭaka* is supported by the following example from the Aṣṭasāhasrikā Prajñāpāramitā Sūtra:

> *teṣāṃ ca saptaratnamayānāṃ prākārāṇāṃ jāmbūnadasya suvarṇasya khoḍakaśīrṣāṇi pramāṇavanty upodgatāni / sarvasmiṃś ca khoḍaka-śīrṣe saptaratnamayo vṛkṣo jāto nānāvicitrai ratnamayaiḥ phalaiḥ phalavān /*
> 'Their [= the walls'] well-founded copings slope into the golden river Jambu. And on each coping grows a tree, made of the seven precious things, laden with various fruits, also made of precious substances.' (translation by Conze 1958: 203)

I think, copings or cornices are a more appropriate place for trees to grow on than turrets.

If we assume that translators of the Kṣudrakavastu used *cog* in order to translate *khoṭaka*, in accordance with the Mahāvyutpatti and the example

10 The Sanskrit text of this part of the Vinayavastu is not extant, therefore our only Sanskrit source is the Divyāvadāna.

from the Vinayavastu quoted above,[11] then our passage is to mean 'city with cornices (*khoṭaka*) and arches (*toraṇa*)'. In that case, we can compare it with the following passage from the Lalitavistara:

> *parikhā**khoṭakatoraṇāś** ca mahatā prākāra ucchrāpitā*[12] (Vaidya 1958: 139)
> 'And high walls with moats, **cornices and arches** were erected.'

Another option is to suggest that *cog*, in accordance with the dictionaries, means 'tower, turret'. In that case, we can reconstruct the beginning of our stanza as follows, for example:

> **yasyāḥ pādatale dṛśyaṃ nagaraṃ sāṭṭatoraṇam*
> 'She on whose sole a city with towers and arches is seen'

Reconstructing the word *dṛśyam* 'seen' is supported by the parallel from Utpala's Samudra, as well as by the Tocharian version, which also has *lkāl* 'seen'.

Both these suggestions — that the original text had either *khoṭaka* 'coping of a wall' or *aṭṭa* 'tower' — struggle to explain why the Āgamakṣudrakavyākhyāna uses the word *rtsig pa* (walls) instead. Could it be that the original text had walls, cornices/towers and arches all at the same time and each version omitted at least one of those things?[13] I am unable to find room for three long words *prākāra*, *khoṭaka* and *toraṇa* within two pādas. If we choose *aṭṭa* 'tower', however, we might get something like this:

11 Different teams worked on the Tibetan translations of the Vinayavastu and the Kṣudrakavastu, although the Indian scholar Vidyākaraprabha was part of both teams.

12 *mahatā prākāra ucchrāpitā* is for standard Sanskrit *mahāntaḥ prākārā ucchrāpitāḥ*, cf. Edgerton (1953/1985: 103) for *mahatā* and ibid. (55–56) for the shortening of *-ā* in nom. pl. masc.

13 Chinese *chéng* 城 means both 'wall' and '(walled) city', which could explain why Yijing's translation lacks walls: a phrase 'city with walls' might have seemed tautological to him. I thank the anonymous reviewer for pointing this out.

**yasyāḥ pāde 'sti nagaraṃ sāṭṭaprākāratoraṇam*
'She on whose foot there is a city with towers, walls and arches.'

The second pāda of this reconstruction finds a good parallel, for example, in the Rāmāyaṇa's Sundarākāṇḍa, verse 53.26:

dagdheyaṃ nagarī laṅkā sāṭṭaprākāratoraṇā
'Burned is this city of Laṅkā, with its towers, walls and arches.'

Finally, the last option is to go with the Āgamakṣudrakavyākhyāna and reconstruct 'city with walls and arches', i.e. something like:

**yasyāḥ pādatale dṛśyā pūḥ saprākāratoraṇā*
'She on whose sole a city with walls and arches is seen.'

As Hirakawa's list shows, Chinese *lóugé* could translate *toraṇa* 'arch', and for the lack of 'walls' in the Chinese version see note 9. Inexplicable remains the rendering of 'walls' with ཅོག *cog* in Tibetan (it being a corruption of རྩིག *rtsig* 'wall' would be too bold of an assumption).

As I tried to show, because of the discrepancies found in our sources, possibilities for reconstructing our original verse are quite numerous, yet not infinite. If we suppose that the Kṣudrakavastu and the Tocharian version are close enough, *kāw-* might either correspond to Sanskrit *aṭṭa* 'tower, turret', *toraṇa* 'arch', *khoṭaka* 'coping or cornice of a wall' or *prākāra* 'wall, rampart'. Given that *kāw-* is something which not only cities, but also houses can have (see A 459 a3), I think that we can exclude *khoṭaka*. However, just like in the case of *kāṅkuk*, there is a possibility that the Tocharian version deviates here from the Kṣudrakavastu and *kāw-* means something else.

After the verses are ended, the Brahmin's words continue in lines A 429 b8 – 431 a1:

tämyo-k /// [c]waṃ n(e)ñci wätkā[lts] sne sañce caṣ cmo(laṃ) ///
'For this very reason... you have (roots of virtue?) in you. For sure, without a doubt, (in) this birth (you shall become a queen?).'

Line a2 reads:

/// m tsātsäwṣuräṣ riyac kälk s[ā]m penu ///

The absolutive *tsātsäwṣuräṣ* is said to belong to an otherwise unattested root *tsāw-* in Poucha (1955: 390) and Malzahn (2010: 976). However, this form is phonologically anomalous, as the sequence *äw* is impossible in Tocharian A. Therefore, I think that we have a mistake — made by the scribe or, less likely, Sieg and Siegling — for *tsātsä<r>wṣuräṣ*, a causative absolutive of *tsārw-* 'to be glad, comforted' (alternatively, the *r* might have been lost due to damage). Then we should understand the phrase *///* *(tā)m tsātsä<r>wṣuräṣ riyac kälk* as '…having comforted her (= Mālikā), [the Brahmin] went to the city', which suits the narrative pretty well. The next phrase, *s[ā]m penu ///* 'And she…' probably refers to Mālikā.

To conclude, here is the final reading of A 429 a2 – 431 a2 with my conjectures:

A 429 a2 */// (mahā)nāmes warpiśkeyac ysi osāt okā[k] ///*
A 429 a3 */// s t[ā]k(a)ṣt tā pat ysi onus naṣt tā ///*
A 429 a4 */// (pä)k[l]yoṣ u[p]ādhy(ā) riyäṣ kakmus tākā tm· ///*
A 429 a5 */// (mahā)nāme (krä)tolāñcāṃ y[ā]msāt-(ñ)i ///*
A 429 a6 */// (m)ā[c]ar kuc [p]ā(ca)r – [c]e ///*
A 429 a7 */// ñuk krätol[ā](ñc) ///*
A 429 b2 */// sam-ci tm-äk ///*
A 429 b3 */// s ṣ(o)treyäntu täm pälkorä(ṣ) ///*
A 429 b4 */// || maitraṃ || käṅkuk yo cākrä pässā(k) ///*
A 429 b5 */// (ta)tmus tāṣ • ṣakk ats sny-ālak-wkäṃ sām ///*
A 429 b6 */// (wä)ll oki śkaṃ nusmāṃ tāṣ • wkän penu sā(m) ///*
A 429 b7 */// (śa)l-penaṃ msāṣ lkāl tāṣ-äṃ : ri śla kāwas ///*
A 429 b8 */// lānt śäṃ mäskatär : 3 || tämyo-k ///*
A 431 a1 */// [c]waṃ n(e)ñci wätkā[lts] sne sañce caṣ cmo(laṃ) ///*
A 431 a2 */// m tsātsä<r>wṣuräṣ riyac kälk s[ā]m penu ///*

Translation:

Narrative (A 429 a2): (The Brahmin) went to Mahānāman's garden, until…

BRAHMIN (A 429 a3): ...were you? And where are you going? (And) where...?

MĀLIKĀ (A 429 a4–5): Listen, teacher. I have come from the city... Mahānāman made me [his] slave-girl.

BRAHMIN (A 429 a6): ...(what about your) mother, what [about your] father...

MĀLIKĀ (A 429 a7): ...I, slave-girl...

BRAHMIN (A 429 b2): ...I... you.

NARRATIVE (A 429 b2–3): Right afterwards... signs. Having seen that...

BRAHMIN (A 429 b4 – 431 a1): In the Maitraṃ tune:

(She on whose palms) a hook (?), a wheel and a garland (are seen, even if she) is born... she will surely, undoubtedly (become a king's wife).

(She who... and) cries like the king (of geese), even if she (is born... she will surely, undoubtedly become a king's wife).

(She on the) soles of whose feet a city with *kāwas* is seen, (even if she is born... she will surely, undoubtedly) become a king's wife.

For this very reason... you have... in you. For sure, without a doubt, (in) this birth (you shall become a queen?).

NARRATIVE (431 a2): ...having comforted her, he went to the city. And she...

[RECEIVED: AUGUST 2021]

Novatorov Street 34, bldg. 7, app. 6
119421 Moscow
Russia
sjerjozha@yandex.ru

References

BHSD = Franklin Edgerton. 1953. *Buddhist Hybrid Sanskrit Grammar and Dictionary, vol. II: Dictionary.* New Haven (Conn.): Yale University Press.

Burlak, Svetlana A. 2000. *Istoričeskaja fonetika toxarskix jazykov.* Moskva: Rossijskaja Akademija Nauk, Institut Vostokovedenija.

Carling, Gerd. 2009. *Dictionary and Thesaurus of Tocharian A. Vol. 1: A–J*. In collaboration with Georges-Jean Pinault and Werner Winter. Wiesbaden.

Conze, Eberhart Julius Dietrich. 1958. *The Perfection of Wisdom in Eight thousand Slokas*. Calcutta: Asiatic Society.

Cowell, Edward B. & Robert A. Neil. 1886. *The Divyāvadāna. A collection of early Buddhist legends. Now first edited from the Nepalese Sanskrit mss. in Cambridge and Paris*. Cambridge: Cambridge Univ. Press.

Edgerton, Franklin. 1953/1985. *Buddhist Hybrid Sanskrit Grammar and Dictionary. Vol. I, Grammar*. Madras.

Hirakawa, Akira. 1997. *Bukkyo Kan-Bon daijiten [Buddhist Chinese-Sanskrit dictionary]*. Tokyo: Reiyukai.

Johnston, Edward Hamilton. 1932. *The Saundarananda or Nanda the Fair. Translated from the original Sanskrit of Aśvaghoṣa by E. H. Johnston*. London: Humphrey Milford.

Karunaratne, T. 1976. "The Significance of the Signs and Symbols on the Footprints of the Buddha". *Journal of the Sri Lanka Branch of the Royal Asiatic Society*, 20, new series, 47–60.

Malyshev, Sergey V. 2018. "The Tocharian A version of the Mahauṣadha-Jātaka". *Tocharian and Indo-European Studies* 18: 105–126.

Malzahn, Melanie. 2010. *The Tocharian Verbal System*. Leiden/Boston: Brill.

Malzahn, Melanie. 2014. "Tocharian A *śorki* "fear" and two other TA scary words". *Tocharian and Indo-European Studies* 15: 87–94.

Morris Jones, John. 1913. *A Welsh Grammar, Historical and Comparative*. Oxford: Oxford University Press.

Peyrot, Michaël. 2013. *The Tocharian subjunctive. A study in syntax and verbal stem formation*. Leiden/Boston: Brill.

Poucha, Pavel. 1955. *Thesaurus linguae Tocharicae dialecti A*. Praha.

Rockhill, William Woodville. 1884. *The life of the Buddha and the early history of his order. Derived from Tibetan works in the Bkah-hgyur and Bstan-hgyur, followed by notices on the early history of Tibet and Khoten*. London: Trübner & Co., Ludgate Hill.

Roerich, Nikolay Y. 1986. *Tibetan-Russian-English Dictionary with Sanskrit parallels*. Moscow: Nauka Publishers. Central Department of Oriental Literature.

Rotman, Andy. 2008. *Divine Stories. Divyāvadāna. Part 1*. Boston: Wisdom Publications.

Schiefner, Anton. 1849/1851. "Eine tibetische Lebensbeschreibung des Çākyamuni's, des Begründers des Buddhatums, im Auszuge mitgeteilt". *Mémoires présentés à l'Académie Impériale de Sciences de St.-Pétersbourg par divers savants et lus dans ses assemblées*, 6.3: 231–333.

Schiefner, Anton and William Ralston Shedden Ralston. 1906. *Tibetan tales, derived from Indian sources*. London: K. Paul, Trench, Trübner.

Sieg, Emil and Wilhelm Siegling. 1921. *Tocharische Sprachreste, I. Band. Die Texte. A. Transcription*. Berlin/Leipzig: de Gruyter.

Skilling, Peter. 1996. "Symbols on the Body, Feet, and Hands of a Buddha. Part II—Short Lists". *Journal of The Siam Society*, Vol. 84, Part 1, 5–28.

T = Taishō Tripiṭaka (https://21dzk.l.u-tokyo.ac.jp/SAT/)

Vaidya, Paraśurāma Lakṣmaṇa. 1958. *Lalitavistaraḥ*. Mithila: Institute of Post-Graduate Studies and Research in Sanskrit Learning.

Wut, Tai Shing (屈大成). 2019.《四分律•藥揵度》注釋 [*On the Bhaiṣajya-skandhaka of the Dharmaguptaka-vinaya*]. Taiwan: 佛陀教育基金會 [The Buddha Educational Foundation].

Zysk, Kenneth G. 2016. *The Indian System of Human Marks. With editions, translations and annotations*. Volume 1 and 2. Leiden/Boston: Brill.

Notes on Tocharian A *o(k)* 'snake', A *oram* and B *sorromp* 'down', B *oṣno*, B *nanāmo* 'recognising', B *pāwe*, and B †*səwm*- 'trickle'[1]

Michaël Peyrot

This article is a collection of short notes on several Tocharian words. It is suggested that the TA cognate of TB *auk* 'snake' is attested as *o(k)*; that TA *oram* and TB *sorromp* 'down' are etymologically related; that TB *oṣno* is a word, perhaps from *ot ṣ no* 'and then'; that *kakāmau* 'taken' in the so-called Petrovskij Buddhastotra is rather to be read as *nanāmo* 'recognising'; that TB *pāwe* is an adjective, perhaps meaning 'clean', while *ṣāwo* 'bath' is a ghost word; and that TB *səwm*- 'trickle' is a ghost word too.

In this article, I present short notes on the following Tocharian words: 1. TA *o(k)* 'snake', 2. TA *oram* and TB *sorromp* 'down', 3. TB *oṣno*, 4. TB *nanāmo* 'recognising', 5. TB *pāwe*, 6. TB †*səwm*- 'trickle'.

1 TA *o(k)* 'snake'

Sieg & Siegling (1921: 245) read line b5 of A 455 as follows:

//// lodaroraga • *wär kats̱\ o* ////

In his personal copy (available at CETOM), Wilhelm Siegling has later noted that the <a> of *kats̱* should rather be <ā>. Indeed, the correct reading is in my view:

/// lodaroraga • *wär k[ā]ts̱\ o* ///

---

1 I thank Ilya Itkin (Moscow) for comments on an earlier draft. This research was supported by the European Research Council (ERC-2017-STG 758855).

With this correction, it becomes evident that Tocharian A *wär* 'water' translates Sanskrit *jala-*, while *kāts* 'belly' renders *udara-*. These equations prompt us to take *o ///* to be the translation of *uraga-* 'snake'. No restoration of the fragmentary *o ///* would have been feasible if we had had no Tocharian B cognate. However, in view of Tocharian B *auk* 'snake', the obvious restoration is *o(k)*. The reading of the whole line so becomes:

/// (ja)lodaroraga • *wär k[ā]tṣ͇͟ o(k)* ///

As pointed out to me by Sergey Malyshev (p.c.), it remains to be seen how the apparent *jalodaroraga* 'water-bellied snake' (?) is to be interpreted.[2] It is conceivable, for instance, that it is a mistake for *jalodaro rogaḥ* 'water-belly disease', which is attested in the Cīvaravastu of the Mūlasarvāstivādavinaya (MSV 1,07, 247a). However, in A 455 b5 a reading or restoration *(ja)lodaro roga* is only possible against the manuscript: <raga> can be read without any problem. I therefore assume that if *(ja)lodaroraga* is indeed a mistake, this corruption of the text was carried over into the Tocharian A translation.

2 TA *oram* and TB *sorromp* 'down'

The Tocharian B adverb *sorromp* 'down' is not frequent, but nevertheless relatively well attested, in clear contexts, and its meaning is not controversial or uncertain. I think this adverb is a cognate of the Tocharian A hapax legomenon A 79 a2 *oram*, translated by Sieg (1952: 13) as "nieder" (cf. also Carling 2009: 91b, "down"). While the semantic connection is quite obvious, the formal side needs to be commented. As for the vowels, I think that it is a good example of the correspondence B *o* : A *o* in the first syllable and of B *o* : A *a* in the second, as among many other examples

2 Sergey Malyshev also raised the valid objection that there is already a word for 'snake': TA *ārṣal*. This is obviously to be acknowledged, but since Tocharian B *auk* is also found next *arṣāklo* 'snake', there was apparently a difference in meaning between the two words. Quite likely, this difference in meaning in Tocharian A was similar to that in Tocharian B.

in B *oṅkolmo* 'elephant' : A *oṅkaläm* (Burlak & Itkin 2003). As for the consonants, the correspondence B *rr* : A *r* may simply be due to degemination in Tocharian A, while the final *-p* may have been lost in Tocharian A, as final *-mp* is rare there,[3] and final *-p* is lost in the pronoun *säm*, if that is, as I believe, cognate with Tocharian B *samp*.

The obvious obstacle to the connection is the mismatch of the initial: there is no parallel whatsoever for the presence of the initial *s-* in Tocharian B and the lack of it in Tocharian A. Probably, this difference has to be explained from wrong segmentation in the phonological phrase, like in the case of E. *adder* < **nadra-*, which lost its *n-* to the preceding article. The converse happened in Dutch *nonkel* 'uncle'. The question is whether the *s-* was lost in Tocharian A or added in Tocharian B, and which phonological context may have been the source of such resegmentation.

The only example in Tocharian A is the following:

A 79 a2

anaprä pesā oram pä(ṣtam)[4]
'Bow down in front of my feet!' (Carling 2009: 91b)

In Tocharian B there are more examples. In all cases, *sorromp* is found together with *klaya-* 'fall', and in most cases it precedes the verb and is found at the beginning of a phrase:[5]

3 In fact, it seems to be found only in *kump** 'pot', where it may have been restored on the basis of the paradigm, e.g. the loc.sg. *kumpaṃ*, which is attested, and *kumpa-kump* 'in crowds', where it may have been restored in the second member on the basis of the first.

4 I find Sieg's restoration of the following imperative verb form as *pä(ṣtam)* questionable in view of the phraseology in Tocharian B (for which see immediately below). Also, the associated meanings 'stand up' and 'stand still' of *käl̂-* 'stand' do not fit a downward movement. However, I admit that *päklā* 'fall!' (if that is what the imperative looked like) is not a very likely restoration either.

5 The following fragmentary attestations may belong here too: THT 630 a1 /// *(so)rromp kakl(āyau)* /// 'having fallen down' (this reading with *rr* is the correct one, rather than the *(so)romp* of Sieg & Siegling's 1953: 401); THT 1334.c a1 /// *sorrom klayāre* /// 'they fell down'; and perhaps THT 406 /// *(sorro)m*

PK AS 13F a4

/// – – – – śaumoṃ śaumoṃ so(r)r(o)mp klyoyomane

'… each man … falling down …'

PK AS 15C a5

/// -ttsai weśeññaisa bodhisatveṃ kwāmane sorromp klāya taur āṣsa ktāte

'… calling the Bodhisattva with a … voice, he fell down and strew dust over his head.'

THT 1285 [etc.] a2

(ar)h(ā)nteś śem sorrom painene kl(āya)

'… he came to the arhat [and] fell down at [his] feet.' (Ogihara 2012: 156)

THT 90 a4

/// yane aruṇāvati riś sorromp ka(klāyau)

'… … to the town Aruṇavatī. (Having) fallen down …'

THT 1363.e b3

/// tme tumeṃ sorromp pä·k· ///

'… them. Thereupon …[6] down …'

THT 22 a8

(ri)tāte akālk sorro(mp) k(l)āya poyśintse

'He cherished the wish [and] fell down before the omniscient.'

In the phrases occurring in these examples, there does not seem to be any context in which resegmentation could have possibly occurred. The best I can think of would be words like _se_ 'he' or _tusa_ 'thus' placed in front of an original _s_-less _*orromp_, e.g. _*s⁄⁄ orromp klāya_ 'he fell down' or _*tus⁄⁄ orromp klāya_ 'thus he fell down'. However, resegmentation seems

klāya. The last two examples are pointed out to me by Ilya Itkin, who also notes the very fragmentary THT 3626.b a2 _/// (so)rromp ///_ '… down …'.

6 _pä_ is probably not the beginning of an imperative in view of the preceding _tumeṃ_ 'thereupon'. One could think of _pälkāte_ 'he looked', but the middle of this preterite is very rare.

improbable to me here since *se* and *tusa* are not in any specific way linked to *sorromp* and should therefore have remained recognisable.

The few examples where *sorromp* is not found phrase-initially seem to have marked, non-default verse word-order:

THT 22 b6
eñcwaññai kentsa (k)l(āya) sorromp läklessu
'The sorrowful one fell down on the iron earth.'

THT 49 a7
/// s· mācer śem-neś eś lmausa 7 klāya[7] *soysa so(rromp) ///*
'… [his] blind mother came to him. She fell down before [her] son …'

IOL Toch 251 b3
/// ·ene sorro(mp) ///
'… down …'

THT 2593 a1[8]
/// t· pain(e)ne so(r)r(omp) ///
'… down at [his] feet …'

In view of the repetitive phraseology, we may perhaps restore IOL Toch 251 b3 */// ·ene sorro(mp) ///* as *(pain)ene sorro(mp)* '… down at [his/her] feet …'. It thus appears that *sorromp klaya-* 'fall down' may be combined with a locative in the sense 'fall down at', e.g. 'fall down at someone's feet', or with a perlative in the sense 'fall down before', e.g. 'fall down before somebody'. The genitive THT 22 a8 *sorro(mp) k(l)āya poyśintse* 'he fell down before the Buddha' is in this light unexpected, but with such a small number of examples it is impossible to decide whether that is a mistake for the perlative *poyśintsa*. Another collocation with the perlative is obviously found in THT 22 b6 *kentsa (k)l(āya) sorromp* 'he fell down on the earth', where the perlative is used as with *klaya-* if it is not accompanied with *sorromp* (Carling 2000: 79).

7 Sieg & Siegling (1949: I, 71) printed *klāysa*, obviously a typographical error. Thomas has corrected this reading in Sieg & Siegling (1983: 86).
8 This example has been brought to my attention by Ilya Itkin.

No relevant wrong resegmentation is possible with a preceding locative, but the perlative is actually promising. If, in Pre-Tocharian B, the perlative had the shape *-*sa*, as in the historical language, and *sorromp* had the shape **orromp*, like in Tocharian A, the sequence *-*sa orromp* would have been contracted to *-*s⫽ orromp*. At this stage, renewal of the perlative ending would have yielded the necessary *-*sa sorromp*.[9] It is difficult to envision a scenario in which Tocharian A *oram* could have lost its initial *s*- to a preceding perlative suffix, because the perlative has no *s*-element in Tocharian A, and this is most probably the original, Proto-Tocharian situation.

An explanation based on the perlative has the advantage that this is the case used in the only occurrence in Tocharian A, *pesā oram* 'down at [my] feet', and that there are two possible constructions with the perlative in Tocharian B, 'fall down on something' and 'fall down before somebody'. At the same time, it requires that the default order of such expressions was "perlative complement + *sorromp* + *klaya*-". This seems natural enough, especially for 'fall down on something', but it would be different from what we find in the prose example with the locative: THT 1285 [etc.] a2 *sorrom painene kl*(*āya*) 'he fell down at [his] feet'.

The ultimate etymology of the so reconstructed Proto-Tocharian **orromp* eludes me, but it obviously contains *omp* 'there' as the second element. On the evidence of the longer *ompe* and *ompek*, this *omp* must have been shortened from *ompe* (Adams 2013: 125), while *omte* and *omteṃ* 'there' are from *omp* plus the neuter pronouns *te* and *teṃ*, respectively, with loss of *p* in the cluster -*mpt*- (Adams 2013: 214–215). It follows that the meaning 'down' is contributed by the initial element **orr*-.

It is likely that Tocharian B *ñor* 'below, down' contains PIE **ni*- 'down' followed by an element *-*or*, but it is unclear to me if that should be the

9 It is conceivable, but as far as I see impossible to prove, that the mismatch between the perlative *pesā* in Tocharian A and the locative *painene* in Tocharian B is to be explained as a case where the perlative was not renewed. Thus, a Pre-Tocharian B **painesa orromp* would have developed into **paine sorromp*, at which stage the nom.-obl. *paine* was replaced with the locative *painene* rather than the perlative *painesa*.

same as the **orr-* of **orromp*. One might expect an adverb **ni-* 'down' to be enlarged with an adverbial suffix, denoting location or motion (depending on the original meaning), but not with another element meaning 'down'.

3 TB *oṣno*

In THT 591 b7 there is a difficult passage that was transliterated by Sieg & Siegling (1953: 377) as follows: **:** *oṣ no [m]i – n ma arañc*$^{ä}_{\searrow}$ *[k](ā)ṯ(ḵ)ạṣṯäṟ*$_{\searrow}$. They proposed to restore and correct to **:** *op no mi(t wa)t mā arañc k(ā)t(k)ästär*. No image of the fragment is currently available, but clearly the large number of emendations does not inspire confidence. Accepting Sieg & Siegling's correction to *op*, Adams (2013: 122) connects this *op* with the allative *opiś* in THT 433 a17, apparently a foodstuff, and he suggests that it means 'fat'. According to him, the passage in THT 591 b7 would mean 'however neither *op* nor honey gladdens the heart'.

In THT 1554 + 3112 b3, Ogihara (2012: 182) reads */// (bodhi)[s](a)tve weṣ̱ṣ̱ạṃ k*$_{u}$*ce [p̱ạ]knāṣṣīṯạṟ*$_{\searrow}$ *[y]āmtsi cai [s]· (·)[ṣ]· ñ*$^{ä}_{\searrow}$ *om no*. The first part is to be translated as: 'The bodhisattva says: "What did you [pl.] intend to do? …'. It is the last part of the line that is difficult. Although I have no proposal to make for the difficult part *[s]· (·)[ṣ]· ñ*$^{ä}_{\searrow}$, obviously the correct reading of the last akṣaras is *oṣno* rather than *om no*.

The clear reading of *oṣno* in THT 1554 + 3112 b3 makes an emendation to *op no* in THT 591 b7 unadvisable. However, at present, I cannot interpret either passage and the meaning of *oṣno* cannot be established at this point. If it is a noun, it would have a remarkable, but not an impossible structure. However, the positioning in the beginning of the verse in THT 591 b7 suggests to me that it is a sentence adverbial. Without being able to prove it, I would therefore suggest that it is shortened from *ot ṣp no*, and I would guess that the meaning is 'and then'. If this interpretation is correct, it could also be written *oṣ no* in two words.

4 TB *nanāmo* 'recognising'

The end of the first line of the famous Petrovskij Buddhastotra, SI 1903 a1 (formerly P1), is read by Pinault (2016a: 7, 14) as *t̠a̠ryā-ykne ymentse śmoñaṣṣe mā[ñ](··) kakām[au ·]* 'having taken on the serv(ant) of the establishment of the threefold consciousness'. In my view, the reading of the last word[10] is problematic: the third akṣara is quite clearly <mo>, not <mau>, and the preceding two syllables do not look like <kakā>, but rather like <nanā>. I think we should read this sequence as *nanāmo*, which is in fact the reading already proposed by Leumann (1900: 16). In my view, *nanāmo* needs no correction, as it can simply be the nom.sg.m. of the verbal adjective of *nana-* 'recognise, appear'. As pointed out to me by Ilya Itkin (p.c.), the obl.sg.f. of the same verbal adjective is attested in THT 1398.b a3 */// nanāmñai ///*.

Unfortunately, I have no suggestion to make for the object of SI 1903 a1 *nanāmo*, i.e. for the two akṣaras transliterated as *mā[ñ]*(··) and interpreted as *māñ*(*ye*) 'servant' by Pinault. The relevant passage is too damaged in the current state of the fragment. In my view, Pinault is right that Thomas' restoration of these two akṣaras as (*pekwe*) 'ring' (1964: 58) is excluded as the consonant of the first akṣara can be read as *[m]*. However, rather than Pinault's reading *mā*, I would opt for *m[au]*. Nevertheless, I am not able to offer a suitable restoration of the word, which should be disyllabic according to the metre. With this caveat, my translation is: *täryā-ykne ymentse śmoñaṣṣe mau – nanāmo [·]* 'recognising the *mau* – of the basis of the threefold consciousness'.

Verbal adjectives in *-mo* are regularly derived from the present stem. However, *nana-* 'recognise' forms a $^{\textit{ṣṣə}}/_{\textit{ske}}$-present |naná$^{\text{ṣṣə}}/_{\text{ske}}$-| of class 9, and thus *nanāmo* is apparently instead derived from the subjunctive stem |naná-|. As in other cases like *weñmo* and *päknāmo* (Winter 1977: 147; Malzahn 2010: 343–344), the reason obviously is that |naná-| was in origin a present, not a subjunctive stem. This is further confirmed by the second-syllable accent of |naná-|, instead of the typical first-syllable

10 On this word, see also Pinault (2016b: 225).

accent of regular subjunctives, and by the Tocharian A cognate nasal present |knānā-|, which both clearly point to a Proto-Tocharian present **knana-* (Peyrot 2013: 762).

5 TB *pāwe* (†*ṣāwo* 'bath')

Hesitantly, Adams (2013: 715) posits a noun *-ṣāwo* 'bath', occurring only in the compound *särwāna-ṣawo* in Or.6402A/1.1 (W 13) a6 *särwāna-ṣawo masketar* '… becomes a face-bath'. There are two obvious problems. On the one hand, Adams supposes that *ṣawo* is the unaccented compound variant of *ṣāwo**, while there is evidently no compound accent effect in the alleged first member *särwāna*, for which in a compound *särwanā-** may be expected. At the same time, the first syllable of *ṣawo* cannot be accented, since it would then have to be /ṣə́wo/, which would rather be written ***ṣuwo*. On the other hand, there seems to be no basis for the supposed meaning 'bath' in the context.

However, more serious are problems with the reading. The reading given by Adams is from Filliozat (1948: 69), who, using "( )" and "[ ]" for currently common "[ ]" and "( )" respectively, reads the line as

× (ṣ̱arwāna ṣa)wo [mask]etaṟ e × tene *su*m̱aṣ̱ṣalle eśa ×

I think the correct reading is rather:

– – rwāna [p]awo[n]a m̱a̱[sk]enṯa̱ṟ˴ e[ś]anene s[t]am̱a̱ṣ̱ṣ̱a̱lle eśa ·e

The second part can without further problems be interpreted as *eśanene stamäṣṣälle*[11] *eśa(n)e* 'It is to be placed on the eyes. The eyes …'. For the first part, the restoration of *(sä)rwāna* 'face' is likely, but the reading *ṣawo* is excluded because there is a further akṣara, which is probably *[n]a*, while the first akṣara rather looks like *[p]a*. The resulting *[p]awo[n]a* is obviously the f.pl. of an adjective, and a word *pāwe* is indeed attested.[12] Since

11 For *stəm-*$^{caus.}$ 'place' vs. *səwm-* 'trickle', see below (§4).

12 The paper is damaged exactly where the horizontal closure of the akṣara should have been if it had been <ṣa> rather than <pa>. A reading *[ṣ]awo[n]a*

on account of THT 405 b3 *kaklaiksauwa särwana* 'a dry face', *särwāna* is a plurale tantum (Hilmarsson 1989: 85), *(sä)rwāna pawona mäskenträ* can be translated as 'the face becomes *pāwe*'. The entry *-ṣāwo* in Adams' dictionary is thus to be deleted: no such word exists.

The idea that *pāwe* is a noun meaning 'powder' goes back to Sieg (1955: 74). Sieg has not included *[p]awo[n]a* in his discussion. As it turns out, *pawona* is not compatible with a noun *pāwe*, as there is no such noun class, but, as pointed out above, formally *pawona* looks like the feminine plural of an adjective *pāwe*. The following, difficult attestations of *pāwe* are known to me:

W 8 a3
[p]āwe ā(r)[kw](i)
'… *pāwe* [and] white'

Or.6402A/1.6 (W 18) a3
lak̲\ pāwe yamaṣ̲a̲ṃ [e]śanene
'… makes it *pāwe*. On the eyes …'

W 30 a5
ṣ̲a̲rwāna • p̲a̲ścane kātso • po kektseñ$^{ä}_{[\backslash]}$ • *ārkwi pāwe yama(ṣ̲ṣ̲a̲ṃ)*
'… the face, the breasts, the belly, the whole body it makes white [and] *pāwe*' (Sieg 1955: 74: "Puder (macht) [es] weiß")

W 6 b2
pāwesa or *pāwe sa*, too fragmentary to translate

Or.6402A/1.5 (W 17) b2
nastukārm̲\ eśanene kartse pāwesa ṣ̲p̲a̲ nestsi[13]
'a nasal medicament in the eyes in order to be good and *pāwe*' (?) (Sieg 1955: 74: "als Klistier für die Augen gut, auch [gut], als Puder (?) (zu dienen)"

is therefore not completely excluded, but since no adjective *ṣāwe* is attested otherwise, *[p]awo[n]a* is clearly preferable.

13 The word *nestsi* has been omitted by Filliozat (1948: 71). Sieg (1955: 74) proposes to restore it, but it is in fact clearly readable.

Apart from the form *[p]awo[n]a*, I see the following arguments to take *pāwe* to be an adjective:

- In Or.6402A/1.6 (W 18) a3, *pāwe* is not in the right position of the sentence to be the subject of the verb *yamaṣäṃ* 'does, makes'. At the same time, for semantic reasons it can hardly be a noun 'powder', because what would be the subject in that case? The easiest here is to take it as an object complement, i.e. 'it makes it *pāwe*'. Obviously, *pāwe* is then best analysed as an adjective.
- In W 30 a5, the same holds true. Sieg translates "Puder (macht) [es] weiß", but this requires the supposed object complement *ārkwi* to come before the supposed subject *pāwe*. Much more straightforward is to take *ārkwi* and *pāwe* as coordinated object complements.
- In W 30 a5 *ārkwi pāwe*, in Or.6402A/1.5 (W 17) b 2 *kartse pāwesa ṣpä* and possibly in W 8 a3 *[p]āwe ā(r)[kw](i)*, the word *pāwe* is found next to another adjective. In Or.6402A/1.5 (W 17) b 2 *kartse pāwesa ṣpä*, the two are even explicitly coordinated with the conjunction *ṣpä*.

The occurrence of the perlative *pāwesa* in Or.6402A/1.5 (W 17) b2 and possibly in W 6 b2 is not in favour of *pāwe* being an adjective, but the construction in Or.6402A/1.5 (W 17) b2 is difficult, and not any easier if *pāwesa* is taken to be a noun. In particular, *kartse* 'good' could in that case not modify it, because it is nom.sg.m.

It seems to me that *pāwe* has a positive meaning: it appears to describe good results of medical treatment, for instance on the face. It is further coordinated with 'white' and with 'good'. A possible meaning may be 'clean', 'clear' or 'bright'. In all three cases, there would be a similar term, like *astare* 'clean', *takarṣke* 'clear', *lak$_u$tse* 'bright', etc., and since it is confined to medical texts, it is apparently a more specific term.

If the proposed meaning is approximately correct, it is suggestive to think of a connection with Lat. *pūrus* 'clean', Ved. *pávate* 'becomes clean', etc. (cf. e.g. de Vaan 2008: 500–501). In that case, the most straightforward reconstruction for Tocharian would be **ph$_2$uo-*. If the formation was thematicised later, **peh$_2$u-* would also be possible. It is theoretically conceivable that a *w* was lost after *p*, i.e. *pāwe* < **pwawe* < **puH-uo-*,[14] but there is no parallel in Indo-European or Tocharian for this peculiar formation.

6 TB †*səwm-* 'trickle'[15]

A verb *səwm-* 'trickle' is posited by Adams (2013: 761–762, his notation is "*sum-*"; likewise Malzahn 2010: 950 and Peyrot 2013: 835) on the basis of these two occurrences:[16]

Or.6402A/1.1 (W 13) a6
eśane sumäṣṣälle
'[it is] to be trickled in the eyes'

W 42 b1
/// slaṅkälya satkentampa sumäṣälya
'it is to be pulled out and together with medicines [it is] to be trickled'

The meaning 'trickle' and the addition of the second occurrence are due to Krause (1952: 300), who changed Filliozat's reading *sukäṣälya* (1948: 79) into *sumäṣälya*. Both the meaning and the change of Filliozat's reading must have been based on a draft of Sieg's posthumously published 1955 article (see Sieg 1955: 74, 78).

Above (§3), I have presented my revised reading of the first occurrence: *e[ś]anene s[t]am̱a̱ṣ̱ṣ̱a̱lle* 'is to be placed on the eyes'. Thus, the existence of the verbal root *səwm-* now depends on the second occurrence. As it turns out, Krause's correction of Filliozat's reading is not warranted. I am hesitant to propose a reading myself, but Filliozat's reading is obvi-

14 A parallel for this reduction is offered by *maścītse* 'mouse', which probably derives from **mwas-* < **muHs-* (Beekes 2010: 985).

15 My attention to this verb has been drawn by Federico Dragoni in the context of his study of the word *sumo* 'libation' in his PhD thesis (2022: 216–217).

16 I keep Adams' translations and readings, except for the confusing *sumäṣṣalle*, *slaṅkalya* and *sumäṣalya*, which I have corrected to *sumäṣṣälle*, *slaṅkälya* and *sumäṣälya*, respectively.

ously better than that of Krause, as the second akṣara is rather *k̲a̤*, and in any case not *m̤a̤*. However, the reading of the first akṣara is difficult too. Perhaps the word should be read *[ṣ]u[k̲a̤]ṣ̲a̤lya* (cf. the quite similar akṣara *pu* in line b3, with the same relatively low upper left knob), but this is not certain and does not immediately yield a comprehensible translation: 'is to be dangled' (?).

Thus, Or.6402A/1.1 (W 13) a6 *sumäṣṣälle* is to be read *stamäṣṣälle* and W 42 b1 *sumäṣälya* may have to be read *ṣukäṣälya*. Neither of these forms can possibly be from a root *səwm-* (*sum-*), which is, therefore, a ghost.

[RECEIVED: SEPTEMBER 2021]

Leiden University Centre for Linguistics
Universiteit Leiden, Postbus 9515
2300 RA Leiden, The Netherlands
m.peyrot@hum.leidenuniv.nl

References

Adams, Douglas Q. 2013. *A dictionary of Tocharian B.* Second edition, revised and greatly enlarged. Amsterdam / New York: Rodopi.

Beekes, Robert S.P. 2010. *Etymological dictionary of Greek.* With the assistance of Lucien van Beek. Leiden: Brill. [2 vols]

Burlak, Svetlana A. & Il'ja B. Itkin. 2003. "A sound change that never happened: The fate of Proto-Tocharian **o* (B *o*) in Tocharian A". *Tocharian and Indo-European Studies* 10: 17–35.

Carling, Gerd. 2000. *Die Funktionen der lokalen Kasus im Tocharischen.* Berlin / New York: Mouton de Gruyter.

Carling, Gerd. 2009. *Dictionary and Thesaurus of Tocharian A. Part 1: A–J.* Compiled by Gerd Carling, in collaboration with Georges-Jean Pinault and Werner Winter. Wiesbaden: Harrassowitz.

CETOM = *A comprehensive edition of Tocharian manuscripts.* www.univie.ac.at/tocharian

de Vaan, Michiel. 2008. *Etymological dictionary of Latin and the other Italic languages.* Leiden: Brill.

Dragoni, Federico. 2022. *Watañi lāntaṃ. Khotanese and Tumshuqese Loanwords in Tocharian.* PhD thesis Leiden.

Filliozat, Jean. 1948. *Fragments de textes koutchéens de médecine et de magie. Texte, parallèles sanskrits et tibétains, traduction et glossaire.* Paris: Adrien-Maisonneuve.

Hilmarsson, Jörundur. 1989. "West Tocharian *särwāna* 'face'". *Tocharian and Indo-European Studies* 3: 77–90.

Krause, Wolfgang. 1952. *Westtocharische Grammatik. Band I. Das Verbum.* Heidelberg: Winter.

Leumann, Ernst. 1900. "Über eine von den unbekannten Literatursprachen Mittelasiens". *Mémoires de l'Académie Impériale des Sciences de St.-Pétersbourg,* VIIIe série, IV/8.

Malzahn, Melanie. 2010. *The Tocharian verbal system.* Leiden / Boston: Brill.

Ogihara Hirotoshi. 2012. "Tokarago B "Avadāna shahon" ni tsuite — The "Avadāna manuscript" in Tocharian B"". *Tōkyō Daigaku Gengogaku Ronshū — Tokyo University Linguistic Papers* 32: 109–243.

Ol'denburg, S. 1893. "Kašgarskaja rukopis' N. Ḟ. Petrovskago". *Zapiski Vostočnago Otdělenīja Imperatorskago Russkago Arxeologičeskago Obščestva* 7 (1892): 6–7.

Peyrot, Michaël. 2013. *The Tocharian subjunctive. A study in syntax and verbal stem formation.* Leiden / Boston: Brill.

Pinault, Georges-Jean. 2016a. "The Buddhastotra of the Petrovskii Collection". *Written Monuments of the Orient* 2016, issue 1: 3–20.

Pinault, Georges-Jean. 2016b. "Glossary of the Tocharian B Petrovsky Buddhastotra". *Tocharian and Indo-European Studies* 17: 213–247.

Sieg, Emil. 1952. *Übersetzungen aus dem Tocharischen II.* Aus dem Nachlass herausgegeben von Werner Thomas. Berlin: Deutsche Akademie der Wissenschaften.

Sieg, Emil. 1955. "Die medizinischen und tantrischen Texte der Pariser Sammlung in Tocharisch B". *Zeitschrift für Vergleichende Sprachforschung* 72: 63–83.

Sieg, Emil & Wilhelm Siegling. 1921. *Tocharische Sprachreste, I. Band. Die Texte. A. Transcription.* Berlin / Leipzig: de Gruyter.

Sieg, Emil & Wilhelm Siegling. 1949. *Tocharische Sprachreste, Sprache B, Heft 1, Die Udānālaṅkāra-Fragmente, Texte, Übersetzung und Glossar.* Göttingen: Vandenhoeck & Ruprecht.

Sieg, Emil & Wilhelm Siegling. 1953. *Tocharische Sprachreste, Sprache B, Heft 2. Fragmente Nr. 71–633.* Aus dem Nachlaß hg. v. Werner Thomas. Göttingen: Vandenhoeck & Ruprecht.

Sieg, Emil & Wilhelm Siegling. 1983. *Tocharische Sprachreste, Sprache B, Teil I: Die Texte. Band 1: Fragmente Nr. 1–116 der Berliner Sammlung.* Neubearbeitet und mit einem Kommentar nebst Register versehen von Werner Thomas. Göttingen: Vandenhoeck & Ruprecht.

Thomas, Werner. 1964. *Tocharisches Elementarbuch, II. Texte und Glossar.* Heidelberg: Winter.

Winter, Werner. 1977. “Internal structure and external relationship of two verbal paradigms: Tocharian B *weñ-*, A *weñ-* ‘say’”. *Journal of Indo-European Studies* 5: 133–159.

Telling, explaining, and instructing in Tocharian A: the semantics of the verbs *ākl-*, *āks-*, *en-*, *eśe yäp-*, *kärsā-* (caus.), *ṣärp-*

Maksim Vyzhlakov

This paper deals with a group of six verbs in Tocharian A denoting transmission of information and knowledge, which are often translated in a similar way. Although the amount of information is sometimes quite scarce, the author attempts to specify their semantics by analyzing the verbal arguments, as well as Old Uyghur and Sanskrit parallels. The author argues that only *ākl-* denotes teaching (in the educational sense). On the other hand, *āks-* has such meanings as 'tell', 'explain', and 'preach'. The semantics of the causative of *kärsā-* is more general: the verb focuses more on the recipient than on the theme and can be rendered as 'inform'. The other three lexemes are less close to this group of synonyms. While *en-* refers to correcting someone's behavior by instruction or coercion, *eśe yäp-* is characterized by a special attitude to the patient, expressing either paying attention to it or taking care of it. Finally, the literal meaning of *ṣärp-* is 'point [show something to somebody with a gesture]', while the metaphorical one can be approximately described as 'present, set forth [information]'.

There is a group of verbs[1] in Tocharian A which denote the transmission of information and knowledge. The alleged similarity in their meaning can be seen in the following table summarizing translations occurring in the lexicographical literature:

---

1 Of course, *eśe yäp-* is not a verb per se. However, it is an example of a construction, widely spread in Tocharian A, which can be interpreted as a "compound verb" (Burlak & Itkin 2013: 436). Cf. also Meunier (2013).

	Carling (2009: 28, 29, 72, 77, and 136 resp.)	Malzahn (2010: 521, 522, 540, and 929 resp.)	TEB II: 80, 80, 85, 86, 93, and 149 resp.	Poucha (1955: 16, 17, 38, 41, 70, and 341 resp.)	Itkin (2019a: 82, 82, 93, 94, 105, and 203 resp.)
ākl-	act. 'teach', mid. 'learn'	act. 'lehren; teach', mid. 'lernen; learn'	lernen, lehren	docere, discere	учить
āks-	announce, proclaim, instruct, teach (= Skt. *ā-deśaya-*)[2]	verkünden, lehren; announce, proclaim	verkünden, lehren	docere, tradere	преподавать
en-	teach, rule, punish	unterweisen, anordnen, beherrschen, bestrafen; instruct, rule, punish	unterweisen, befehlen	iubere, punire[3]	наставлять, советовать[4]
eśe yäp-/ yām-[5]	make aware, bring to awareness	-	wahrnehmen	aspectabiliter, manifeste[6]	обучать, просвещать
kärsā- (caus.)	let know, tell, announce[7]	wissen lassen, erkennen lassen, lehren; make know(n), teach[8]	wissen[9]	scire[9]	знать[9]

2 The stem is given as *ākṣiññ-*.
3 The stem is given as *e(n)-*.
4 Marked as causativum tantum (Itkin) or just causativum (Poucha).
5 For the sake of brevity, I will denote *yäp-/yām-* just as *yäp-* throughout the paper.
6 The meaning of *eśe* only.
7 The stem is given as *kärsā-*.
8 The stem is given as *kärs⁽ā⁾-*.
9 The meaning of the base verb.

	Carling (2009: 28, 29, 72, 77, and 136 resp.)	Malzahn (2010: 521, 522, 540, and 929 resp.)	TEB II: 80, 80, 85, 86, 93, and 149 resp.	Poucha (1955: 16, 17, 38, 41, 70, and 341 resp.)	Itkin (2019a: 82, 82, 93, 94, 105, and 203 resp.)
ṣärp-	—	hinweisen, unterweisen, erklären; indicate, explain, instruct	hinweisen	demonstrare, instituere, docere[4]	указывать[4]

It can be argued that each dictionary has a different translation for each lexeme. However, I cannot agree that they show the difference in their semantics clearly enough. For example, if Carling (2009) provides a translation 'teach' for *ākl-*, *āks-*, and *en-*, does it mean that these three verbs denote different kinds of teaching? Does it mean that *ākl-* is a hypernym in relation to *āks-* and *en-*? Are *āks-* and *en-*, which have additional meanings, really polysemic?[10] Besides this, how should we treat the fact that sometimes the cited scholars quite significantly disagree with each other? (Cf., for instance, translations of *en-* and *ṣärp-* by Malzahn (2010) and Itkin 2019a.) In my opinion, all such minor details make the apparent differences in the semantics of the discussed verbs rather questionable. That is why, in this paper, I would like to verify these translations and, to the extent that the data allows, determine what sets the meanings and usage of these lexemes apart.

Speaking of the composition of this word list, due to the partial overlapping in their translations, I treat the discussed verbs as near-synonyms

10 While someone may consider these problems insignificant within Tocharian studies, they may become more serious outside this field. Cf., for example, a complaint by the authors of a lexicostatistical database *NorthEuraLex*: "experts have a tendency to provide long lists of all the words that can be used for some concept, instead of focusing on the single most salient one" (Dellert et al. 2020: 288). In my opinion, such situations as the one presented in the table can hardly help if we search for the "most salient" word for the concept of teaching.

(not as full synonyms or sense synonyms)[11] which denote transmission of information and knowledge. Also, this group is not homogenous because not every verb overlaps with each other. (For example, *en-* and *kärsā-* (caus.) have a common meaning, but the latter does not overlap with *ākl-* and *āks-*, at least, according to Carling 2009.) Moreover, as we will see after the verification, some of these words should not belong to this group at all.

My approach to synonym analysis is close to the tradition and practice of the so-called Moscow school of semantics and the Moscow Lexico-Typological group.[12] For instance, linguists associated with this tradition compare the contexts within which the analyzed lexemes occur in order to find general differences between them as well as looking for stable collocations. Special attention is given to the syntactic constructions where the lexemes occur: in my case, I focus on the structure and the semantics of the verbal arguments (cf., for instance, Rakhilina et al. 2009: 72 ff.; Bonch-Osmolovskaya et al. 2009: 118–120; Rakhilina & Reznikova 2013: 9–10). Another important instrument in my analysis is the comparison of the Tocharian A lexemes with their counterparts in Old Uyghur and Sanskrit parallel texts. It should be emphasized that the analysis of each Tocharian A lexeme is not aimed at finding the "best" English word(s) to render it in every passage where it occurs. Instead, I try to generalize the preserved evidence[13] and to define each lexeme in the least vague way which can be applicable to this lexeme in (ideally) all of the contexts where it is attested[14] and which (ideally) can provide plausible scenarios

11 The terminology is according to Murphy (2003: 146 ff.).

12 The full implementation of their methods would be impossible because the object of my research differs both qualitatively and quantitively, as scholars in this tradition usually study living languages.

13 This, of course, means that this study can be heavily affected by even a small piece of new data. However, it is an inevitable drawback of every induction-based research, especially in the case of Tocharian A with its fragmentary and small corpus.

14 Thus, such generalization should not be understood as simple searching for the aforementioned "best" English words and then listing them as the meaning of the lexeme. It also seems that in many cases (especially those

of colexification, at the same time, allowing us to distinguish this lexeme from the others.[15]

In order to reduce misunderstanding in the interpretation of certain meanings and to have some reference point to which the semantics of the analyzed verbs can be compared, I will use the concepts and definitions of CONCEPTICON.[16] This choice can also be justified by the fact that these concepts and definitions are used (Rzymski et al. 2020: 2 ff.) in the *Database of Cross-Linguistic Colexifications* (CLICS), the data from which will be adduced in this paper as well.

Finally, it should be noted that I will cite a large number of passages in Tocharian A (as well as in Old Uyghur and Sanskrit). It should be emphasized that the main aim is to illustrate the contexts in which the discussed lexemes occur. (Cf. also fn. 14.) This means that on some occasions (when citing a translation made by another scholar, for instance) the rendering of a discussed lexeme in a specific translation may differ from my interpretation. In such cases, I will provide my rendering of said lexeme and leave it to the reader to judge whether this rendering fits the context appropriately. (In other words, my interpretations provide, first of all, the evidence of possibility of a given rendering in a given passage.)

Before we go any further, the Tocharian B cognates should also be listed for the sake of comparison (according to Adams 2013: 40, 41, 87, 112, 176, and 718 resp.):

ākl- bv.[17] 'learn', caus. 'teach';
āks- 'tell, announce, proclaim, instruct, issue [a proclamation or official document], recite, interpret [a sign]';
en- 'instruct, teach; punish';

---

which lack a good Old Uyghur parallel or a particularly unambiguous context) finding the "best" translation, based on considering whether it fits the passage or not, can be quite problematic.

15 In my opinion, such approach corresponds to the long-known definitional criterion of polysemy (see Geeraerts 2016: 237).

16 In case my definition is close to that of the chosen concept but does not coincide with it entirely, I will use ~ before the name of this concept.

17 Base verb.

aiśai yām- 'take care, take care of, handle, treat (of), pay attention to';
kärs- (caus.) 'make know(n), announce, teach';
ṣärp- 'explain to, inform; teach; indicate, guide, point (to)'.

ākl-

An analysis of this verb should distinguish between its lexicalized gerundive *ākälṣäl* and all the other forms. The former is significantly more frequent than the latter (33 and 17 tokens respectively). The meaning of *ākälṣäl* is 'disciple, pupil' (Carling 2009: 27), and I have found no cases where it is used in gerundive function. Thus, it can be excluded from the analysis. It is worth noting though that, among the analyzed words, there are no other forms or derivatives meaning 'disciple' or 'pupil'. This itself can point to the primary role of *ākl-* in the semantic domain of teaching.

As for the verb itself, it shows both transitive and ditransitive behavior. Its theme is marked by the accusative[18] and the recipient by the genitive. Take for instance the following passages:

A 302 b2

: *krant märkampal klyosäṃseñc* ***ākälsanträ*** *pikänträ* :
'... they hear, **learn** and write the good Law ...'[19]

A 213 b2

• *kospreṃ puklyi ko(s)pr(eṃ) manarkāśśi śāsträntu* ***ākläṣ*** •
'... how old is he? How many Śāstras does he **teach** to the Brahmin youths? ...'

In fact, the number of examples providing sufficient context and/or supported by the Old Uyghur parallels is not so particularly extensive

18 In this paper, I refer to the case denoting direct object as to 'accusative' instead of 'oblique'.

19 The translations I use for this paper follow the CEToM database (which is based on different sources), unless a different source is mentioned. The symbols in **my** translations are: (...) means reconstructed text; [...] means additional text which is needed for better understanding the phrase; <...> means other additional notes; (?) means questionable translation.

(there are eight of them), but they confirm the overall interpretation of this lexeme (provided in the table). These examples show that the transitive pattern is connected with the middle forms, expressing the concept of LEARN defined as "[t]o acquire, or attempt to acquire knowledge or an ability to do something", while the ditransitive pattern is connected with the active forms expressing the concept of TEACH, i.e., "[t]o pass on knowledge and skills".[20] Note that, according to the preserved data, both meanings tend to be narrower than these concepts, representing only the educational aspect of teaching and learning and thus excluding such understandings of 'learning' as 'learning from one's mistakes' or 'finding out'. (In other words, there is an opposition of conscious or volitional acquisition of knowledge and accidentally acquiring knowledge.) This educational aspect is supported by the fact that the theme objects of this verb belong to either elements and text of the Buddhist teaching (*märkampal* 'law, dharma', *śāsträ* 'shastra, teaching', *piṭaka*s (the baskets of sutras) or general *knānmune* 'wisdom':

A 32 b4

(///) ***ākluṣ*** *piṭak sutä(rṣi) ///*

'... they **have learned** the collection of sūtras ...'

A 222 b1

/// ***āklu*** *ysomo tri päräs*[21] **:**

'... **having learned** altogether the three piṭakas'. (the translation is mine)

A 260 b6

/// knānmune ***äkälseñc*** *(omä)skenäṣ älsanträ* •

'they **teach** wisdom, they keep away from the evil.'

The middle 'learn' can be seen as a semantically regular derivation from the active 'teach' and should be understood as 'to teach oneself', focusing on a special involvement or interest of the subject in the action, which

20 To be precise, the different transitivity patterns are mentioned in Carling (2009: 28).

21 "*tri-päräs* = *tripiṭakäntu*" (Couvreur 1956: 71).

is one of the primary functions of the Tocharian middle (see Malzahn (2010: 103) and Burlak & Itkin 2013: 420).

As for the verbal abstract, *ākälyune*, it has been attested only three times (two of which are in the parallel passages) and does not provide any new information:

A 213 b6–7 = YQ II.5 b2–3

|| *kus ne yas ṣome tosäṃ pärkluneytu pärkcär tmäṣ wākär ṣome ṣñi ṣñi* ***ākälyuneyaṃ*** *śla a(mokäntu) veda vyākaraṇa • lokāyana • horagaṇita • nakṣacarita purāṇä kₐpāraṃ mā(skyās sa)ñceyntu sākät kälymāṃ pältsäkyokk ats (lyu)krā särki ppärksāc-äṃ •*

'When [lit. who] some of you [pl.] have asked the questions mentioned, then some [others] on their part, each according to his **educational training**[22], in connection with skills as … Veda, grammar [*Vyākaraṇa*], materialism [*Lokāyatana*], horoscope and astrology [*Horāgaṇita*], dancing and acting [*Nāṭyacarita*], legends [*Purāṇa*], must ask him, one after the other, deep and difficult questions, quietly kept in your minds only.' (transl. Ji et al. (1998: 91, 93) and Peyrot 2013a: 645)

YQ II.12 a4–5

/// *(kā)mluneyaṃ* ***āklyuneyā*** *waṣtäṣ läntässi āklye yāmu pälkā*$_{a5}$*(t)* ///

'… **by being taught** (even in his mother's womb), having acquired the insight to go away from the house, he saw (?)'.

In the latter case, one of the reviewers suggested the rendering 'having acquired insight' because the presented translation seems quite unnatural. It is true that Maitreya could hardly be educated by someone in his mother's womb. However, if we interpret it simply as 'learning' (generally acquiring knowledge), it does not appear as outlandish. The same inter-

22 One of the reviewers offered 'discipline' or 'doctrine' instead. In my opinion, if we interpret these renderings as 'the way someone has been taught', then it would not be very different from 'training' or 'teaching' (as 'result of teaching'). Otherwise, I do not think this opinion holds true because there is no additional evidence or even indirect proof of it.

pretation can be applied to *āklye yāmu* (this word group will be treated below).[23]

In addition to that, there is an example of this lexeme as part of the compound *(ākä)lyune-ṣäññum* 'having learned independently, by oneself (?)'[24] (Itkin 2019a: 82):

A 251 + A 252 + A 306 + THT 1493 2–3

/// (: 1 ***ākä****)***lyune***-ṣäññumänt suträ vi(ny a)*$_3$*bhidharmaṃ ptāñkte wewñunt* **:**

'It is the one **who taught** (?) **himself** what is said by Buddha-god in Sūtra, Vinaya, and Abhidharma' (joined and transl. Itkin (2018: 125, 130), restoration (ibid.) and Carling 2009: 27).

We get a hint of new information from another derivative of *äkl-*, *āklye* 'study, instruction' = Skt. *śikṣā-*[25] (Carling 2009: 29). While Carling (ibid.) mentions it as a part of the construction *āklye yäp-* (mid.), meaning 'study'[26] and being presented in the form of acc. sg. only, it seems to be generally overlooked that there is no evidence of any independent usage of *āklye*. It is attested as a part of the construction with *yäp-* in 12 cases out of 16. The other three tokens are too damaged and it is only the fourth, A 353 a2, where *āklye /// mä(r)k(am)p(a)läntu*[27] corresponds to Skt. *śaikṣā dharmā* and the collocation with *yäp-* is less likely. In this case, independent usage can neither be proved nor ruled out (meaning that *āklye* can be a part of a periphrastic expression, as suggested in Ogihara 2009: 273). (This passage and its parallel will be described in the paragraph *The Sanskrit parallels*.) Returning to *āklye yäp-*, it should be noted that it does not have a theme nor a recipient, thus, 'study' should be understood as 'engage in study, grow in knowledge/skill by studying'. (This

23 There is an Old Uyghur parallel, MaitrHami 2, 13 b12–18. However, while it contains similar information, it does not precisely correspond to the Tocharian A original.

24 'самостоятельно изучивший (?)'.

25 For the analysis of Sanskrit counterparts, see the last paragraph.

26 Cf. Meunier (2013: 174): 'étudier, s'entraîner'.

27 Restoration Ogihara (2009: 271).

does not entirely match to the definition of STUDY, "[t]o follow a course of study; to be enrolled at an institute of learning".) In other words, this allegedly compound verb (cf. fn. 1.) semantically broadens the paradigm of *ākl-*, adding to the active ditransitive 'teach' and middle transitive 'learn' a third variant, namely, the middle intransitive 'study'. The only unclear detail is the collocation of this verb with objects in the locative. Cf.:

A 434 a1–2

> (/// *śā*)$_{\mathrm{a2}}$*snaṃ* ***ākle yal*** **:**
>
> '… [one] **should study** from (?) … the (do)ctrine…' (restoration Siegling, personal copy: 238;[28] the translation is mine).

YQ II.10 a5–6

> /// (*mahāka*)*lps*(*aṃ*) *ptāñäktaśśi kapśiṃñās pälkāluneyaṃ* ***āklye yāmu*** *āṣānik me*$_{\mathrm{a6}}$(*trak*) ///
>
> '… the venerable Metrak, **having been taught** by seeing the bodies of Buddhas in … great eons, …'
>
> My interpretation: '… **having studied** seeing the bodies …'

The amount and quality of the material is not enough to distinguish what semantic role is expressed by the locative here (stimulus? manner? instrument?). There is an Old Uyghur parallel for this passage, but it does not seem to be useful in this regard:

MaitrHami 2, 11 a30–b2

> .. *sansaz tümän maxaklpta bärü burxanlaray körü körü* ***ögränmiš*** *üčün siziksiz otyuraq uqtï* ..
>
> 'Weil er (d.i. Maitreya) gewohnt war, seit zahllosen Myriaden von Mahākalpas die Buddhas zu sehen, verstand er klar (Hend.)' (Geng & Klimkeit 1988: 152–155).[29]

28 https://www.univie.ac.at/tocharian/images/TS_Siegling/TS_Siegling_Page_238.png

29 Note that Old Uyghur passages and dictionary entries, cited in this paper, can use different systems of transcription. For instance, *ï* usually corresponds to *ı*, *γ* to *g*, *q* to *k*, *x* to *h*, *j* to *y*.

According to J. Wilkens (p.c.), the passage is not entirely clear, but the more literal translation of *burxanlaray körü körü ögränmiš* is 'he had learned to see the Buddhas one after the other'. In general, the semantics of OU *ögrän-*[30] seems to be close to the proposed interpretation of *āklye yäp-*: 'to study, to obtain skills' (DTS: 380). (The examples provided in (DTS: 380) show that the verb can be used both transitively and intransitively.) In any case, the OU passage does not give us enough information to understand TA *pälkāluneyaṃ āklye yāmu* with more precision.

As for *äkl-*, the Old Uyghur parallels support the previously described interpretation. The verb is quite consistently reflected with two related OU verbs, *bošgur-* (= *bošyur-*) 'to teach, to instruct' and *bošgun-* (= *bošyun-*) 'to learn, to study, to apprehend' (DTS: 113–114, cf. also Clauson 1972: 379–380). For A 260 b6, the parallel is:

MaitrHami 16, 13 b6–9

> .. *adnayuy [ay]ıy yawlaq törüdin tidip ädgü bilgä bilig* ***bosyursarlar*** ..
> 'andere am schlechten (Hend.) Gesetz hindert, welche Wesen gute Weisheit **lehren**' (Geng & Klimkeit 1985: 89, 109)[31]

A 286 b5

> – – *ñc pāpṣune pāsanträ knānmune* ***ā(kälsanträ)*** ///
> 'they preserve the morality and **learn** the knowledge'.

MaitrHami 16, 13 a28–30 = MaitrSengim Taf. 162 a17–19

> .. *bur[xan no] mınta süzük köngül[in busı b]irip čxsaput küzädip b[ilgä bilig]* ***bosyunsarlar*** ..
> 'und in der Lehre des Buddha mit reinem Herzen [Almosen gibt], die Gebote hält und Weisheit **lernt**'. (Geng & Klimkeit 1985: 89, 109; see also Tekin 1980: 141)

30 Hereinafter, the Old Uyghur headwords are given in the transcription as per Wilkens (2021). If the transcription in the cited source is different, the source variant is provided in the parentheses.

31 As for the other correspondences, see A 213 b2 = MaitrHami 2, 6 a3–5 and YQ II.11 a6 = MaitrHami 2, 12 b13–15.

Despite the fact that in the latter case the TA verb is almost entirely reconstructed, the reconstruction is highly plausible, because neither *bošgur-* nor *bošgun-* are attested among the renderings of the other analyzed TA verbs.

āks-

This verb is the most frequent one among the analyzed lexemes. It is represented by at least 78 examples, as well as by five[32] tokens of the verbal abstract *ākṣiñlune.*

Its first difference from *ākl-* is that *āks-* has only active finite forms and corresponds only to the 'teaching' side of *ākl-*. Just like the active paradigm of *ākl-*, *āks-* is mainly ditransitive, and its theme is marked by the accusative, whereas and the recipient is marked by the genitive. Cases where either the theme or the recipient are omitted can be treated as ellipsis. Cf.:

A 9 a3–4

|| *tmäṣ yaṃtrācāre käṣṣi lānt«a»c kälk cam wram lānt* ***ā(kṣi)***$_{\text{a4}}$***ññā***

'Thereupon the master mechanic went to the king and this matter to the king he **told** [saying]'.

A 217 a4–5

: *wärpā*$_{\text{a5}}$*(t* ***ā)ksissi*** *krañcäṃ märkampal mā =ryu praṣtaṃ okñäṣ ñäktas napenäs säm oṅkraci* **:**

'He [i.e., the Buddha] has consented **to teach** the good Law[33] [and] within a short time he will promote immortality for gods and humans.'

My interpretation: '**to preach**'.

A 231 b6

/// (pä?)rkäntär käṣṣiṃ ṣāmnāñ ***ākṣiñiṣ*** *wasäṃ pttāṃñkät* **:**

---

32 Although one of them, A 392 a2, is almost completely restored.

33 The recipient is omitted and should be 'to the world'. Cf. the previous sentence, A 217 a3: *ārkiśoṣṣis krant märkampal āksis(s)i* 'to teach the good Law to the world'.

'...the monks will (ask?) the teacher: "**Let** the Buddha-god **explain** [this] to us." ' (translation mine)

The passages A 9 a3–4 and A 231 b6 represent the other common renderings, 'to tell, to report' and 'to explain'. The former can also be illustrated by the following examples:

A 66 b6

/// (täm kaklyuṣuräṣ ārtañ) v(i)dehak riyäṣ lcär cam wram ṣñi ṣñi ypeyac kälkoräṣ lāñcäśśi ***ākṣiññār***

'(After having heard that, the envoys) went out from the city Videhaka [and] having come each to [their] countries, they **announced** that matter to the [respective] kings.'

My interpretation: '**told / reported**'.

A 261 b2 = YQ II.12 b7

upādhyāy pādharis caṣ wram ***(ākṣ)iññam*** *mänt ne täm ṣurmaṣ dakṣiṇāpath kälymeyaṃ (///)*

'... I **am going to report** this matter to Bādhari the teacher, therefore (I would like to go) to the land of Dakṣiṇāpatha.' (Ji et al. 1998: 127)

YQ II.12 b6–7

/// (kär)sor täṣ tñi kus ne was „pādhyāy caṣäk wram ***āksi***$_{b7}$***(ssi)*** *///*

'... it is known to you that we (have **to**) **report** this precise thing to (our) teacher!'

In fact, all of these different translations of the verb in question can be reduced to one rendering, 'to tell', provided we understand it as "[t]o talk about a story giving its details; to give a detailed account of" (the concept TELL). It should, however, be mentioned that there are no passages that present an equivalent of 'telling' as in 'telling a tale'. We are only left with cases that deal with the reporting of an event. From this standpoint, the link to the meaning 'to explain' is fairly transparent, even to the point where we cannot tell one from the other with full certainty. Cf. the concept of EXPLAIN: "[t]o inform about the reason for something, how something works, or how to do something". We can make out the difference if we assume that TELL focuses on the telling of a story and EXPLAIN focuses on accounting for details. It would seem logical to assume that, for the passages expressing TELL, the detail in common would be the absence of a recipient in situations being reported. In case of the examples with EXPLAIN, this detail is irrelevant. In all the following passages, the rendering 'to explain' seems more likely (cf. also the full context in A 65 b3–5 and PK NS 1 b1–3):

A 65 b3–5

kāru$_{b4}$*(ṇik nātäk se* ***pākṣi*****)*****ññā*****-ñi kucne tu wsār pälkoräṣ weñāṣt kupprene tsmāraṃ mā tāppus tāṣ mänt nu wsār tsmāraṃ tā*$_{b5}$*(ppus tākiṣ •)*
'Oh compassionate (lord, [my] son, **exp**)**lain** me what you said concerning the wheat: "If it is not consumed at the root." But how (could) the wheat be (consumed) at the root?' (CEToM, with corrections from Peyrot 2013a: 648).

PK NS 1 b1–3

: 1 ṣotre $_{b2}$ ***ākṣñam****-ci ṣpäṃ lyākaṣt āmsiṃ tarpas ṣtāmäntu āsunt sne* $_{b3}$ *oko :*
'The sign I **will teach** you. In a dream you saw ponds, grass, [and] trees dried out [and] without fruit.' (CEToM, with corrections by I.B. Itkin, p.c.).

My interpretation: '**will explain**'.

YQ II.4 b3–4 = A 212+216 b5

tmäk yas cami kapśiññaṃ taryāk $_{b4}$ *(wepi lakṣaṇäs lkā)tsi päskāyäs (ku)s ne tom yasäṃ śāsträntwaṃ nṣā* ***ākṣiññunt***
'then you go (and try to see) on his body the 3(2 marks) which **have been described** to you by me in [my] teachings' (based on Ji et al. 1998: 83).

My interpretation: '**have been explained**'.

YQ II.6 a4

/// v·kṣ«†ä» märkampalṣi kär paräṃ ***pākṣñā****-m pācar :*

'… **tell** us, oh father, the dignity and glory of the Law!'

My interpretation: '**explain**'.

There is also a relatively large group of examples where the theme object of *āks-* is *märkampal* 'law, dharma'. Going through this group, we can also find an intransitive-like construction without either theme or recipient. This construction does not appear to be elliptic, as would be the case of TELL and EXPLAIN:

A 217 a4–5

: *wärpā*$_{a5}$*(t* ***ā*)*ksissi*** *krañcäṃ märkampal mā=ryu praṣtaṃ okñäṣ ñäktas napenäs säm oṅkraci* :

'He [i.e., the Buddha] has consented **to teach** the good Law [and] within a short time he will promote immortality for gods and humans.'

My interpretation: '**to preach**'.

YQ III.2 a3–4

• *tmäṣ ptāñkät käṣṣi ṣī märkampal* ***ākṣiṃñā*** *okä*$_{a4}$*(t tmāṃ) /// (pa)räṃ kälpānt* •

'Then Buddha-god the teacher **preached** the Law for the first time, eight(y thousand) … (Śākyas) attained the glory.'

YQ III.2 a4

• *trit* ***ākṣiññā*** *śtwar tmāṃ śākkiñ paräṃ kälpānt*

'He **preached** for the third time, [and] forty thousand Śākyas attained the glory.'

The collocation with *märkampal* and the fact that it occurs in passages which quite clearly describe a situation of sermons allow me to posit that this lexeme does not have the meaning TEACH in these cases, unlike *ākl-*. Instead, I contend that its meaning is PREACH, "[t]o deliver a sermon". It is, in fact, hard to even distinguish whether 'to preach' itself should be considered as an independent meaning, because it can also be rendered as 'to explain (the Law)'. From a typological point of view, colexified pairs of both TELL – EXPLAIN and TELL – PREACH are not unique among the languages of the world, although they are relatively rare. According to CLICS, the former is attested 15 times in 12 languages, while the latter is attested 9 times in 8 languages.[34] It is interesting that one of the few languages combining TELL – EXPLAIN – PREACH in one lexeme is Tibetan, the ancestor of which certainly maintained a certain level of contact with the Tocharian languages.[35]

This leaves us with the question of whether *āks-* presents the meaning of 'to teach' at all. Just like 'tell' and 'explain' are a hard pair to distinguish individually, the difference between 'explain' / 'preach' and 'teach' is not easy to tackle. However, in general, *ākl-* shows a greater level of connection with the semantics of TEACH due to such forms as *ākälṣäl*, the main word for 'pupil, disciple', or the middle paradigm presenting the meaning 'to learn'. I should also mention that in the *Maitreyasamiti-Nāṭaka* there are at least two scenarios which can be labeled as 'teaching'. The first one is the activity taking place in Bādhari's school with his pupils as the recipients. This activity is usually denoted by *ākl-*,[36] but not by *āks-*.[37] The second scenario that may correspond to 'teaching' is propagating or spreading the word about the Law by the Buddha, and it is denoted by *āks-*,[38] not by *ākl-*.[39] Moreover, it is TELL which tends to be the primary concept for

34 The data is far from exhaustive, but it can show at least the relative frequency. For instance, the colexification of TELL and SAY is attested 56 times in 50 languages.

35 I.B. Itkin (p.c.) suggests that both cases might be a calque from Sanskrit. Unfortunately, I have not found any Sanskrit parallels for *ākl-* proper.

36 Four times. More precisely, in A 213 b2, YQ I.2 a7, YQ I.3 a6, and YQ II.11 a6. Note also, that at least in the first and the fourth passages the teacher is certainly Bādhari.

37 The only counterexample is YQ II.4 b3–4. However, the activity described in this passage tends to be more specific than general teaching, connected with considering a particular question (the 32 signs) within Bādhari's "course" (*yasäṃ śāsträntwaṃ* 'in my teachings'). 'Explain' seems more natural here, and it is supported by the Old Uyghur parallel (see below).

38 Nine times, in my estimation.

39 According to one of the reviewers, 'teach' should be the rendering in (YQ III.12 b7–8) /// *(wä)rp[o]räṣ waltsurā tsru caṃ citrarathes märkampal* ***ākṣiññurä***$_{b8}$*(ṣ)* /// 'having received ..., and **having** briefly **proclaimed**

āks- (the contexts containing such usage are usually quite unambiguous and the renderings tend to be irreplaceable by 'explain' or 'preach'). Both TEACH and TELL are fairly general concepts and their colexifications seem to be less likely (at least, CLICS does not contain any such cases). It seems that the closest examples of *āks-* as 'teaching' are those where it used in connection with 'writing', especially the one where *āks-* collocates with *akṣar* 'syllable; system of writing' (Carling 2009: 4):

A 273 b4–6

|| *ratna(śi)kh(i)näṣ ṣu śākya*$_{b5}$*(muni ṣolar māk ptāñktañ käṣṣiñ ñäktas napenäśśi tmānäntu wältsantu kä)ntantuyo māk* **:** *akṣar lame yomuṣ akṣar* ***āksiṣa***$_{b6}$***(ntāñ*** *cemäk nāṃtsuṣ ṣeñc cesmäṣ cam brāhmī ñom akṣar peke piktsi āklye yāmwe näṣ)* ||

'From Ratnaśikhin onwards until Śākya(muni many Buddha-gods, teachers, to many gods and mortals by the ten thousands, by the thousands,) by the hundreds, the ones who have attained the realm of script, (these ones were) the **teach(ers)** of the [proper] script, (from them I have learned to write this script and writing named Brāhmī.)'[40]

My interpretation: '**those who explain**'.

A 311 a5

(///) ***ākṣiññār***-*äm krañś ptāñkte märkampal pekluneṣi pñi* **:**

'the good ones **have taught** us the merit of writing the Law of the Buddha Lord ...'

My interpretation: '**have explained**'.

But even in these cases, the 'explain' rendering does make sense. In the case of A 273 b4–6, the Old Uyghur supports the 'preaching' interpretation (for the correspondence and restoration, cf. Pinault (2013: 215–216); see also fn. 42).

some basic teaching of the Law to Citraratha, ...' Yet, I see the fragment as essentially dealing with the aforementioned propagating of the Law. This makes the rendering 'preach' no less preferable, in my view.

40 While the translation is after CEToM, I have corrected the parentheses to show the restoration in a more precise manner.

The Old Uyghur parallels also invite us to consider 'preaching' as an independent meaning. To render it, Old Uyghur uses the verb *nomla-* 'to preach the law, to preach, to explain a doctrine' or the figura etymologica *nom nomla-* with the same meaning. (DTS: 360–361; see also Clauson 1972: 778) Cf., for instance, the parallels for YQ III.2 a3–4 and YQ III.2 a4 mentioned above:

MaitrHami 3, 2 a14–17

> .. *anta ötrü tngri tngrisi burxan ang ilki bir qurla* ***nom nomlayu*** *yrlï[qamïš]ta säkiz tümän šakilar qutqa tägdi* (.)
> 'Als dann der Göttergott Buddha zum ersten Mal **das Gesetz zu predigen** ge[ruhte], erlangten 80000 Śākyas das Heil.' (Geng & Klimkeit 1988: 174–175)

MaitrHami 3, 2 a19–21

> .. *üčünč qata* ***nom nomlayu*** *yrlïqamïšta tört tümän šakilar qut bultïlar* ..
> 'Als er zum dritten Mal **das Gesetz zu predigen** geruhte, fanden 40000 Śākyas das Heil.' (ibid.: 176–177)[41]

At the same time, the other meanings of *āks-* are covered by the Old Uyghur verbs *ay-* (= *aj-*, '1. to speak, to tell; to make clear, to explain; 2. to call (to name); 3. to give instructions, to make arrangements; to command') and its causative *ayıt-* (= *ajït-*), which can in fact have non-causative semantics ('1. to cause to tell~speak; 2. to ask; 3. to demand an answer; 4. to show, to instruct; 5. to speak, to say'). (DTS: 25 and 29–30 resp.)

A 274 a3

> **: pākṣiññā**-*m käṣṣi ku(s ///)*
> '**Tell** us, o teacher! What...' (Peyrot & Semet 2016: 367–368)

MaitrHami 11, 2 b26–28

> .. *a[nı] amtı biziŋ[ä]* ***ayu*** *beriŋ nä asıg tusu kut kıv siziŋä kälgälir* ..

41 As for the other correspondences, cf. A 257 a2 = MaitrHami 11, 11 a6–11 and A 273 b4–6 = MaitrHami 11, 15 a27 – 16 a3.

'Now **say** this to us: What profit and power are about to come to you?' (ibid.: 359, 362)

For YQ II.4 b3–4, the parallel is:

MaitrHami 2, 5 a3–7
(.) *anta siz-lär ang ilki iki qïrq irü blgü qutïn buyanïn adïrtlayalï uqyalï qataylanïnglar kim siz-lärkä šasatarlarda* ***adartlayu ayïtdïm*** *ärdi ..*
'dann möget ihr euch bemühen, zuerst die 32 guten Zeichen (*lakṣana*) der Würde [des Buddha] zu unterscheiden und zu verstehen, die ich euch aus den Śāstras klar **detailliert beschrieben** habe.' (Geng & Klimkeit 1988: 126–127)

There is also a correspondence with OU *okı-* (= *oqï-*) 'to call (summon)' (DTS: 369). However, a substantial part of the Tocharian A fragment is lost, so we cannot know for sure if the correspondence is precise. For instance, the Tocharian A passage could include a construction of the absolutive and a noun (e.g., 'having issued [lit. 'told'] the call').

YQ II.11 b7
/// ***ākṣiññuräṣ*** *träṅkäṣ ||*
'... **having pronounced**, he says:'

MaitrHami 2, 13 a17–19
.. anta ötrü tngri tngrisi burxan ikilä ol urïlaray ***oqïp*** *inčä tip yrlïqadï ..*
'Dann **rief** der Göttergott Buddha wiederum jene Jünglinge **herbei** und geruhte, so zu sprechen' (Geng & Klimkeit 1988: 160–161).

en-

This verb is represented only by three (or four – see below) examples, as well as 10 tokens of the verbal abstract *enäṣlune* (based on the sbj. II stem) and one token of the adjective *enäṣluneṣi*, derived from it. Besides that, there is one example of the verbal abstract based on the sbj. VII stem, *eñlune*.

All of the preserved examples of the verbal forms are transitive, with only middle finite forms attested:

A 63 b1–2

|| *tmäṣ säm rupyāvate wäl bodhisatveṃ tsopatsäṃ kāruṇaśśäl triwont āṣträṃ knānmuneyo wlyepäṃ* $_{b2}$ *(tsaryo swāräṃ ra)keyo poñcäṃ potoyo puk wrasas ṣya wkäṃ pältsäkyo* ***enäsmāṃ***

'Then this king Rūpyāvata with pure knowledge, mixed with great compassion of a Bodhisattva, with soft (hand and pleasant) speech [kept] **instructing** all beings with all respect and with equal thought.' (CEToM, with corrections by I.B. Itkin and me)

My interpretation: '**edifying**'.

A 256 a4–5

: *pyām yärk krañcäśśi* ***peṃṣār*** *ykoñcä(s yaläntwä)* $_{a5?}$ *ṣ* **:**

'Pay homage to the good ones [and] **punish** the negligent ones (because of [their negligence of their] duties)!'

My interpretation: '**admonish**'.

The meaning of *enäsmāṃ* in A 63 b1–2 can be interpreted quite loosely. For instance, 'teach' could fit here as well. On the other hand, this particular verb is already different from the previous ones due to the fact that it marks the recipient object by the accusative and not the genitive. Unfortunately, the amount of material does not give us enough leeway to judge whether this verb has a theme object at all. Still, considering its argument structure, we can get a hint of a different focus in the semantics than *ākl-* and *āks-*. As for the 'punishing' semantics assumed by the translation of A 256 a4–5, cf. the definition of PUNISH: "To inflict pain, suffering or loss on somebody who has broken a law or done something wrong" (CONCEPTICON). This definition can generally be applied to A 256 a4–5, but it will not work with A 63 b1–2 in that it does not show any alleged focus on any kind of harm to a wrong-doer. Cf. also the following context in A 63 (translation): 'Having acknowledged the good behavior of the beings, attentively the great gods, (the Asuras), [and] the chiefs of the Yakṣas ensured [lit. made] the protection of the country because of the constant performing of ceremonies in that manner.' (CEToM) So we can assume that the behavior of the beings was improper, but king Rūpyāvata mended their behavior through his instructions and then the land received the favor of the gods.

There is also a potential fourth example, if we accept the following conjecture by Geng et al. (2004: 53):

A 256 a3–4

lyukrā kakmusāṃ purpār tkaṃ (***enä***)$_{a4}$***ssi*** *se* **:**

'receive the land that has come (to you) by succession **in order to rule** (it)' (transl. Carling 2009: 73)

Given that the addressee of this imperative is the same as in a4–5 above (Udrāyaṇa), if we accept this conjecture and translation, as well as the translation of a4–5, we may conclude that this lexeme was used within one small fragment with very distinctive meanings, which, however, seems unlikely. (Thus, either the conjecture is wrong or the semantics of *en-* differs at least from one of the interpretations.) But let us now compare this information with the examples of the verbal abstract and the derived adjective:

A 131 b3

/// (trä)ṅkäṣ (mā?) tswāt ***enäṣlune*** *///*

'...says: "[He/she] did (not?) obey the **instruction**...'. (restoration I.B. Itkin, p.c.; the translation is mine)

A 342 a2

tämyo täm ñi kälṣäl caṣäṣ ***enäṣluneṣiṃ*** *erkātune* ||

'Therefore I must bear the vexation **of instruction** from him.' (based on CEToM)

A 353 a6

• *käṣṣiyāp* ***enäṣlune*** *pañitswātsäṃ lutkäsmā(ñcsā) /// (mä)s(ka)l nä(m) taṃne wkä(nyo) āklye yal* ||

'provided with the same instruction, having become one (like) water (and) milk, making splendid the **doctrine** of the teacher [guru-]. It should be learned in this way.' (restoration and translation Ogihara 2009: 272)

A 354 b5
: *pritwä(s) ptāñäkte* ***enäṣluneyaṃ*** :
'Be linked with the **instruction** of Buddha!' (ibid.: 275–276)

A 354 b6
kusne nu caṣ märka(m)p(a)lṣi ***enäṣlun(eyaṃ*** *sn)e (y)korñe tāṣ : wawikuräṣ cmo(lwāṣiṃ sark klopis ākā yäṣ 14)*
'He who in the **discipline** of the law will not be careless, who has taken away the cycle of birth, he will go to the end of sorrow.'
My interpretation: 'Whoever will be not neglectful to the **edification** of this law'.

In general, the recipients of this verb do not show any visible semantic similarities, which is not the case for the agent. The 'instruction' comes from a higher or wiser creature, e.g., the Buddha, a teacher, king Rūpyāvata, prince Udrāyaṇa. As one of the reviewers noted, this can be applied to the act of teaching as well. This is true, but for *äkl-* and its 'teaching' there are no collocations with the political figures attested.

Moreover, there are several additional details which, if they are true, deviate from TEACH. A 131 b3 represents *enäṣlune* as something that can go against the will of the recipient (as he obeys or disobeys). A 342 a2 shows that it can be unpleasant. A 354 b6, if we accept my interpretation of this passage, also focuses on the fact that *enäṣlune* can be accepted or rejected by the recipient. It also imposes on him some demands to be fulfilled (this aspect is not seen in the other verbs). On the other hand, there is no sign of any harmful impact in any of these passages, so the translation 'punish' is probably not completely correct, although, as we have seen above, the "instruction" can have a shade of unpleasantness or assume some kind of coercing the recipient (the recipient is bound to obey). A 63 b1–2 probably focuses on this particular aspect: king Rūpyāvata admonishes living beings, but, unlike a common kind of admonishing, he does this in a very pleasant, unforceful way.

It is certainly possible that the semantics of this verb and the derived noun was separated into two meanings: 'edify' and 'punish', but the preserved material is far too limited to reach such conclusion. It seems then that a better option in these circumstances would be to summarize the overall sense of the verb as 'to correct one's behavior by instruction or coercion'. The focus on correcting someone clearly distinguishes this verb from the others, which represent teaching as transferring knowledge.

As for *eñlune* (sbj. II), Malzahn (2010: 540) posits that it differs semantically from *enäṣlune*, meaning not 'instruction', but 'advice':

A 11 a5

: *kälymeyā* ***eñlune*** *keṃpar eṃtsāt pracri nakt-äṃ kärparäṃ* :

'The proper **advice** from his brother he misinterpreted and the (good) dignity was lost for him.'

The difference between 'instruction' and 'advice' is very subtle and can hardly be assured on the basis of a singular passage or even a singular fragment. On the one hand, if we look at the previous leaf, A 10ext[42], its context clearly shows that Daśagriva asks his retinue for advice: "What should now be done with respect to him[43]?" (CEToM) – to which Vibhīṣana gives his opinion. In addition, it is certain that Vibhīṣaṇa does not possess a higher ranking than king Daśagriva. On the other hand, Vibhīṣaṇa's advice is arguably admonishing: '…(Our) enemy is powerful. (He), however, having got his cause (Sītā), will go away willingly, being joyful. (You are talking) for (your) own harm: "One should not give away (Sītā) to him!" From what has this "wisdom" been born, (which leads) to its own perishing?'[44] (I.B. Itkin, p.c.)[45]. Moreover, in A 11, we can see the

42 A 10 + THT 1646.c + THT 1370.b, joined by I.B. Itkin (p.c.).

43 Rāma.

44 '… (Наш) враг могуществен. (Он), однако, свое дело (т.е. Ситу) получив, радуясь, уйдет сам по себе. Себе во вред (ты говоришь:) "(Ситу) ему не следует отдавать!"! От чего же родилась эта "мудрость", (ведущая) к собственной погибели?'.

45 Pace Sieg (1944: 13), CEToM, and—for A 10 b1—Peyrot (2013a: 277).

same focus on accepting/rejecting the 'instruction' (*eṃtsāt* 'took'), and the a5 passage supports the fact that Vibhīṣaṇa was wiser than his brother.

eśe yäp-

This word group is represented by 12 examples, only half of which have at least some context. It is a combination of the verb *yäp-/yām-* 'to do' and the adverb *eśe* 'aware, into cognizance' (Carling 2009: 77). In fact, as Meunier (2013: 147) shows, the rendering of the latter is based on the semantics of the Tocharian B verb *aik-*, 'to know, to recognize' (Adams 2013: 107; the cognate of *eśe*, TB *aiśai*, is an old action noun derived from *aik-*). Neither TA *eśe* nor TB *aiśai* occur independently but only as a part of one or two constructions respectively. One of these Tocharian B constructions, *aiśai yam-*, as we have seen above, is rendered by D.Q. Adams as 'take care, take care of, handle, treat (of), pay attention to', while he also posits the translation 'take care of, handle, treat' for the Tocharian A counterpart (ibid.: 112), which contradicts both with the opinions evidenced in the initial table and with the opinion of Meunier (2013: 147), who provides a twofold definition (for both verbs), 'prendre connaissance de, prêter attention à'. In order to check whose version is more plausible, let us consider all the relatively well-preserved passages:[46]

A 76+83 b6 + THT 1382.k a2[47]
/// lāntune entse ypeyu ***yśe yatsi*** **:**

46 There is also this ambiguous passage, A 386 a2–3: • *säs prāmodya träṅkträ* • *oktasāṃ ytār* ***yśeś*** *yāmuntāp kus ne säm ṣūrmaṣ tām praṣtaṃ tsārwo kācke kātäṅkāṣ* $_{a3}$ *säm prāmodya plānto träṅkträ* • || 'Dies wird prāmodya genannt: Was dem, der den achtfachen Weg verwirklicht, daraus [wtl. deswegen] zu der Zeit [als] freudige Erregung [und] Sehnsucht entsteht, das wird prāmodya "Freude" genannt.' (Schmidt 1974: 223) Here, *yśeś* is probably a scribal error. If it is an error for *yśe*, then it is the only passage where the 'aware' meaning is undisputable. However, I share Couvreur's opinion (1956: 72), that "*yśeś* (386 a 2) ist verschrieben für *yneś* «deutlich»". Thus, it can be excluded from the analysis.

47 For the joining of those fragments, see Itkin & Malyshev (2021: 62).

'... [I] took the kingship **in order to take care** of the realms.' (translation mine)

A 153 b3

/// wram pättāñkät käṣṣi ***eśe yāmtsāt***

'The Buddha-teacher **comprehended** (this) matter' (Itkin & Malyshev (2021: 69).

My interpretation: '**paid attention to**'.

A 212 b1 = YQ II.4 a7

: *mäṃt ne* $_u$*pādhyāy āklāṣlye* ***eśe yalye*** *täm näṣ yas* ***eśe yāmpe*** **:**

'... to whatever extent pupils **can be brought to awareness** by a teacher, (that) I **have made** you **aware** of ...'

My interpretation: '**can be taken care of ... have taken care of** you'.

A 260 a4

/// p$_u$*kaṃ mā (te) sam kāruṃ c(i) k*$_u$*yal mā* ***eśe yatār****-äṃ 1*

|| '...is your compassion not same to all? Why don't you **take care** of him/her/it?' (restoration Carling (2009: 115); transl. (ibid.) with my addition)

A 371 a1

|| $_i$***śe*** *täṣ* ***pyāmtsār*** *śolasuts tapakäṃte*[48] *ṣäk nidānaṃ śtwar pārāje(s) śäk täryā p(i) saṅgh(āvaśeṣ) ///*

48 The division and meaning of the sequence *tapakäṃte* is unclear.

> '**Pay attention** to it, the venerable[49] one <f.>, *tapakäṃte*, six [passages?][50] in the introduction, four pārājikas[51], thirteen saṅgh(āvaśeṣas)[52]...' (restoration Couvreur 1956: 75 and Siegling, personal copy: 206;[53] translation mine).

Note that all the attested finite forms are middle and are more likely to be transitive than intransitive. However, the gerundive in A 212 b1 = YQ II.4 a7 certainly conveys the passive meaning (while the finite form in the same sentence is transitive). Another problem is that while the patient is always present, the theme (which should be expected if the verb expresses the transmission of information) is either absent or unclear (in other words, to make aware of what?). In A 212 b1 = YQ II.4 a7 and A 371 a1, there are the pronouns *täm* and *täṣ*. In A 153 b3, there is *wram*, '(this) thing'. It makes verifying the 'making aware' meaning particularly difficult.

The only informative evidence we may have access to can be gathered through Old Uyghur parallels. There are two such instances, the first for A 212 b1 = YQ II.4 a7 (cited above, p. 201):

49 "*śolassu* nicht «vitalis», sondern «ehrwürdig» (= skr. *āyuṣmant-*)" (Couvreur 1956: 69).

50 S.V. Malyshev (p.c.) suggests that this can refer to the "list" of six passages in the introduction of the *Prātimokṣasūtra* of the Sarvāstivādins (Einleitung III, cf. von Simson 2000: 159–160) and that this and the following lines resemble the beginning of the final part of the *Prātimokṣasūtra* (cf. passages from A 353–354 below).

51 "the first four items in the list of the monk's code of discipline [...] which forbid sexual intercourse, theft, killing, and boasting of higher states." (Irons 2008: 378)

52 Another set of the monastic rules: "Of the second category of precepts, *saṅghāvaśeṣas*, bhikṣus in all schools have thirteen, whereas *bhikṣuṇīs* in the Dharmagupta and Theravāda have seventeen, and *bhikṣuṇīs* in the Mūlasarvāstivāda have twenty." (EoB II: 668)

53 https://www.univie.ac.at/tocharian/images/TS_Siegling/TS_Siegling_Page_206.png.

MaitrHami 2, 4 b17–19

.. *nä ymä baxšïlarnïng titsilarqa* **qïlγuluq iš ködüg** *ärti ärsär*(,) *alqunï mn tükäl* **qïltïm** (.)

'Was auch die **Tat** sein mag, die ein Lehrer für die Schüler **tun muß**, das **habe** ich alles vollständig **getan**.' (Geng & Klimkeit 1988: 126–127)

Cf. also more literal translation by J. Wilkens (p.c.):

'Whatever the **deeds** (hend.) **one would expect** from teachers **to be done** with regard to (their) pupils, all these I **have accomplished**'.

Here we can find the OU verb *kıl-* (=*qïl-*), both independently and as a part of a pleonastic ('do deeds') construction. It is clear that the semantics of *kıl-* itself[54] is not very useful. However, 'deeds' stresses that the passage deals with a behavioral activity instead of a psychological one.

And the other parallel is for A 260 a4 (cited above, p. 201):

MaitrHami 16, 12 b13–15 = MaitrSengim Taf. 161 b3–5

.. *alquqa tüp tüz yrlıqančučı biligi[n]g ärür .. inčä ọkmu* **körü tutarsn** (.)

Cf. several translations:

'(Obwohl) deine Barmherzigkeit für alle ganz gleichmäßig ist, ***behandelst** du (mich doch aber) gerade so?' (Tekin 1980: 140)

'Deine Barmherzigkeit ist (doch) über alle gleich. Kannst du das wohl **sehen** und **aushalten** (d.h. ohne bewegt zu werden)?' (Geng & Klimkeit 1985: 88, 108)

'Your compassion is the same (hend.) with respect to everybody. Do you **regard** (the issue) like this?' (J. Wilkens, p.c.)

As we can see, the interpretation of this Old Uyghur passage is much less clear. OU *kör-* is '1. to see, to look; 2. to obey, to surrender; 3. to experi-

54 '1. to do, to make, to create, to construct; 2. to do, to act, to behave in a certain way; 3. to turn into someone/something; 4. *fig.* to have an affair with a woman [...]' (DTS: 442).

ence; 4. to listen, to perceive […]' (DTS: 317). Still, Geng & Klimkeit's variant is unlikely (here, *tut-* is an auxiliary verb meaning a continuous action).[55] What we can say about this passage is that it does not deal with 'awareness' either, but is more likely to describe a behavior or an attitude.

Combining the Tocharian and Old Uyghur evidence, we can say that D.Q. Adams's interpretation is more plausible. However, the Old Uyghur translations tend to be too imprecise to help us in further specifying the semantics. If we try to find an interpretation which would fit well at least to all the mentioned Tocharian A passages, I think it is possible to generalize the meaning of the discussed verb as 'to pay attention', both literally (to some information or detail) and figuratively (to pay attention to someone > to take care of him/her). This would not entirely exclude the possibility of a more general meaning like 'to treat' (if we understand this as 'to behave towards someone in a certain way'), but there is no unambiguous evidence which show us, for example, treating someone badly. Thus, we are left only with a "positive" treatment which can be equaled with 'taking care'.

kärsā- (caus.)

This verb is represented by 17 examples. Even at a glance we can distinguish that, from a semantic point of view, the verb tends to be a "true" causative of *kärsā-* (bv.) which means 1) 'to understand, to realize' 2) 'to get to know, to learn'; 3) 'to recognize, to consider A as B' (for the analysis of its semantics and comparison with *knā-*, see Vyzhlakov 2021: 50–63). It seems that *kärsā-* (caus.) corresponds only to the second meaning of the base verb. The situation, however, is made more complex by the voice alternations. Technically speaking, they are not present in the case of this verb, because, among its finite forms, only the active (transitive) ones are attested. Their semantics can be summarized as 'to inform [to make someone aware]'. Unlike the previous verbs, the recipient of *kärsā-* (caus.) is marked by the accusative, whereas the theme ('inform about

55 J. Wilkens (p.c.).

what?') is not expressed at all. (However, there are only few examples preserving enough of the context to allow us to exclude the presence of the theme.) In other words, the distinction between *āks-* and *kärsā-* (caus.) is of a similar nature as the difference between the English *to tell* and *to inform* respectively. Given the different argument structure, it is possible that *kärsā-* (caus.) focuses more on the general fact of informing than on detailed accounting (unlike *āks-*); cf.:

YQ I.7 b2–4

> || *māṇibhadre träṅkäṣ piṣ tu bādhariṃ* ***pśärs*** *nä*$_{b3}$*(ṣ) /// śtwar lāñś tsopatsäṃ ynāñmuneyo ñäkciṃ ārkiśoṣṣäṣ ṣu peṃ winässi wo*$_{b4}$*(tkar-ñi)* /// ||
>
> 'Maṇibhadra says: Go and **tell** Badhari; (I will go to the noble Metrak and tell him that Indra and) the four kings have ordered to (come) from the divine world to honor his feet with great respect, …'
>
> My interpretation: '**inform**'.

YQ III.2 b2–3

> */// ymār ymār śākkeśši lānt* ***śaśärs*** *śākkeśši nātäk śuddhodaṃ wäl penu ca*$_{b3}$*(ṣ) ///*
>
> 'Very quickly she **informed** the king of the Śākyas. The lord of the Śākyas, king Śuddhodana, also this …'

YQ I.7 a5–6 = A 215 b6

> */// (ñäkta)ñ«ṭä» bram ñkät* ***śaśärsār*** *kar • bram ñkät śkaṃ wlāñkät* ***śaśärs*** *wlāñkät śkaṃ* $_{a6}$ *vai(śravaṃ śaśärs) ///*
>
> '… (the Śuddhāvāsa gods) **told** only God Brahmā, and God Brahmā **told** Indra, and Indra (told King) Vai(śravaṇa)'.
>
> My interpretation: '**inform**'.[56]

There are, however, several passages containing different non-finite forms, which, in Tocharian A, are generally neutral with respect to voice. The analysis of these cases leads to two or even three different meanings, which are probably connected with the valency alternations.

56 One of the reviewers suggested this as well.

The first meaning is attested by a single example, being expressed by the infinitive, and it may coincide with what I have proposed for the finite forms. However, the fragment is badly damaged, and its translation depends on its Old Uyghur parallel:[57]

MaitrHami 1, 13 a17–18

*.. antay ärsär tüz-ün maitriq[a] oq **uqïtyalï aymaz** ..*

'Wenn das so ist, warum **teilt** er es nicht gerade dem edlen Maitreya **mit**?' (Geng & Klimkeit 1988: 96–97)

YQ I.7 a4 = A 215 b5

*/// **śärsäs(s)i** (mā wo)tka-m ||*

'… did not (order) us **to make known**?'

My interpretation: '… did not (order) us **to inform**'

The second meaning can be considered as the passive variant of 'to inform [to make someone aware]'. In this role, the infinitive and the past participle are attested. Cf. the following passages:

A 7 a1–2

*tämyo sās ñi ṣñaṣṣeyāp ṣñi lyutār pāk śkaṃ (lkā)$_{a2}$tsi krāṃtso nasluneyā mā yātalyi tuṅ⫽ **śärsässi***

'Therefore this one as [she is] affiliated to my relative and mainly in her being beautiful to look at must not **be made aware** of the love.'[58]

YQ I.1 a3 = A 288 b2

*tāpä«r»k ṣakk ats klyom metrak śuddhavāṣinäs ñäktasā **śaśärsu***

'Now, surely the noble Metrak **was instructed** by the Śuddhāvāsa gods'.

My interpretation: '**was informed**'.

Note that YQ I.1 a3 only displays a recipient while lacking a theme. A 7 a1–2 is probably the only example containing both arguments, but the syntax of the phrase is fairly complex, which makes understanding it

57 I am thankful to one of the reviewers for drawing my attention to this parallel.

58 One of the reviewers suggested that '**informed**' or '**told**' fits better here.

much harder. Nevertheless, if the middle semantics is possible, it does raise the question of whether *kärsā-* (caus.) has the middle paradigm.

The third group is represented by the infinitive and the *m*-participle and expresses the transitive meaning 'to make known':

A 72 a5

/// kä devadattenäṣṣ aci yleṃ krop camä(-k) wram ***śärsäsmāṃ*** *(///)*

'... (der Bodhisattva ging zu) Devadatta und der Gazellenherde, um diese Sache **zu verkünden**.' (Peyrot 2013b: 168)

My interpretation: '**to make known**'

A 215 b3–4 = YQ I.7 a2–3

: *$k_u$yall aśśi täṣ was vaiśravaṃ wäl ptāñkät käṣyāp ārkiśoṣṣaṃ pākär naslune bādhariṃ brāmnā* ***śärsäs(s)i*** *(wotäk ||)*

'Why (did) King Vaiśravaṇa (order) us **to make known** the appearance of the Buddha-god the Teacher on earth through Bādhari the Brahmin?'

A 273 a5

/// (sä)s akṣar puk märkampalntu ***śärsässi*** *āyāto nāṃtsu*

"This script is definitely appropriate **to make known** all the Laws.'[59]

These examples have one detail in common: they lack an explicit recipient, but have an explicit theme, quite the opposite to what we saw in the finite forms and, to some degree, to what we found in the first two non-finite groups.[60] (There is some controversy around A 215 b3–4 = YQ

59 As one of the reviewers pointed out, in both this and the previous passage, the rendering 'inform' is also possible. This is true if they refer to another meaning of 'inform', where its direct object is not the recipient, but the theme (which corresponds to 'make known'). However, in modern English dictionaries, this meaning tends to be marked as 'obsolete' (MerWeb) or 'now rare' (OED). That is why, in order to avoid confusion, I do not use this rendering in this paper.

60 One of the reviewers noted that, in the religious context, the absence of the recipient is possible, and offered such rendering as 'inform' and 'teach'. As for the former, see the fn. 60 above. As for the latter, it is, of course, relevant.

I.7 a2–3 though, which will be discussed below.) The difference between these meanings can correspond to the focus on the arguments with different semantic roles. On the other hand, the problem lies not only in the over-expression of certain arguments in connection with certain meanings, but on the observation that all these meaning are connected with the voice and causation alternations (at the semantic level), which, in their turn, resemble the alternations that are characteristic for the Tocharian conjugational system. This leads me to a cautious suggestion that the third meaning might not be connected with the causative at all, which, however, remains a mere speculation with the current amount of evidence.[61] Note also that there is at least one passage containing an active

However, given the definition of TEACH adapted in this paper, it would coincide with the PREACH side of *āks-*. I can say with some degree of certainty that, A 215 b3–4 = YQ I.7 a2–3 and A 273 a5 allow the PREACH interpretation, but A 72 a5 does not. Combining this with the Old Uyghur evidence (see below), I would adhere to the 'make known' interpretation.

61 There is no factual evidence for it, but only considerations from the semantic point of view. As we can see, the causative of *kärsā-* combines a quite regular transitive causative derived from the base verb, an intransitive passive variant of this causative, and a transitive non-causative (with quite visible link to the semantic of the base verb as well). (The presence of this non-causative sense was already noted by Malzahn (2010: 54) but, as far as I know, was left uncommented.) Given the fact that there are no other forms attested except the non-finite ones, which are derived from the present stem, and that the causative and s-transitive (the term is as per Peyrot (2013: 30); cf. also Antigrundverb in Malzahn 2010: 51) are indistinguishable in Prs VIII (and thus, their infinitives should also be identical), it is tempting to suggest that the A 72 a5, A 244 b2–3, A 215 b3–4 = YQ I.7 a2–3, and A 273 a5 passages do not belong to the causative, but to the third conjugational paradigm, the s-transitive. (The attested preterit finite forms (having the meaning 'to inform') belong to the Prt II class, while the s-transitive is connected with the Prt III class; cf. Malzahn 2010: 51, 64.) From a systemic point of view, there are both pros and cons for this point of view. On the one hand, the base verbs in such three-part systems always have the sbj. V and prt. I classes (Malzahn 2010: 66), to which *kärsā-* (bv.) corresponds perfectly. On the other hand, there is no such combination known, where all the paradigms are transitive. Moreover, it is generally considered that the causative sets including

finite form, which appears to make sense only if we interpret it as 'to make known':

A 244 b2–3

> (1)2 *k(r)ant rakeṣināṃ tsopatsäṃ yonyo kn(āṃ)muneṣi kapśiññis ṣñi* ***śärsäṣt*** *ṣo*$_{b3}$*(kyo ciñcrone* **:**)
> '… 12. Through the great track of the good word … [you] **make known** (the great tenderness) of [your] body of wisdom …' (transl. CEToM with an addition by myself)

In any case, by now the overall picture of the semantic relationships between the verb paradigms (including the alleged active/middle alternation) looks like this:

<table>
<tr><th></th><th>base verb</th><th></th><th>active</th><th>nonfinite (cf. middle?)</th></tr>
<tr><td>act.</td><td>2. to get to know, to learn</td><td rowspan="2">> caus.</td><td>to cause someone to know (= 'inform')</td><td>to be caused by someone to know (= 'be informed')</td></tr>
<tr><td>mid.</td><td>2. to be known [realized], to be learned</td><td>to cause something to be known (= 'make known')</td><td>no data</td></tr>
</table>

Returning to general interpretation of the analyzed lexeme, I should note that the Old Uyghur parallels are quite predictable, showing the same abstract causative semantics in general. At the same time, these passages translate *kärsā-* (caus.) by using different lexemes compared to the other verbs we have analyzed earlier. First, there is *ukıt-* (= *uqït-*), which is the

s-transitives are based only on the intransitive base verbs (Malzahn 2010: 53–54; Peyrot 2013: 31), which is not the case of *kärsā-* (bv.). There is a peculiar case in Tocharian B though, where both the base verb and *s*-transitive are transitive, *tsuk-*, bv. '± suck (out)' (tr.), *s*-tr. '± suckle; foster' (tr.), while TA *tsuk-* only has the base verb attested. (Malzahn 2010: 71) However, there is no evidence of the causative in this case. Moreover, as I.B. Itkin (p.c.) notes, there are just no indisputable cases where we can distinguish between the causative and the *s*-transitive in Tocharian A.

causative of *uk-* (= *uq-*) 'to understand' (DTS: 613). Wilkens (2021: 789) provides a wider range of renderings for *ukıt-*: 'mitteilen, lehren, beibringen, zeigen, demonstrieren, aufzeigen, hinweisen, darlegen, erläutern, manifestieren, zu erkennen geben, definieren'. Cf. the parallel for A 215 b3–4 = YQ I.7 a2–3 (: *$k_u$yall aśśi täṣ was vaiśravaṃ wäl ptāñkät käṣyāp ārkiśoṣṣaṃ pākär naslune bādhariṃ brāmnā śärsäs(s)i (wotäk ||)* 'Why (did) King Vaiśravaṇa (order) us to make known the appearance of the Buddha-god the Teacher on earth through Bādhari the Brahmin?'):

MaitrHami 1, 13 a10–13 = MaitrSengim Taf. 11 b2–8

> *nä oyrïnta nä tïltayïnta biz-ing bägimiz wayširwan ilig tängri tängrisi burxannïng yirtinčüdä blgürmišin badari baramanqa* ***uqïtyalï*** *yrlïqar ärki ..*
>
> 'Aus welcher Veranlassung und aus welchem Grund geruht wohl unser Herr, der König Vaiśravaṇa, dem Brahmanen Badhari das Erscheinen des Göttergottes Buddha in der Welt **mitzuteilen**?' (Geng & Klimkeit 1988: 96–97)[62]

It should be noted that *baramanqa* is in the dative, and in this case it has a twofold function. Besides the obvious recipient semantics, it can also denote the agent if used with causative verbs (Erdal 2004: 369). According to J. Wilkens (p.c.), in this passage rather a "normal" dative is used. This contradicts the TA parallel, A 215 b3–4 = YQ I.7 a2–3, where the recipient interpretation of *brāmnā* (the perlative) seems unlikely. Cf., however, the parallel for YQ I.7 a4 = A 215 b5:

MaitrHami 1, 13 a17–18

> *.. antay ärsär tüz-ün maitriq[a] oq* ***uqïtyalï aymaz*** *..*
>
> 'Wenn das so ist, warum **teilt** er es nicht gerade dem edlen Maitreya **mit**?' (Geng & Klimkeit 1988: 96–97)

There may be some issues with the accuracy of this translation. The construction *-gAlI ay-* (here *-yalï ay-*) means 'to tell to do' and usually dis-

62 The other parallels are A 273 a5 = MaitrHami 16, 15 a14–16, (YQ I.7 a4 = A 215 b5) = MaitrHami 1, 13 a17–18, and (YQ I.7 a5–6 = A 215 b6) = MaitrHami 1, 13 a21–24.

plays different subjects. (Erdal 2004: 409) Thus, a more precise translation should be '…tell [us] **to inform** the noble Maitreya'. If so, the TA YQ I.7 a4 = A 215 b5 and OU MaitrHami 1, 13 a17–18 passages can be considered as very close. This implies that MaitrHami 1, 13 a10–13 = MaitrSengim Taf. 11 b2–8 and MaitrHami 1, 13 a17–18 use the same OU verb governing the same case for rendering different TA meanings ('to make known' in A 215 b3–4 = YQ I.7 a2–3 and 'to inform' in YQ I.7 a4 = A 215 b5). In my opinion, the simplest explanation might be that the OU rendering (the dative in MaitrHami 1, 13 a10–13 = MaitrSengim Taf. 11 b2–8) just differs from the TA original (the perlative in A 215 b3–4 = YQ I.7 a2–3).

Another way of translating *kärsā-* (caus.) into Old Uyghur is *tuyuz-* 'wahrnehmen lassen, wissen lassen, zu Gehör bringen' (Wilkens 2021: 768) and 'to cause, or allow (someone) to become aware' (Clauson 1972: 571). For instance, for YQ I.7 b2–4, there is

MaitrHami 1, 13 b12–17

> *.. bar s(ä)n badari bramanqa tüz-ü tükäti* ***tuyuz-yïl*** *.. [amtï] mn [tüz-] ün maitri tapa barayïn xormuz[ta tngritä] ulatï tört maxarač tngrilärning ayayu ayarlayu yu̥künü äsängüläyü ayïtmïšïn tägüräyin* (.)
> 'Gehe du, **lasse** es den Brahmanen Badhari völlig **verstehen**! [Jetzt] will ich zum [ed]len Maitreya gehen. Ich will das [von Gott] Indra und von den vier Mahārāja-Göttern mit Verehrung (Hend.) und Verneigung (Hend.) Gesagte überbringen.' (Geng & Klimkeit 1988: 98–99)[63]

Thus, even if the Old Uyghur material does not reflect the nuances of voice and causative alternations of *kärsā-* (caus.), it still quite unambiguously shows its general meaning.

ṣärp-

This verb is represented by eleven examples, as well as one involving the compound adjective *ṣoma-ṣärpāṣluneyum*, derived from an unattested

63 The other parallel is YQ III.2 b2 = MaitrHami 3, 2 b11–13.

verbal abstract. It is transitive and active, with no middle forms attested. Its literal meaning can be deduced from the following passages as corresponding to the concept of POINT (WITH FINGER); namely, "[t]o use the finger to show something to somebody", and more generally, as 'to show something to somebody with a gesture'[64]:

A 254 b2–3

|| *täm pälkoräṣ metrakṣiñi wrasañ lyutār me*$_{b3}$*(maṣ klopasuṣ nāntsuṣ tosäm) ñemiṣinās risaṃ ñemiṣinäs skāksaṃ ṣtāṅksaṃ kuccatāksaṃ kälymāṃ nirmitṣinās ris* ***ṣärpäsmāṃ*** *tränkiñc*

'Dies gesehen habend, (sind) die Lebewesen des Maitreya über alles Maß (leidvoll geworden); [auf] diese trügerischen Städte-[Bewohner], die sich in den Juwelen-Städten, in den Juwelen-Balkonen, -Palästen, -Türmen befinden, **zeigend**, sagen sie' (Geng et al. 2004: 55).

YQ III.12 b5

/// prāryo ***ṣärpäsmāṃ*** *tränkäṣ plamäs •*

'**pointing** with his finger, says: Sit down!'

Cf. also:

A 175ext[65] b4

/// (ṣi)k toräṣ (na)ndeṃ ***ṣä(rpä)sm(āṃ)*** *karemāṃ akmalyo ālam w(c)ac (tränk)i(ñc) ///*

'…walking <lit. stepping>, **pointing** at Nanda, with a smiling face, [they] say to each other…'[66] (joined and transl. in Itkin 2019b: 288).

64 As one of the reviewers noted, YQ III.12 b5 points to the fact that 'with finger' is not part of the verb semantics proper, with which I have to agree. As indirect support for this, cf. Tocharian B: PK AS 17I a4–5 || *tane sumana tseññai uppāltsa supriyeṃ* ***ṣär[p]s[e]m(a)n[e]*** *priya*$_{a5}$*sundariṃś weṣṣäṃ* || 'Here Sumanā **pointing** at Supriya with a blue lotus says to Priyasundarī'. (I am thankful to I.B. Itkin for drawing my attention to this passage.)

65 = A 175 + A 178 + THT 2968.g + (?) THT 2530 + (?) THT 2518+2410. (Itkin 2019b: 288–290)

66 '…шагая, на Нанду **указывая**, со смеющимся лицом друг другу говорят…'

If the conjecture is correct, then the overall context (Nanda is in the center of attention) does not exclude the 'pointing' interpretation here. Also, note that all three passages contain explicit themes (which are pointed at), but not explicit recipients (to whom something is shown).

It is possible that this lexeme can be linked to another, more general concept, SHOW ('[t]o have somebody see something'), but there no any other contexts attested which would display a wider usage than ~POINT (e.g., 'to demonstrate', 'to show how one does something'). While it can be compared to a certain extent[67] with the rendering 'point out' offered by Peyrot (2013a: 828), I do not find that very fortunate because of another meaning of this English lexeme, '[t]o draw attention to the fact; to explain or show (that something is the case)' (OED), which is not attested in the case of *ṣärp-*. Instead, it has another, figurative meaning, which is connected to showing in a more abstract way and without such (important in the case of *point out*) detail of the semantics as 'drawing attention'. Because it is attested only in the manuscripts representing Tocharian A translations from Sanskrit, I will discuss it further in the section on Sanskrit parallels.

The Sanskrit parallels

Most of the identified Sanskrit parallels are found in the *Prātimokṣasūtra*, corresponding to the Tocharian A manuscript A 353–354. Cf.:

67 While lexicological research on English verbs lies far beyond the scope of this paper, it seems that, comparing with *point (at)*, *point out* has a more visible accent on distinguishing an object and on explicit mentioning of a recipient. Cf. *point* 'To indicate position or direction by, or as if by, extending the finger; to direct attention *to* or *at* (something) in this way.' (OED), 'to indicate the position or direction of something especially by extending a finger; to direct attention' (MerWeb) and *point out* 'To direct someone's gaze or attention towards (with, or as with, the finger, etc.); to remark on; to distinguish or separate, to draw attention to.' (OED), 'to direct someone's attention to (someone or something) by pointing', especially the example "He *pointed* his girlfriend *out* (to me) in the crowd." (MerWeb).

A 353 a1–2

*/// (ṣaṣä)**rpuṣ** nṣā taryāk tärkāluneyumināñ wärkṣantāñ mä$_{a2}$(rkampaläntu : ṣaṣärpuṣ nmuk wärkṣantāñ märkampa)lä(n)tu (ṣaṣärpuṣ śtwar **ko**)**rpā āksiṣlaṃ** märkampaläntu : **ṣaṣärpuṣ** käṣtär **āklye** (///)*[68] *märkampalänt(u :)*

'...the thirty demanding dismission [and] turning down (?)[69] rules **have been presented** by me, (the ninety turning down (?) rules have been presented, the four) rules **which are to be** confessed [lit. **told/ explained in return**] (have been presented), a lot of rules (connected with?) the **teaching have been presented**' (restoration Schmidt 1989: 74; the translation is mine).

PrMoSū (Schlussteil I)

***uddiṣṭās** trayodaśa saṃghāvaśeṣā dharmā uddiṣṭau dvāv aniyatau dharmau uddiṣṭās triṃśa(n n)iḥsargikāḥ pātayantikā dharmā uddiṣṭā navati pātayantikā dharmā uddiṣṭāś catvāraḥ **prat**(**i**)**deśanīyā** dha(r) m(ā) **u**(**ddi**)**ṣṭ**(**āḥ**) saṃbahulā(ḥ) **śaikṣā** dharmā*

'ich habe die dreizehn Saṃghāvaśeṣa-Fälle **vorgetragen**; ich habe die beiden Aniyata-Fälle vorgetragen; ich habe die dreißig Niḥsargika-Pātayantika-Fälle vorgetragen; ich habe die neunzig Pātayantikā-Fälle vorgetragen; ich habe die vier **Pratideśanīya**-Fälle **vorgetragen**; ich habe die zahlreichen **Śaikṣa**-Fälle vorgetragen' (restoration and translation von Simson 2000: 258, 316).

A 353 a4–6

*ta(ṃ) n(e wkä)nyo kus /// ālak penu märkampalis tāskmāṃ märkampal tmaṃ nu yasā ṣyak ṣo$_{a5}$ma ārtlune pältskumäñcsā plaṃtmāṃñcsā mā k$_u$ñaś ypamāñ(cs)ā /// (pä)ltskumäñcsā • **ṣoma***

68 5 akṣaras missing (Schmidt 1989: 74).

69 This probably means going down morally (Peyrot 2013: 821, fn. 852), while the main meaning of the verb is probably 'turn (tr.)' (Malzahn 2010: 888–889). However, given the fact that the punishment for a *saṃghāvaśeṣa* offence was time-limited—six or more nights—and required a ceremony of 'calling back' the punished monk (Clarke 2002: 387–388), I would suggest that here *wärk-* may mean 'return' (to the saṅgha or to the full-rights status).

***ṣä(r)p(ā)ṣluneyumäñcsā** 3 • sas wär mal(k)e nā(ṃ)tsuñc*$_{a6}$*sā • käṣṣiyāp enäṣlune pañitswātsäṃ lutkäsmāñ(csā)*[70] */// (mä)sk(ä)l näm taṃ ne wkänyo **āklye yal** ||*

'In this way, what (?) … also another dharma similar to [this?] dharma. Then you should become … [those] who think together only about approval, who rejoice, who do not do a conflict, who thinks … , who have the only **exposition** [of the doctrine], who are united [as] water [and] milk, who make splendid the precept of the teacher. It **should be studied** in this way.' (restoration by Schmidt 1989: 74; the translation is mine[71] with an addition from Itkin 2019b: 283)

PrMoSū (Schlussteil I)

*iti yo (v)ā (pu)nar anyo 'p(y āga)cched dharmasyānudharmas tatra vaḥ sahitaiḥ samagraiḥ saṃmodamānair avivadamānair ekāgr(ai)r **ekoddeśair** ekakṣīrodakībhūtai(ḥ) sukhaṃ phā(ṣaṃ) v(iha)rtavyam iti **śikṣā karaṇīyā** ||*

'Darin oder aber in dem, was es sonst noch an Regeln gibt, die der Lehre entsprechen, sollt ihr vereint, alle zusammen, einvernehmlich, ohne euch zu streiten, auf ein Ziel ausgerichtet, einer **einheitlichen Lehre** folgend, (gleichsam) zu einer einheitlichen Mischung von Milch und Wasser geworden, glücklich und zufrieden leben: Das **sollen wir lernen**.' (restoration and translation von Simson 2000: 258, 316)

A 353 b4

*– – (ptāñä)kte **enäṣlune** 3 :*

'/// It is the **doctrine** of Buddha.' (Ogihara 2009: 273)[72]

PrMoSū (Schlussteil II 3)

*etad buddhasya **ś(āsa)nam** 3*

70 The Sanskrit parallel fragment lacks this passage (so there is no counterpart of *enäṣlune*).

71 I am thankful to I.B. Itkin and S.V. Malyshev (p.c.) for counselling me about this passage.

72 The same correspondence is attested in A 354 a3 = PrMoSū (Schlussteil II 7) and A 354 b5 = PrMoSū (Schlussteil II 13).

'Das ist das **Gebot** des Buddha.' (restoration and translation von Simson 2000: 260, 316)

A 354 b3

: *ptāñäktes tsraṣisā tsopats āñmatsumäñcsā* : *prātimokäṣ* ***ṣaṣärpu āksiññu*** *śkaṃ tsopa(tsäṃ riṣaknā 11)*

'...Under the Buddhas, under the powerful ones, under the noble-hearted ones, and under a great (sage), the Prātimokṣa **has been explained and taught** (11).' (restoration and translation Ogihara 2009: 274–275)

PrMoSū (Schlussteil II 11)

saptabhir lokanāyakair buddhavīrair mahātmabhiḥ prātimokṣaḥ ***samuddiṣṭo nirdiṣṭaś*** *ca maharṣiṇā 11*

'11. Die sieben Anführer der Menschheit, die edlen Buddhahelden, **haben** den Prātimokṣa in seiner Allgemeinheit **verkündet**, und der große Seher **hat** ihn im Einzelnen **gelehrt**.' (von Simson 2000: 317)

A 354 b6

: *13 kus ne nu caṣ märka(m)p(a)lṣi* ***enäṣlun(eyaṃ*** *sn)e (y)korñe tāṣ* : *wawikuräṣ cmo(lwāṣiṃ sark klopis ākā yäṣ 14)*

'Who will be careful **about the teaching** of this law, having removed the cycle of the births, he will go to the end of the pains. 14' (restoration and translation Ogihara 2009: 276).

PrMoSū (Schlussteil II 14)

*yo hy asmiṃ dharma****vinaye*** *apramatto bhaviṣyati prahāya jātisaṃsāraṃ duḥkhasyāntaṃ sa (y)āsyati 14*

'14. Wer hinsichtlich der Lehre und der **Disziplin** ohne Nachlässigkeit ist, der wird den Kreislauf der Geburten hinter sich lassen und das Ende des Leidens erreichen.' (restoration and translation von Simson 2000: 263, 318)

Besides that, there is a TA gloss *trikärsālune ākṣi(ñlu)n(e)* translating a Skt. compound *traividyāpadeś ///* in the Sanskrit fragment SHT 1821 a2 (as per Wille & Bechert 2000: 18), in which TA *ākṣi(ñlu)n(e)* corresponds to Skt. *upadeśa-* (as per Carling 2009: 30). Also, there are two Tocharian fragments containing the translation of *Udānavarga*, A 218 and A 391, from where we can extract two more correspondences: Skt. *ādeśayantaḥ* – TA *āksisamāṃ* and Skt. *pradeśitaḥ* – TA *(āk)ṣ(i)ñus* respectively (as per Carling 2009: 29–30, for the respective Sanskrit fragments, cf. Bernhard 1965: 197, 280).

Finally, I would like to summarize the TA-Skt. correspondences in the following table:

TA lexeme	Skt. gloss	English meaning according to BHSD, s.v.[73]	German meaning according to SWTF, s.v.
āklye yal	*śikṣā karaṇīya*	'1. instruction; 2. morality' + 'affair, business, duty (thing to be done)'	'Schulung, Unterweisung; Anweisung' + 'zu tun, zu machen; zu bewirken; hervorzubringen; zu betreiben; zu handeln; das, was zu tun ist: Pflicht; Aufgabe; Angelegenheit'
āklye ///	*śaikṣa*	'[…] 2. [with dharma] (rule) of good behavior'. Cf. also (MW: 1089): '[…] in accordance with right teaching or with rule, correct'	'[…] 2b. *śikṣā* betreffend: Śaikṣa; (Bez. des 7. Abschnitts [~*ā dharmāḥ*] des Prātimokṣasūtra, in dem alle Regeln auf "*ṣikṣā karaṇīyā*" enden'

73 Unless another source is mentioned.

TA lexeme	Skt. gloss	English meaning according to BHSD, s.v.[73]	German meaning according to SWTF, s.v.
āks-	*ādeśayantaḥ*	Cf. *ādeśayati* 'causes (*dakṣiṇā*, the profit from gifts or works or merit) to be assigned (to someone else)'	Cf. *ā-diś* '1. (den Lohn guter Taten, *dakṣiṇā*) zuweisen, übertragen; 2. caus. zeigen, verkünden'
	nirdiṣṭa	Cf. *nirdeśa* '1. elucidation (particularly of religious or philosophical questions)' and *nirdeśana* 'explanation, exhibition, revealing, making clear [...]'	'erklärt, dargelegt'
	prati-deśanīya[74]	'requiring confession'	'(reuig) zu bekennend, ein (reuiges) Bekenntnis erfordernd'
	pradeśita	Cf. *pradeśeti* 'exhibits, displays'	'gezeigt, aufgewiesen'
ākṣiñlune	*upadeśa-* in *traividyā-padeś ///*	'of a type of Buddhist literature, one of the pravacana [...], lit. instruction'; cf. also *upadeśeti* 'exhibits, displays'	'1. Belehrung, Unterweisung [...]'

74 = TA (*ko*)*rpā āksiṣlaṃ*.

TA lexeme	Skt. gloss	English meaning according to BHSD, s.v.[73]	German meaning according to SWTF, s.v.
enäṣlune	*vinaya* in *dharma-vinaya*	'discipline'	'[…] 2. (bezüglich der *adhikaraṇaśamathā dharmāḥ*:) disziplinarisches Verfahren; (oder:) das Erkennen (auf); 3. (Korpus des) Vinaya; Ordenszucht'
	śāsana	'punishing, a punisher, chastiser; teaching, instructing, an instructor; an order, command, edict, enactment, decree, direction' (MW: 1068-1069; see also other meanings in compounds and derivatives)	'Anweisung; Lehre'
ṣärp-	*uddiṣṭa*	Cf. *uddiśati* 'poses, proposes (a mathematical problem)'.	'gelehrt; dargelegt; rezitiert'
	samuddiṣṭa	Cf. *samuddiśati* = *uddiśati*. Cf. also (MW: 1168): 'fully pointed out or declared or indicated, shown, explained, enumerated, particularized'	'in vollem Umfang dargelegt, rezitiert, verkündet'
ṣärpāṣlune	*uddeśa* in *ekoddeśair*	'exposition, explanation, setting forth (of a doctrine)'. Cf. also Pāli *ek'udesa* 'a single repetition' (Rhys Davids, Stede 1921: 136)	'1. Unterweisung; Darlegung; Rezitation; 2a. Hinweisung; kurze Angabe; Erklärung in Kurzform; 2b. Bezeichnung; Erwähnung (eines Dings bei seinem Namen); Kennzeichen […]'

The Sanskrit counterparts of *āklye* and *enäṣlune* do not add much to the general picture. In the case of *enäṣlune*, these parallels only suggest that *en-* could have the 'punishing' component in its semantics,[75] although it should be noted that *śāsana* in all four cases is not used with the meaning of 'punish'. Instead, it only seems to be used with the meaning of 'instruction' or 'doctrine'. This being the case, I find no reason to change the interpretation of *en-* proposed in the respective paragraph.

As for *āks-* and *ṣärp-* and their counterparts, the Sanskrit material does not help us, and instead it makes the situation even more obscure due to the fact that all seven Sanskrit lexemes are derived from the same root and they semantically intersect with each other. In this instance, we have to test a Tocharian A group of synonyms the distinction between which is not entirely clear against a Sanskrit group of synonyms, the distinction between which is not entirely clear either. It seems, though, that the counterparts of *āks-* have two main meanings which can be reduced to EXPLAIN and SHOW (cf. 'exhibit', 'display'), but the latter are not reliably supported by the Tocharian material, unlike the former. Moreover, the Sanskrit material and definitions seem to point to EXPLAIN more strongly than to TELL, thus, leaving the problem of the primary meaning of *āks-* unsolved. As for the counterparts of *ṣärp-* and *ṣärpāṣlune*, they tend to have a stronger focus on presenting or setting forth the information (arguably a logical figurative variant of its literal meaning). Finally, the most important passage, A 354 b3, containing the collocation *ṣaṣärpu ākṣiññu*, would make perfect sense if we interpret it as 'fully presented and explained'. Thus, given the attested material and its quantity, its figurative meaning can be defined as '~to present, to set forth [information]'. Probably, the only case where the semantics *ṣärp-* may be closer to 'explain' is *ṣoma ṣä(r)p(ā)[ṣ]luneyumäñcsā* in A 353 a4–6, although even in this case the interpretation of 'exposition' as an 'introduction' (to the doctrine) is possible. On the other hand, here we deal not with the verb itself, but with the verbal abstract, which may develop additional meanings

75 As I.B. Itkin (p.c.) notes, this would resemble the Russian *наказать* which means both 'to punish' and 'to bid'.

(cf., for example, *yātā-* and various renderings of *yātlune*). Finally, all the Tocharian A forms in these correspondences have passive semantics, but are non-finite. This leaves the question about the existence of the middle paradigm of *ṣärp-* unresolved.

Conclusion

While further Tocharian A material would be very welcome for a more grounded interpretation of the semantics of these verbs, the general distinction between their meanings can be outlined even in the present situation. Thus, *ākl-*, *āks-*, and *kärsā-* (caus.) can be considered as the main verbs for expressing transmission of information and knowledge, where the first verb denotes the teaching in its common understanding (with such prototypical figures as teacher and pupils), the second verb rather focuses on a particular mode of transmission (explaining, detailed account), and the third verb focuses on the very fact of transmission (mostly neglecting. As for *en-*, it stays at the border of this group, focusing on behavioral consequences of transmission of information. The verb *ṣärp-* deals with the said transmission to the least extent, only in its figurative meaning, focusing on presenting information. Finally, *eśe yäp-* probably does not belong to this group at all, denoting a behavioral activity (thus, supporting D.Q. Adams's interpretation).

Besides this, this study has allowed to create more systematized definitions, for which cf. the following table:

lexeme	active	middle
ākl-	TEACH: to pass on knowledge and skills (ditr.)	LEARN: to acquire, or attempt to acquire knowledge or an ability to do something (tr.)
āklye y-		~STUDY: to engage in study, grow in knowledge/skill by studying (intr.)

lexeme	active	middle
āks-	1. TELL: to talk about a story giving its details; to give a detailed account of; 2. EXPLAIN: to inform about the reason for something, how something works, or how to do something; 3. PREACH: to deliver a sermon (ditr.)	—
en-	—	to correct someone's behavior by instruction or by coercion (tr.)
eśe yäp-	—	1. to pay attention to something/someone; 2. to take care of someone (tr.)
kärsā- (caus.)	to cause someone to know (= 'inform', 'make aware') [more focusing on the action, than on the theme] (tr.)	to be caused by someone to know (= 'be informed', 'be made aware') [more focusing on the action, than on the theme] (intr.)
	to cause something to be known (= 'make known'; tr.)	—
ṣärp-	1. ~POINT (WITH FINGER): to show something to somebody with a gesture; 2. ~to present, to set forth [information] (tr.)	—

[RECEIVED: AUGUST 2021]

Palacký University Olomouc
Tř. Svobody 26
779 00 Olomouc, Czech Republic
m.v.vyzhlakov@gmail.com

Abbreviations

BHSD = Edgerton, Franklin. 1953 (1985 reprint). *Buddhist Hybrid Sanskrit grammar and dictionary, Vol. 2: Dictionary*. New Haven: Yale University Press.
CEToM = *A Comprehensive Edition of Tocharian Manuscripts*.

www.univie.ac.at/tocharian/ [retrieved: Jan. 4, 2022].
CLICS = Rzymski, Christoph, Tiago Tresoldi et al. 2019. *The Database of Cross-Linguistic Colexifications, reproducible analysis of cross-linguistic polysemies.* https://clics.clld.org/ [retrieved: Nov. 13, 2021].
CONCEPTICON = List, Johann Mattis, Christoph Rzymski, Simon Greenhill, Nathanael Schweikhard, Kristina Pianykh, Annika Tjuka, Carolin Hundt & Robert Forkel (eds.). 2021. *CLLD Concepticon 2.5.0* [Data set]. Zenodo. https://concepticon.clld.org/ [retrieved: Nov. 15, 2021].
DTS = Nadeljaev V. M., D. M. Nasilov, È. R. Tenišev & A. M. Ščerbak (eds.). 1969. *Drevnetjurkskij slovar'*. Leningrad: Nauka, Leningradskoe otdelenie.
EoB II = Buswell Jr., Robert E. (ed.). 2004. *Encyclopedia of Buddhism. Volume II: M–Z*. New York: Macmillan Reference USA.
MerWeb = Merriam-Webster.com. 2021. www.merriam-webster.com [retrieved: Nov. 11, 2021].
MW = Monier-Williams, Monier. 1899. *A Sanskrit-English Dictionary: Etymologically and Philologically Arranged with Special Reference to Cognate Indo-European languages.* Oxford: Clarendon Press.
OED = *OED Online*. 2021. Oxford University Press. www.oed.com [retrieved: Nov. 12, 2021].
Siegling, personal copy = Siegling, Wilhelm. Personal and annotated copy of *Tocharische Sprachreste / Herausgegeben von E. Sieg und W. Siegling, Bd. 1. Die Texte*. Berlin; Leipzig, 1921.
SWTF = Waldschmidt, Ernst et al. 1973–2018. *Sanskrit-Wörterbuch der buddhistischen Texte aus den Turfan-Funden*. Göttingen: Vandenhoeck und Ruprecht.
TEB II = Thomas, Werner & Wolfgang Krause. 1964. *Tocharisches Elementarbuch, Band II. Texte und Glossar*. Heidelberg: Winter.

References

Adams, Douglas Q. 2013. *A Dictionary of Tocharian B. Revised and greatly enlarged. 2nd edn.* Amsterdam / New York: Rodopi.
Bernhard, Franz. 1965. *Udānavarga. Band I. Einleitung, Beschreibung der Handschriften, Textausgabe, Bibliographie*. Göttingen: Vandenhoeck & Ruprecht.
Bonch-Osmolovskaya, Anastassia, Ekaterina Rakhilina & Tatiana Reznikova. 2009. "Conceptualization of Pain: A Database for Lexical Typology". In Peter Bosch, David Gabelaia & Jérôme Lang (eds.), *Logic, Language, and Computation. 7th International Tbilisi Symposium on Logic, Language, and Computa-*

tion, TbiLLC 2007, Tbilisi, Georgia, October 1–5, 2007, Revised Selected Papers. Berlin / Heidelberg: Springer, 110–123.

Burlak, Svetlana A. & Ilya B. Itkin. 2013. "Toxarskie jazyki". In Ju. B. Korjakov & A. A. Kibrik (eds.), *Jazyki mira: Reliktovye indoevropejskie jazyki Perednej i Central'noj Azii.* Moskva: Academia, 386–485.

Carling, Gerd. 2009. *Dictionary and thesaurus of Tocharian A. Volume 1: A–J.* Compiled by Gerd Carling in collaboration with Georges-Jean Pinault and Werner Winter. Wiesbaden: Harrassowitz Verlag.

Clarke, Shayne. 2002. "One rule for all? *Saṃghāvaśeṣa* indemnity for the Sarvāstivādin monastic hierarchy". In *Buddhist and Indian Studies in honour of Professor Sodo Mori.* Hamamatsu: Kokusai Bukkyōto Kyōkai, 387–398.

Clauson, Gerard, Sir. 1972. *An etymological dictionary of pre-thirteenth-century Turkish.* Oxford: Clarendon Press.

Couvreur, Walter. 1956. "Bemerkungen zu Pavel Pouchas Thesaurus linguae tocharicae dialecti A". *La Nouvelle Clio* 7–8: 67–98.

Dellert, Johannes, Thora Daneyko, Alla Münch et al. 2020. "NorthEuraLex: a wide-coverage lexical database of Northern Eurasia". *Language Resources & Evaluation* 54: 273–301.

Erdal, Marcel. 2004. A *Grammar of Old Turkic.* Leiden / Boston: Brill.

Geeraerts, Dirk. 2016. "Sense individuation". In Nick Riemer (ed.), *The Routledge Handbook of Semantics.* London / New York: Routledge / Taylor & Francis, 233–247.

Geng, Shimin & Hans-Joachim Klimkeit. 1985. "Das 16. Kapitel der Hami-Version der Maitrisimit". *Journal of Turkish Studies* 9: 71–132.

Geng, Shimin & Hans-Joachim Klimkeit. 1988. *Das Zusammentreffen mit Maitreya. Die ersten fünf Kapitel der Hami-Version der Maitrisimit. Teil I: Text, Übersetzung und Kommentar.* Wiesbaden: Harrassowitz.

Geng, Shimin, Jens Peter Laut & Georges-Jean Pinault. 2004. "Neue Ergebnisse der Maitrisimit-Forschung (II): Struktur und Inhalt des 26. Kapitels". *Studies on the Inner Asian Languages* 19: 29–94 [+ plates III–XIII].

Irons, Edward A. 2008. *Encyclopedia of Buddhism.* New York: Facts on File.

Itkin, Ilya B. 2018. "Prolog v četyrëx s polovinoj variacijax: k rekonstrukcii načal'nyx strok teksta «*Maitreyasamiti-Nāṭaka*»". *Voprosy Jazykoznanija* 2: 122–131.

Itkin, Ilya B. 2019a. *Ukazatel' slovoform k neopublikovannym toxarskim A tekstam iz sobranija Berlinskoj biblioteki.* Moscow: Institut vostokovedenija RAN.

Itkin, Ilya B. 2019b. "Toxarskaja A rukopis' 144–211 iz Šorčuka: novye dannye. II". *Vestnik Instituta vostokovedenija RAN* 3: 275–292.

Itkin, Ilya B. & Sergey V. Malyshev. 2021. "Notae Tocharicae: *apälkāts*, *pärsā(n)ts*, *letse* et autres addenda et corrigenda-4". *Voprosy Jazykoznanija* 3: 47–75.

Ji Xianlin, Werner Winter & Georges-Jean Pinault. 1998. *Fragments of the Tocharian A Maitreyasamiti-Nāṭaka of the Xinjiang Museum, China. Transliterated, translated and annotated by Ji Xianlin in collaboration with Werner Winter, Georges-Jean Pinault*. Berlin / New York: de Gruyter.

Malzahn, Melanie. 2010. *The Tocharian Verbal System*. Leiden / Boston: Brill.

Meunier, Fanny. 2013. "Typologie des locutions en *yam-* du tokharien". *Tocharian and Indo-European Studies* 14: 123–186.

Murphy, M. Lynne. 2003. *Semantic Relations and the Lexicon: Antonymy, Synonymy and other Paradigms*. Cambridge: Cambridge University.

Ogihara, Hirotoshi. 2009. *Researches about Vinaya-texts in Tocharian A and B [Recherches sur le Vinaya en tokharien A et B]*. PhD thesis École Pratique des Hautes Études.

Peyrot, Michaël. 2013a. *The Tocharian subjunctive. A study in syntax and verbal stem formation*. Leiden / Boston: Brill.

Peyrot, Michaël. 2013b. "Die tocharische *Daśakarmapathāvadānamālā*". In Yukiyo Kasai, Abdurishid Yakup & Desmond Durkin-Meisterernst (eds.), *Die Erforschung des Tocharischen und die alttürkische Maitrisimit*. Turnhout: Brepols, 161–182.

Peyrot, Michaël & Ablet Semet. 2016. "A comparative study of the beginning of the 11th act of the Tocharian A *Maitreyasamitināṭaka* and the Old Uyghur *Maitrisimit*". *Acta Orientalia Hungarica* 69: 355–378.

Pinault, Georges-Jean. 2013. "Contribution de *Maitrisimit* à l'interprétation de textes parallèles en tokharien". In Yukiyo Kasai, Abdurishid Yakup & Desmond Durkin-Meisterernst (eds.), *Die Erforschung des Tocharischen und die alttürkische Maitrisimit*. Turnhout: Brepols, 183–234.

Poucha, Pavel. 1955. *Thesaurus Linguae Tocharicae Dialecti A*. Praha: Státní Pedagogické Nakladatelství.

Rakhilina, E. V. & T. I. Reznikova. 2013. "Frejmovyj podxod k leksičeskoj tipologii". *Voprosy Jazykoznanija* 2: 3–31.

Rakhilina, Ekaterina V., Tatiana I. Reznikova & Olga Yu. Shemanaeva. 2009. "Dealing with Polysemy in Russian National Corpus: The Case of Adjectives". In Peter Bosch, David Gabelaia & Jérôme Lang (eds.), *Logic, Language, and Computation. 7th International Tbilisi Symposium on Logic, Language, and Computation, TbiLLC 2007, Tbilisi, Georgia, October 1–5, 2007, Revised Selected Papers*. Berlin / Heidelberg: Springer, 69–79.

Rhys Davids, Thomas William & William Stede. 1921. *Pāli-English Dictionary*. London: Pāli Text Society.

Rzymski, Christoph, Tiago Tresoldi, Simon J. Greenhill et al. 2020. "The Database of Cross-Linguistic Colexifications, reproducible analysis of cross-linguistic polysemies". *Scientific Data* 7: 13.

Schmidt, Klaus T. 1974. *Die Gebrauchsweisen des Mediums im Tocharischen*. PhD Universität Göttingen.

Schmidt, Klaus T. 1989. *Der Schlußteil des Prātimokṣasutra der Sarvāstivādins. Text in Sanskrit und Tocharisch A verglichen mit den Parallelversionen anderer Schulen*. Sanskrittexte aus den Turfanfunden XIII. Göttingen: Vandenhoeck & Ruprecht.

Sieg, Emil. 1944. *Übersetzungen aus dem Tocharischen I*. Berlin: Akademie der Wissenschaften.

Tekin, Şinasi. 1980. *Maitrisimit nom bitig. Die uigurische Übersetzung eines Werkes der buddhistischen Vaibhāṣika-Schule. 1. Teil: Transliteration, Übersetzung, Anmerkungen. 2. Teil: Analytischer und rückläufiger Index*. Berlin: Akademie-Verlag.

von Simson, Georg. 2000. *Prātimokṣasūtra der Sarvāstivādins. Teil II. Kritische Textausgabe, Übersetzung, Wörtindex sowie Nachträge zu Teil I*. Göttingen: Vandenhoeck & Ruprecht.

Vyzhlakov, Maksim V. 2021. *Specifying semantics of synonymous verbs in Tocharian A as a part of working on a Tocharian A basic word list*. PhD Palacký University, Olomouc.

Wilkens, Jens. 2021. *Handwörterbuch des Altuigurischen*. Göttingen: Universitätsverlag Göttingen.

Wille, Klaus & Heinz Bechert. 2000. *Sanskrithandschriften aus den Turfan-Funden. Teil 8. Die Katalognummern 1800–1999*. Stuttgart: Steiner.

TOCHARIAN AND INDO-EUROPEAN STUDIES (abbreviated TIES) was founded in 1987 by Jörundur Hilmarsson and appeared under his editorship in Reykjavík, Iceland, until his death in 1992. Vol. 6 appeared posthumously in 1993 under the editorial finish of Guðrún Þórhallsdóttir who also supervised the continuation of the Supplementary Series up to vol. 5 in 1997. Vols. 7 to 10 were published by C. A. Reitzel Publishers Ltd., Copenhagen. Subsequent volumes are published by Museum Tusculanum Press in Copenhagen.

Orders and correspondence concerning distribution should be directed to:

Museum Tusculanum Press
Rådhusvej 19
2920 Charlottenlund
Denmark
info@mtp.dk

Manuscripts for publication and other correspondence on editorial matters should be directed to:

Mail: Georges-Jean Pinault
École Pratique des Hautes Études, PSL
4–14, rue Ferrus
75014 Paris
France

Email: ties@hum.ku.dk

Milton Keynes UK
Ingram Content Group UK Ltd.
UKHW051803140424
441124UK00001BA/30